D0984436

WITHDR

THE FORGOTTEN
NETWORK

September, 1949

THE FORGOTTEN NETWORK

DUMONT AND

THE BIRTH OF

AMERICAN

TELEVISION

David Weinstein

 Temple University Press
PHILADELPHIA

About the Author

David Weinstein is a Senior Program Officer at the National Endowment for the Humanities.

Temple University Press, Philadelphia 19122
Copyright © 2004 by Temple University
All rights reserved
Published 2004
Printed in the United States of America

⊗ The paper used in this publication meets the requirements of the American National Standard for Information Sciences—Permanence of Paper for Printed Library Materials, ANSI Z39.48–1984

Library of Congress Cataloging-in-Publication Data

Weinstein, David, 1967–
   The forgotten network: DuMont and the birth of American television / David Weinstein.
    p. cm.
   Includes bibliographical references and index.
   ISBN 1-59213-245-6 (cloth : alk. paper)
   1. DuMont Television Network—History. 2. Du Mont, Allen B. (Allen Balcom), 1901–1965. I. Title.

PN1992.92.D86W45 2004
384.55′23′0973—dc22

2003067203

On frontispiece: A neon sign atop the DuMont receiver plant in East Paterson, New Jersey. *Source: The Raster,* September 1949, Allen B. Du Mont Collection, Archives Center, National Museum of American History, Smithsonian Institution.

2 4 6 8 9 7 5 3 1

Contents

A Note on Spelling

Allen B. Du Mont spelled his name "Du Mont." I have retained this "Du Mont" spelling when referring to Allen Du Mont in this book. Allen Du Mont's company was generally spelled "DuMont" in the contemporary press, and historians have continued to use the "Du-Mont" spelling for DuMont Laboratories and the DuMont Television Network. I follow this practice, referring to the company and the network as "DuMont."

Preface and Acknowledgments

The Forgotten Network examines television and life in America during the 1940s and 1950s, the years when TV moved from the laboratory to the living room. In 1946, only 8,000 television sets were in use nationally and radio was the favored entertainment medium in the American home. Within ten years, America had become a television nation. By 1956, nearly 35 million families, about 71 percent of all Americans, had purchased television sets. As historian James L. Baughman wrote, "No other household technology, not the telephone or indoor plumbing, had ever spread so rapidly into so many homes."[1] This book tells the story of television's phenomenal growth from the perspective of DuMont Laboratories, one of the pioneering companies in receiver manufacturing and network broadcasting.

Today, the postwar television boom seems all the more remarkable considering the primitive state of TV technology in these years before home theater, high definition television, and digital cable. Viewers watched hour after hour of flickering, fuzzy, black and white images. There were only two or three stations operating in most markets, while the entire country had only four national networks: ABC, CBS, NBC, and DuMont. Despite technological limitations, however, the novelty of the medium and the tremendous assortment of programing offered by early broadcasters induced millions of Americans to purchase television receivers. The four networks, and their partners at local stations, offered something for everybody. Over the course of a typical day, stations scheduled shows on everything from current affairs to cooking. Crime dramas aired alongside variety shows, wrestling, religious sermons, and programs for children featuring TV cowboys and puppets. Most of this programing was produced live from local or network studios.

Throughout this book, I note the continuing influence and legacy of the early programs that aired on DuMont and other networks. Program genres and production techniques familiar to modern viewers were established through trial and error during television's first decade. In addition, DuMont and the other networks introduced viewers to the sorts of stock characters that continue today: ditzy wives, blustery husbands, ingratiating daytime hosts, tough cops, righteous social and political commentators, and off-the-wall late-night comedians. The people who worked in television during the 1940s and 1950s were skillful in determining the types of programs for which the medium was most suited. It is no wonder that three of the four networks responsible for much of this programing continue to occupy prominent spots on cable converter boxes today. The fourth pioneering network, DuMont, folded in 1955 and is largely forgotten. Yet DuMont was instrumental in bringing television to America and setting the stage for what has followed.

DuMont aired approximately 200 different series, plus numerous news and sports specials, from 1946 to 1955. Rather than attempting to catalog or analyze every DuMont program, I focus on the shows that earned the highest ratings, ran for the longest period of time, attracted the most press coverage, and influenced the scheduling, advertising, and production techniques of other local and network broadcasters. To determine the DuMont programs that were most memorable and significant, I also spoke with people who worked in the television industry during the 1940s and 1950s. DuMont crew members and talent described the thrill of working with Jackie Gleason as he created his best-known characters, including Ralph Kramden of "The Honeymooners." Cameramen and engineers explained how they experimented with camera and lighting techniques to create programs like *The Plainclothes Man*, a gritty detective show that was shot from the first-person perspective of the lead character. Many former DuMont employees were most proud of *Captain Video*, a quirky children's adventure set in outer space. Through my conversations, I learned about the thrill, and occasional frustration, of working on live productions during the birth of commercial television.

The search for copies of programs from the 1940s and 1950s represents a great challenge for television historians. DuMont's most popular and influential programs were broadcast live from the network's New York studios. In the days before videotape and reruns none of the television networks preserved their programs. Occasionally, however, broadcasters made kinescopes, which were created by filming television monitors that showed the programs as they aired live. These kinescope films were shipped to affiliated stations across the country that did not broadcast the programs live. While DuMont aired thousands of programs from 1946 to 1955, only about 400 kinescopes have survived. Many of these are available for viewing at the Museum of Television and Radio in New York and Los Angeles, and the UCLA Film and Television Archive in Los Angeles. Some series are better represented in the archives than others. For example, there are only four extant episodes of *The Plainclothes Man*, a weekly police drama that ran for nearly five years, but UCLA holds a near-complete run (74 episodes) of *The Morey Amsterdam Show*, which aired on DuMont for eighteen months. A few additional kinescopes of various programs have made it into the hands of collectors. Through a combination of travel to archives and extensive sleuthing through the world of film and television collectors, I was able to view at least one episode from each of DuMont's most prominent series.[2]

This book would not have been possible without the help of many television industry veterans who shared their memories and their memorabilia. They helped me understand a time, a place, and a company that was long gone by the time I was born. Les Arries Jr., Norman Baer, Ted Bergmann, Edward Bobley, Bishop Edwin Broderick, Judy Crichton, Hal Cooper, Olga Druce, Stan Epstein, Arthur Forrest, Thomas T. Goldsmith, Don Hastings, Dave Hollander, Wes Kenney, Marvin Pakula, Irwin Rostin, Howard Rubin, Don Russell, Mary Kay Stearns, and Chris Witting were unfailingly generous with their time and with precious photographs and scrapbooks documenting their work. Special thanks to Bruce DuMont and Yvonne DuMont Stelle for their insightful stories and observations about Allen B. Du Mont.

In the course of my research, I was fortunate to encounter writers, collectors, and Web masters who shared my interest in DuMont and early television. Clarke Ingram, Charles Grant, Jerry King, and Alan Ruiter offered valuable information about DuMont's personnel, programing, and business operations. Mike Berro, Dave Goldin, Tom Kleinschmidt, Bob Reed, Bruce Simon, and Richard Warner loaned me an assortment of materials, from program guides to audio tapes. I am especially grateful to Rory Coker for tutoring me on the wonders of *Captain Video* and reviewing a draft of the *Captain Video* chapter.

Thomas Doherty served as a constant source of inspiration through his own work and his discussions with me about television history and the publishing business. David Marc shared several fascinating interviews that he conducted with television pioneers as part of an oral history project at the Center for the Study of Popular Television, Syracuse University. Paul Feldman, a basketball buddy who also practices law, gave me lots of helpful advice. James L. Baughman, Virginia Field, Don Godfrey, Jeffrey Miller, and Michael Socolow reviewed this manuscript at various stages of development. I cannot thank them enough.

I remain indebted to many passionate and knowledgeable librarians and archivists. Thanks to John Fleckner, David Haberstich, Rueben Jackson, Kay Peterson, Deborra Richardson, and Wendy Shay at the Archives Center of the Smithsonian Institution, National Museum of American History in Washington; Tom Connors, Michael Henry, and Chuck Howell at the Library of American Broadcasting, University of Maryland; Jane Klain at the Museum of Television and Radio in New York; Zoe Berman at the UCLA Film and Television Archive. Howard Mandelbaum (Photofest), Muriel Reis (Fox Television), and Thomas Rockwell (Norman Rockwell Family Agency) facilitated the use of several photos and illustrations.

The National Endowment for the Humanities granted two Independent Study, Research, and Development (ISRD) awards that provided me with time to research and write this manuscript. I have been fortunate to be surrounded by smart and supportive NEH colleagues willing to chat about DuMont and more general issues regarding historical research and writing.

Thanks to Micah Kleit, my editor, for recognizing the potential of a book on DuMont, trusting me to write the book, and providing constant guidance along the way.

Friends and family patiently allowed me to ramble about DuMont and early television for nearly four years. Chief listeners were Jonathan Markovitz, Diane Frendak, and Greg Wahl, who had the good sense to tempt me away from DuMont when I needed a vacation, a hockey game, or a beer. Jonathan and Greg also read drafts of this manuscript.

As children of the 1940s and 1950s, my parents, Judy and Steve Weinstein, shared their thoughts and memories and offered gentle encouragement.

Most of all, I thank Rachel Weinstein, my partner in this book and in life.

Allen B. Du Mont examines a cathode-ray tube.

Source: Allen B. Du Mont Collection, Archives Center, National Museum of American History, Smithsonian Institution.

1

My Father Was an Engineer

For a generation of Americans, the name "DuMont" stood for innovation, entertainment, and an exciting new medium called television. After World War II, when television took a rapid hold of the country, many people first watched TV on DuMont brand sets, the best receivers that money could buy. While it made its mark as a manufacturer, DuMont Laboratories was most familiar to Americans as the parent company of the DuMont Television Network. In 1946, DuMont used its New York and Washington, D.C., stations as the foundation for one of America's first television networks. The DuMont network eventually reached from coast to coast. Jackie Gleason got his big break on DuMont, where he and his writers created "The Honeymooners." Other DuMont stars like Bishop Fulton Sheen and Morey Amsterdam, along with fictional characters like detective Rocky King and the children's space hero Captain Video, helped Americans make sense of the postwar world and shaped the television programing that followed.

By the middle of 1955, DuMont Laboratories was in shambles and the network ceased operations. Allen Du Mont was forced to relinquish control over the company that he founded in 1931. No other company challenged the three-network oligopoly of NBC, CBS, and ABC until 1985, when Rupert Murdoch purchased six stations as the foundation for his new Fox Television Network. The DuMont story concerns money, power, politics, business, and the birth of commercial television in America. It shows how three large radio networks took control of television broadcasting from 1946 to 1955. Like pioneering entrepreneurs in other industries, from automobiles to computer software, Du Mont and his company were swamped by bigger, tougher competitors. But CBS, NBC, and ABC were not the only parties responsible for the DuMont network's extinction. The Federal Communications Commission (FCC), Paramount Pictures, DuMont's executives, and Allen Du Mont himself all played important roles in the network's many successes and its ultimate demise.

Like much on early television, DuMont programs displayed a charming and somewhat innocent faith in the power of television to enhance the lives of viewers and to help bring about a safer and happier world. This optimistic view of television was most clearly articulated by Allen Du Mont, the head of the company and one of the people most responsible for the postwar introduction of television. The key to understanding how the DuMont network operated, including its successes and failures, begins with the man on top of the DuMont Laboratories television empire. Trained as an engineer, Allen Du Mont had a gift for working with electronics, starting with his first jobs as a production manager at Westinghouse and then at the De Forest Radio Company during the 1920s. Facing unemployment in 1931, Allen Du Mont started DuMont Laboratories with $1,000. He operated out of the basement of his Upper Montclair, New Jersey, home. Initially, DuMont developed cathode-ray tubes used to display electronic images in instruments. In 1937, the company bought a new factory and moved into television. DuMont's tubes, which could display a TV picture without quickly burning out, made commercial television possible. Historian Les Brown explained that "Du Mont transformed the cathode-ray tube from a fragile, short-lived device to a reliable piece of equipment around which practical TV receivers could be built."[1] In 1938, DuMont began to license its picture tubes to other manufacturers and added a line of receivers to its electronic instruments, establishing itself as one of the country's first manufacturers of TV sets. During World War II, DuMont also built an experimental station in New York which served as the DuMont network's flagship when commercial television was introduced to the country after the war.

DuMont's slogan, "First With the Finest," referred mostly to the company's receivers, which had a reputation as "the Cadillac" of television sets, but DuMont also manufactured high-quality equipment, such as cameras and transmitters, used by television stations.[2] By 1950, DuMont Laboratories had annual sales of $76 million (approximately $580 million in 2003 dollars).[3] Allen Du Mont became a folk hero, widely praised for his accomplishments as an inventor and manufacturer of high-quality television equipment. He was also a prototype of the successful American entrepreneur, demonstrating, in the words of *New Yorker* writer Robert Rice, "perseverance, equanimity, intelligence, physical energy, loyalty to associates, devotion to his family, and the strength of mind to be able to refrain from taking more than one cocktail at lunch."[4] Du Mont was a favored speaker at luncheons for professional associations and businessmen. As an executive, he also won awards from a variety of outfits, including *Forbes* (Outstanding Business Leader, 1951) and the American Schools and Colleges Association (Horatio Alger Award, 1949). Du Mont's alma mater, Rensselaer Polytechnic Institute, awarded him an honorary Doctor of Engineering degree in 1944. Throughout the 1940s and early 1950s, magazine articles widely credited Du Mont as a technology guru who also understood the business of TV.

Despite his prominence, Allen Du Mont was not a gregarious or magnetic leader. A typical magazine portrait cautioned that "if one expects to meet the dominant, loud tycoon type, he will be disappointed, for Du Mont is mild, retiring, friendly." The *Popular Boating* profile also noted that Du Mont was not physically imposing. The "short, stocky man" walked with a noticeable limp, left by a childhood polio attack.[5] Even when he started to make money from DuMont Laboratories, Allen Du Mont was not flashy. As the *New Yorker* observed in 1951, "Extreme conservatism governs almost everything he does. He has owned automobiles [from] the same manufacturer (Chrysler) for twenty-five years and has seldom driven any one of them more than fifty miles an hour . . . For the last couple of years, his wife has been urging him to redecorate his office, which contains the same furniture that he has used for years."[6] According to Du Mont's daughter, Yvonne DuMont Stelle, her father did not entertain people from work or bring company business to the family's northern New Jersey home at the end of the day.[7] He also did not frequently venture into Manhattan to see a Broadway show, a night-club act, or a live television production, even though Du Mont would have received royal treatment as the head of the network and a minor celebrity in his own right. According to his close friend, Thomas T. Goldsmith, Du Mont enjoyed the local theater around Montclair, New Jersey, but his physical disability sometimes made it difficult for him to travel into the city.[8] Instead, Du Mont spent many evening and weekend hours in the electronic research laboratory located a few hundred yards from his home.[9]

Other than television, Allen Du Mont's passion was boating, something he did alone or with a select group of friends and relatives. Du Mont's boat, the *Hurricane III*, afforded him an opportunity to practice engineering and navigation on the seas. He excelled in "predicted log races," in which boaters calculated the exact time at which they would pass predetermined marks in a course which might run from 35 to 150 miles. The races required participants to consider a number of variables, including the current, tide, and winds. One boating magazine noted that "Du Mont does not win often but he is remarkably consistent and seldom, if ever, has a bad race." As a measure of Du Mont's dedication to boating, he won the American Power Boat Association's national championship for accumulating the most points in races in three consecutive years: 1953, 1954, and 1955.[10] Around the time of the World Series, Du Mont would take his annual cruise from Long Island to Florida, frequently accompanied by Goldsmith, DuMont's longtime head of research. Even on vacation, the two scientists indulged in their shared passion for television during these journeys. Du Mont had a TV on board which he would use to watch the ball games while Goldsmith steered the ship. "We learned a lot about television broadcasting there because we would get signals from distant stations, and we'd survey the performance of television from Maine clear down to the tip of Florida," Goldsmith said.[11] Boating provided a welcome element of risk and excitement in Allen Du Mont's otherwise conservative life outside the office. As Du Mont told Edward R. Murrow in a 1955 interview on *Person to Person* (CBS), "I find that when you get out in the ocean, the problems level off. In other words, any problems that you have in you business, when you're out in the ocean, wondering if you're going to get back or not, why, they don't seem so important."[12]

Many friends and colleagues described Allen Du Mont as gentle and naive, suggesting that these qualities may have hindered the entrepreneur, especially in dealing with his business partners at Paramount Pictures.[13] "If anything, his problem was trusting people and taking them at their word," said his daughter Stelle. "He gave his word and it was always good, and he expected other people to be the same, and they're not."[14] Ted Bergmann, a former DuMont executive, learned about his boss's ethics when Du Mont asked him to replace Chris Witting as the head of the Broadcasting Division in early 1954. Bergmann explained to Du Mont that there were no Jewish network presidents. "Doc, the major advertisers and advertising agencies do not have Jewish executives and they don't do business with Jewish executives."

"What are you talking about?" Du Mont replied. "There's [David] Sarnoff and there's [William] Paley."

"They don't contact advertisers," Bergmann explained. "At NBC it's Pat Weaver, at CBS it's Jack Van Volkenberg, and at ABC it's Bob Kintner. You won't find a Jew in any of those top spots."

Du Mont then looked at Bergmann and said, "Ted, if any of these companies don't want to do business with us because you're Jewish, I don't want their business."

"You've got to love a man who says a thing like that," said Bergmann. "And I did."[15]

The DuMont network needed people like Bergmann, who knew the entertainment business. Even though Allen Du Mont was the president and founder of one of the leading television companies, he had little interest in fundamental aspects of postwar network broadcasting, such as production techniques, aesthetics, scheduling, or advertising sales. Science was his genius and his passion. "My father was an engineer," remembered Stelle. "He never intended to be president of a major company."[16] His friend Goldsmith agreed that Du Mont's "real love was in the laboratory. He was happiest when he was doing technical things."[17] If Du Mont watched TV, it was mostly to study reception and other technical matters, rather than programing. In a 1951 *New Yorker* profile, author Robert Rice quipped that "Du Mont is always stimulated by Milton Berle's horizontal resolution, if not his jokes."[18] Larry Israel, the first sales manager of DuMont's Pittsburgh station, WDTV, remembered watching television with Allen Du Mont during one of Du Mont's trips to the station. The company president repeatedly fiddled with the back of the set to adjust the picture. When Israel pointed out that they were watching a wonderful program, Du Mont was not the least bit interested, according to Israel.[19]

Given Du Mont's strengths and weaknesses, it was probably good for the network that he did not try to implement a particular programing style. Du Mont showed little aptitude for, or interest in, running a television network. Even more experienced competitors like William Paley of CBS and David Sarnoff, head of NBC's parent company, RCA, did not know how to fill airtime when they began the monumental job of selling television to the public after World War II. Networks adapted genres and techniques from theater, film, radio, and print magazines, but everything had to be reconfigured. Management turned to young and ambitious executives, producers, directors, and talent on both sides of the camera. Nowhere was this more true than at DuMont.

Working through its national network—including owned-and-operated stations in New York, Pittsburgh, and Washington, D.C.—DuMont was an early leader in television production and distribution. Its programs addressed many of the pressing issues of postwar urban life: crime, communism, faith, gender roles, ethnic identity, and the search for community in old cities and new suburbs. During DuMont's greatest burst of creativity, from 1949 to 1952, the network introduced viewers to a fantastic range of people and programs. On DuMont, a confident daytime television host flirted with his pretty co-host while proclaiming his devotion to mothers everywhere. A space-age superhero confronted intergalactic bullies. A little Jewish comic with snappy one-liners enjoyed fame for a little while, before a big Irish comedian came along to overshadow him, and everybody else on television, with a cavalcade of sketches and characters. Hard-boiled detectives taught criminals that crime doesn't pay, and a Catholic priest showed viewers how stronger faith and morality could solve the world's problems.

The best word to describe television before 1952 on all networks, especially DuMont, is "giddy." Regardless of the genre, DuMont programs celebrated the greatest postwar innovation, television itself, with a playful self-reflexivity and enthusiasm, as if the people making the shows were inviting the home audience to join the amazing new world of television. Whereas the other networks sometimes transferred older and more experienced radio executives and directors into television, most of the staff at DuMont were not yet professionally established. They were entranced by the magic of television and enthusiastic over the prospect of entering a new industry on the ground floor. DuMont's programs conveyed the excitement that network personnel felt living in New York City and working in the fledgling television business.

The story of how DuMont and three other companies created network television is relevant and inspiring today, given the state of the contemporary television industry. Advances in digital and satellite distribution have created almost unlimited viewing options, but, more than ever before, television executives are prisoners of history and convention, stuck in a losing game. They copy the latest hit shows while desperately trying to craft a unique and recognizable network brand or identity that will stand out amidst the sea of channels. Program genres and visual styles shift slightly from time to time, and channel to channel, but not much is new. DuMont is a reminder of what television was like when everything was new.

Allen Du Mont (left) with his friend David Sarnoff, president of RCA, circa 1944.

Source: The Raster, January 1945, Allen B. Du Mont Collection, Archives Center, National Museum of American History, Smithsonian Institution.

2

From Basement to Broadway

One day in 1912, William Du Mont, an executive with the Waterbury Clock Company, bought a new radio kit for his son, Allen, who was home sick. The eleven-year-old boy was confined to the bedroom in the family's Brooklyn home, suffering from a polio attack that left him with a severe limp for the rest of his life. By the time Allen B. Du Mont returned to school almost a year later, he had built a radio receiver and a transmitter. At the age of twelve, Du Mont was hooked on electronic engineering. "Maybe this attack of polio I had was a blessing in disguise," he later said.[1] In 1912, radio was a novelty. Guglielmo Marconi, a young Italian inventor, had patented a successful wireless apparatus and formed the world's first radio company only fifteen years earlier. Throughout the 1910s, a network of amateur operators built radios and shared engineering tips in clubs that they formed across the country. Members did not even have to leave their bedrooms to participate: meetings took place "in the air," on a prearranged wavelength. Since the technology for sending voices over the air had not yet been developed, radio operators generally communicated via Morse code and attempted to send and receive signals over long distances. Hugo Gernsback, editor of *Modern Electrics* magazine and an officer in the Wireless Association of America, estimated that 122 wireless clubs and 400,000 "wireless experimenters and amateurs" were active in 1912.[2] Radio fired the imagination of Du Mont and thousands of others, introducing them to the magic of instant communication via invisible electromagnetic waves.

After Allen's recovery from polio, the Du Mont family moved to Montclair, New Jersey, where the young man continued to experiment with radio. At the age of fifteen, he earned his wireless license from the government by passing a set of exams that tested his ability to assemble, operate, and repair radio equipment.[3] Du Mont spent every summer vacation from 1916 to 1924 working as a radio operator on merchant ships that took him around the world. These dual passions for broadcast engineering and boating remained with Du Mont for his entire life. In 1924, the promising scientist graduated from Rensselaer Polytechnic Institute in Troy, New York, and took a job with the Westinghouse Lamp Company in Bloomfield, New Jersey. When Du Mont started at Westinghouse, the company was making only 500 radio tubes a day. As demand for receivers continued to boom through the 1920s, Du Mont redesigned the plant and increased output to 50,000 tubes a day. For his efforts, Allen Du Mont earned a Westinghouse employee award and a hefty $500 bonus in 1927.

In 1928, Du Mont left Westinghouse for a position as chief engineer of the De Forest Radio Company, headed by the legendary radio inventor and entrepreneur, Lee De Forest. Allen Du Mont's few years at De Forest marked the last time until 1960 that he would work in a company bearing someone else's name. De Forest was in the process of reorganization in 1928 and had not produced anything for a year. Applying some of the skills that he honed at Westinghouse, Du Mont helped the De Forest plant produce up to 30,000 tubes a day. He was rewarded with a promotion to vice-president in charge of engineering and manufacturing for the company. Du Mont also had the opportunity to direct De Forest's experimental research in mechanical television, conducting a few early TV transmissions through station W2XCD.[3] In 1931, Allen Du Mont returned from a vacation in Bermuda to find himself out of work and De Forest Radio on the verge of collapse. Perhaps taking a cue from Lee De Forest, Du Mont decided to start his own enterprise, rather than looking for a new job at another firm. The young engineer applied his aptitude for electronics and management to develop cathode-ray tubes for a variety of devices, including television.

DuMont Laboratories Before Television

At the age of thirty, during an economic depression, with a wife and a two-year-old son to support, Du Mont formed the Allen B. DuMont Laboratories. Although the new company was the riskiest venture of Allen Du Mont's life, he ran the business with typical caution. DuMont Laboratories started with $1,000 and a three-person staff. The boss saved overhead by operating from the basement of his Upper Montclair, New Jersey home, and supported his family with occasional work as an expert witness in patent litigation cases. Still, Du Mont made sacrifices to keep his electronics firm afloat, borrowing money from relatives and other sources, including his life insurance policy. The entrepreneur later estimated that he invested at least $30,000 (more than $400,000 in 2003 dollars) in his company during its first four or five years.[4]

Du Mont initially focused on the design and sale of cathode-ray tubes. In these years before television's commercial introduction, DuMont Laboratories' biggest item was the oscillograph, used for testing electrical equipment. University and government research laboratories were the main purchasers of DuMont's oscillographs.[5] As demand for oscillographs increased, the company moved out of the Du Mont family basement and into a row of five stores that served as a small research and production facility. In 1935, Allen Du Mont formed a partnership with Mortimer Loewi, an investor who stayed in DuMont management through 1953, and formally incorporated DuMont Laboratories. Du Mont celebrated by paying himself a modest salary for the first time. Two years later, DuMont Laboratories sold RCA the rights to one of Allen Du Mont's inventions: a cathode-ray instrument, known as the "magic eye," which was used to tune radio (and later TV) receivers. DuMont invested the $19,750 that the company received from RCA in a new corporate home, purchasing a plant that had previously served as a pickle factory in Passaic, New Jersey.[6]

Still, the firm was small. In 1938, DuMont Laboratories had $1,428.16 in cash on hand, and an approximate net worth of about $60,000 (less than $1 million in 2003 dollars), with most of its assets in plant facilities and patents.[7] Despite its size, DuMont was a leader in the growing cathode-ray industry. In addition, DuMont's tubes could easily be adapted from oscillographs to serve as picture tubes in television receivers. Rather than merely licensing its patents and selling tubes to other manufacturers,

Du Mont and Loewi saw the opportunity to build on the company's expertise in cathode-ray technology by moving into the emerging industry of receiver manufacturing. They desperately searched for capital to build receivers for home viewers and transmitters for stations. "We felt that it was certainly an advantage to have [additional financing] soon," Du Mont remembered. "Because the longer you waited, the less opportunity to get in on the ground floor" of television.[8] Broadcasting was a secondary concern for Du Mont, intended primarily to make sure that consumers would have programing to watch on the DuMont TV sets. Allen Du Mont also believed that if his company started telecasting, it would stimulate others, who would not want to give DuMont Laboratories the competitive advantage of being the first, or only, TV operator in a particular city. As one of the few corporations ready to sell transmitters, cameras, and other TV equipment, DuMont stood to benefit from a boom in station construction.[9] However, raising money for television during the economic depression was not easy. The company's early financing efforts, including a public stock offering, were not successful. "Very few people had any faith in television," Du Mont later explained.[10]

In July 1938, a major film studio, Paramount Pictures, made DuMont an offer that it couldn't refuse. Paramount was primarily interested in DuMont's research and engineering capacity, which it planned to draw on for its own broadcasting plans. "The purpose of the investment was to develop an organization [with] which we could get equipment of the type we desired to continue our investigation in television, and to invest in a company which we thought had great potentialities for growth as television turned out to be successful," said Paul Raibourn, vice-president of Paramount in charge of television, at a 1952 FCC hearing.[11]

DuMont Laboratories' subsequent operations, based upon the July 26, 1938, contract, were a source of constant scrutiny by the FCC over the years, as the regulatory body assessed whether Paramount "controlled" DuMont. The agreement certainly gave Paramount a number of ways to check Allen Du Mont's power. It divided DuMont's common stock into two classes: A stock (owned by Allen Du Mont, his associates, and anyone else who wanted to buy it on the over-the-counter stock market) and B stock (owned exclusively by Paramount). The Class A stock holders elected three of the company's six directors plus the president and vice-president. Paramount had the power to choose the other three directors, along with the secretary, treasurer, and assistant treasurer. In exchange for its stake in DuMont, Paramount supplied a total of $200,000 in cash and loans (about $2.5 million in 2003 dollars).[12]

Allen Du Mont later regretted giving Paramount so much influence. Over the years, the studio contributed little to DuMont beyond its initial investment, and the FCC prevented the DuMont network from expanding because of Paramount's interest in DuMont Laboratories. Nevertheless, when Paramount made its offer, DuMont had little cash and limited options to finance its expansion into television. The small Passaic tube manufacturer was not operating from a position of strength.[13] The Paramount deal enabled DuMont to withstand a $95,000 loss in 1939, when the company began marketing receivers to a public that had no experience with home television.[14] Moreover, Paramount's resources, and its implicit confidence in the small electronics firm, attracted the attention of the trade press and distinguished Du-Mont as an industry leader on the eve of commercial television's unveiling. DuMont Laboratories was no longer a family business.

Steady Wartime Progress

With the Paramount agreement sealed, DuMont produced demonstration models of receivers for New York and New Jersey department stores by the end of 1938.[15] Still, there was little public awareness of the invention, and no programing, until the following year. RCA, the parent company of the NBC radio network, used the 1939 New York World's Fair to introduce its commercial television service. The fair's "Building the World of Tomorrow" theme provided the perfect occasion for RCA president David Sarnoff's announcement that NBC would begin telecasting a regular slate of programs for people to enjoy on new TV sets. The sets would be available at department stores and radio dealerships. Thousands of fair-goers watched Sarnoff and NBC's subsequent programs on receivers displayed in the massive RCA Hall of Television.[16] Sarnoff's telecast focused much of the public and trade press on RCA and New York City, but RCA was not the nation's first, or only, television company. Firms in Philadelphia (Philco, Farnsworth), Los Angeles (Don Lee Broadcasting), and Schenectady, New York (General Electric) had experimented with television throughout the 1930s, and additional stations in Los Angeles and Chicago came on line between 1939 and 1941.[17]

NBC operated the only New York television station (experimental W2XBS, later WNBT) after the inaugural World's Fair telecasts in the spring of 1939. DuMont obtained a permit to build its own experimental station, W2XWV, in April 1940. It officially inaugurated New York's second TV outlet with coverage of the 1940 elections. DuMont built a small studio and offices for station and network personnel on the 42nd floor of 515 Madison Avenue, a midtown office building. Production soon moved to a larger studio on the second floor, while corporate offices remained on the top level until DuMont moved to its own building in 1954. On July 1, 1941, CBS brought New York's third station (WCBW, later WCBS) on line.[18] NBC, DuMont, and CBS dominated television in New York and the rest of the East Coast through the late 1940s.

Programing on all stations was sporadic and even RCA's W2XBS went dark for two months, starting on August 1, 1940.[19] After America entered World War II, stations broadcast civil defense training programs and government films on topics such as victory gardens and food conservation. Lighter offerings included the occasional ball game, quiz show, variety program, or drama.[20] Compared to film and radio, the typical early television show was awkward and low-budget. The engineers who operated the station labored in DuMont's Passaic factory, building tubes and receivers during the day. They commuted into New York for television duties on Wednesday evenings and Sunday afternoons, the two days that W2XWV broadcast. In addition, anxious to promote the development of television after the war, DuMont lent its facilities to radio broadcasters like WOR and ABC, which were interested in learning about the new medium but did not yet own experimental stations. For example, *Billboard* described the start of a 1943 show called *WOR's Television College.* The program aired over DuMont's W2XWV, but was produced by WOR personnel. "Camera lenses opened on three girls lined up against a curtain backdrop. Why they were there, who they were, or what they were supposed to do remained a mystery for the first ten minutes of the program, though they appeared again and again in the same position, smiling self-consciously and obviously ill at ease."[21]

During World War II, only about 8,000 TV sets were in circulation nationally.[22] The goal of wartime telecasting was not to attract viewers. The

problem of creating and maintaining audiences became an industry obsession only after the war. Instead, telecasters used the delay in television's commercialization, brought on by the war, to test equipment, practice production techniques, and introduce sponsors to television. Almost
from the inauguration of its first experimental station, DuMont's sales
department devised creative deals for advertisers. Starting in the summer
of 1943, DuMont ran a midweek special: on Wednesdays, sponsors could
use the studio for commercial experimentation, without charge. In order
to stimulate interest in cameras and other technical equipment, DuMont
also encouraged "out of town radio station operators, who might be con-
templating television stations of their own," to visit W2XWV.[23] These
offers demonstrated an ambition and vision that the other stations lacked.
At the time, CBS and NBC had eliminated studio operations and simply
ran a few films, of little interest to advertisers, to satisfy the FCC's re-
quirement that they remain on the air 4 hours a week.[24] Sponsors eagerly
accepted the free airtime on W2XWV, trying everything from short, animated cartoons used as "fill-ins" between shows—a forerunner of the
commercials that are standard today—to sponsored news program with
live product pitches.[25] By the end of 1943, CBS and NBC followed Du-
Mont's example with their own advertising.

Between 1941 and 1945, electronics firms placed a priority on military
research and defense production; however, television research conducted
during the war improved the medium and strengthened the leading television broadcasters and manufacturers. Military contracts generated profits that put several firms, including RCA and DuMont, in a stronger position to finance postwar expansion.[26] Although DuMont was still a small
firm, with sales of $176,000 in 1940, business took off during the war
years. Staring in October 1940, DuMont manufactured portable radio
transmitter-receiver units and cathode-ray tubes for radar and loran navi-
gational instruments. In 1944, as the company's wartime production
peaked, DuMont sales surpassed $9 million ($91 million in 2003 dollars).
DuMont had 120 employees at the end of 1940, and more than ten times
that number in June 1945. When it was impossible to build onto the original Passaic facility, DuMont leased a second plant from the U.S. government in nearby Clifton, New Jersey. The factories were later converted
to produce television tubes for consumers.[27] By the end of the war, Du-
Mont and its competitors were prepared to launch network television.

Network Television Begins

In late 1945, DuMont began to experiment with television in Washington, D.C., through its second station, W3XWT. At the time, a total of seven prewar stations were regularly operating a few evenings each week in five different markets: Los Angeles, Chicago, New York City, Philadelphia, and Schenectady, New York.[28] On February 12, 1946, DuMont was ready to conduct a landmark transmission: the first telecast from Washington to New York since the earliest days of mechanical television in the late 1920s. DuMont gave the city's power brokers the first opportunity to become television celebrities. The program included interviews with Paul Porter, Chairman of the FCC, and Sam Rayburn, Speaker of the House. Viewers saw segments from three different remote locations: Capitol Hill, DuMont's downtown Washington studio, and the Lincoln Memorial, where General Eisenhower placed a wreath at the foot of the Lincoln statue as part of a commemorative service.[29] All three New York stations—WABD (DuMont), WNBT (NBC), and WCBW (CBS)—aired the Washington broadcast.

The FCC licensed Washington's Channel Five to DuMont in April 1946. This was the foundation for a permanent network between Washington and New York. At the time, only NBC was further along in developing network television. NBC and Philco, owner of station WPTZ in Philadelphia, had conducted sporadic transmissions between New York (WNBT), Schenectady (WRGB), and Philadelphia (WPTZ) starting in 1939. Stations in all other markets operated independently because of the difficulty and expense of conducting regular network broadcasts. DuMont signaled its intention to move network television out of the experimental era on April 15, 1946, unveiling its new studios located in the auditorium of the John Wanamaker department store in downtown Manhattan and transmitting the opening ceremonies via coaxial cable to Washington. The mayor of New York City, William O'Dwyer, and the governor of New Jersey, Walter Edge, were among the guests for a telecast that featured a few ceremonial speeches about the promise of television along with a short play, a quiz show, and a dance routine. The program also included a segment from Washington with various politicians and the acting FCC Chairman, Charles Denny. *Newsweek* panned the debut of "the country's first permanent commercial television network,"

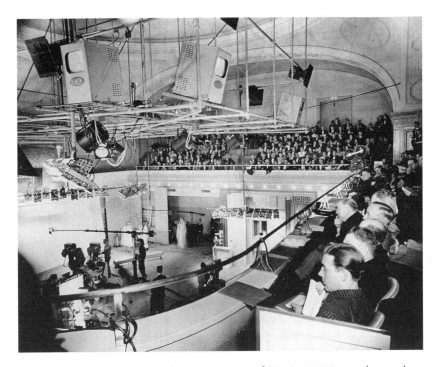

The view from the balcony at the inauguration of DuMont's Wanamaker studio, April 15, 1946.

Source: Allen B. Du Mont Collection, Archives Center, National Museum of American History, Smithsonian Institution.

writing that the speeches were too long and the entertainment "went off with all the enthusiastic gaucherie of high school productions."[30] Still, DuMont forged ahead. WABD continued to feed programing to the Washington station, which was granted commercial status as WTTG on November 29, 1946.[31] NBC also solidified its network plans in October 1946 by signing a formal agreement to share programing with WPTZ.[32] By early 1947, the New York flagship stations of both DuMont and NBC were airing a few hours of programs, three or four nights a week, for local viewers and affiliates in other Northeast cities.[33] Network television had begun.

The FCC and Network Television

While several companies announced network plans after the war, the leaders were NBC, DuMont, CBS, and ABC. Through its policy of allocating

TV stations from 1945 to 1952, the FCC ultimately determined which local and national firms would own valuable station licenses and which networks would prosper in the coming years. DuMont was not favored by the FCC. In fact, the commission's allocation system severely hindered the DuMont network and prevented any other firm from starting a fourth network until the mid-1980s.

The FCC allocated a different number of stations to each city. It then invited applications from companies that wanted to build and run these stations. Many of the first TV station operators were department stores, radio broadcasters, or newspaper publishers that were moving into television. Corporations like DuMont Laboratories that wanted to build a television network also applied for local TV station licenses. To ensure diversity of ownership, the FCC did not allow any company to own more than five station licenses. Except for these five stations per company, the FCC did not grant television stations directly to networks.

As they went on the air through the late 1940s, stations filled airtime with a mixture of their own local shows and programs that were produced by the national television networks. DuMont, NBC, CBS, and ABC competed with each other to build a network of stations that would air its productions. A network's survival depended on a strong affiliate line-up, since broadcasters had no means of distributing their programs from city to city without these affiliates. However, most cities were allocated fewer than four stations by the FCC. As a result, there were not enough stations in most markets for each of the four networks to have a "primary affiliate" that was likely to accept all of the programs that it offered. In Boston, for example, the four networks fought for time on only two stations.

The number of channels in each market was limited because of the technology by which television signals were transmitted from stations to home television receivers. Television signals traveled as electromagnetic waves that operated on particular frequencies, or channels. It was the FCC's job to regulate these airwaves and assign frequencies. In June 1945, the commission decided to set aside only thirteen television channels in the VHF (very high frequency) portion of the electromagnetic spectrum. However, no city had more than seven stations because the FCC could not assign adjacent channels (except for channels four and five) in the same city. Stations operating on identical or nearby frequencies interfered with each other. In fact, the FCC found that even stations 150 miles apart had problems if they were operating on the same channel.[34] FCC engineers understood that the only solution was to assign VHF channels that were spaced far away from one another. So, for example, the commission allocated the city of Washington, D.C., four stations: channels four, five, seven, and nine. Because of the problems of adjacent-channel interference, that left nearby Baltimore only three channels: two, eleven, and thirteen.

The FCC further reduced the number of VHF stations in May 1948, designating channel one for safety and emergency use. By the fall of 1948, the FCC recognized that the twelve VHF channels were insufficient to meet the television demands of consumers and potential station licensees. On September 23, 1948, the commission issued an order, soon known as "the freeze," that halted new authorizations while the FCC examined its plan for assigning stations.[35] The television industry did not come to a total stop during this time. The 123 stations that had already been authorized were allowed to retain their channel assignments. Thirty-seven were already broadcasting, the others were at varying stages of construction. Eventually, 108 actually went on the air before the freeze was lifted in April 1952.

For DuMont, the decision regarding the number of stations in each market was crucial. DuMont needed the FCC to allocate at least four stations in each city, so that each of the four leading networks would have the opportunity to sign a primary affiliate. During the freeze, the FCC decided that the best way to add stations would be to open a new band of frequencies, the UHF (ultra high frequency) band. One option was simply to add several UHF stations in each market, while retaining the existing VHF stations. The advantage of this plan was that it would not have interrupted service or caused major changes for the 108 stations that were operating by 1952, along with the fifteen million national households that had already purchased VHF television receivers.[36] The disadvantage was that the plan depended on the new UHF band to increase the number of stations in each market. In order to watch UHF, consumers would have had to purchase new "all-channel" receivers or special UHF converters. If people could watch VHF stations anyway, there was no guarantee that they would go to the effort and expense of reconfiguring their TV sets for the new UHF stations.

A powerful coalition of local station owners lobbied the FCC to retain the extant VHF stations, with additional UHF channels added as needed.[37] They did not want to move their channels, reconvert engineering operations for UHF, and face increased competition. On the other side, DuMont proposed a more radical system that would not have "intermixed" UHF and VHF stations in a single market. Some cities would have had multiple UHF stations, but no VHF; others would have been VHF-only markets. DuMont expected that the new UHF stations allocated under its plan would have been successful because they would not have been competing against the VHF stations. Without VHF alternatives, consumers in these cities would have purchased new UHF TV sets and converters. Ultimately, DuMont's plan would have created more stations in each city and a more viable multi-network system: eighty-eight of the top one hundred markets would have had four or more stations.[38]

In its Sixth Report and Order, issued on April 11, 1952, the FCC ended the freeze with a plan that maintained the existing VHF system, despite its limitations, as the primary tool for providing the country with television. In many markets, the FCC authorized additional UHF stations, which were expected to compete with the VHF stations.[39] No established stations were moved to UHF. The commission allocated four or more commercial VHF stations in only seven of the country's top one hundred markets.[40] The FCC ultimately "took the familiar regulatory protectionist policy of not wishing to upset the applecart, not wanting to change the status quo and disrupt service to the public," wrote economic historian Barry Litman.[41]

As Allen Du Mont and others predicted in their testimony before the FCC, UHF stations did not challenge the VHF's. Some went out of business. Others never even made it on air. With so many VHF stations established, the public did not purchase UHF receivers. In May 1954, for example, *Business Week* estimated that there were approximately 26 million VHF receivers and only 2 or 3 million UHF sets in use.[42] Historian James L. Baughman explained, "Many early UHF tuners were poorly designed and all cost more than the sets providing only VHF . . . As a result, the typical UHF station manager found that his outlet enjoyed only five to twenty percent of the total audience his VHF competitor commanded."[43] A 1958 Senate report recognized the prescience

and value of DuMont's earlier allocation proposal before the FCC, praising its "breadth of understanding of the problem and [its] professional
quality. This comprehensive project . . . saw with lucidity the fatal dangers of intermixture." The report recognized the FCC's 1952 ruling as
a "major factor" in the DuMont network's demise.[44] But by 1958, it was
too late for the FCC to change its allocation system. Frieda Hennock, an
FCC commissioner when the Sixth Report and Order was released, later
told a congressional subcommittee investigating the FCC that the real
reasons for the allocation decision were not given in the FCC's official
notices. Instead, she attributed the flawed plan to the powerful industry
lobbyists who "can come in and see this commission day and night and
can honeycomb our offices and our staff legally and that is where you get
intermixture and all the evils that your [UHF] debacle stems from."[45]

The Radio Networks Move into Television

During the nearly four years of the freeze, the emerging networks—
ABC, CBS, DuMont, and NBC—scrambled to persuade the relatively
few telecasters on the air to carry their programs. As 1949 began, only
about fifty stations were operating in the entire country. Of the twenty-
eight cities with television, twenty-one had only one or two stations.
These stations usually designated one network as its primary supplier
of programing, even though it picked the best programs from all four
national broadcasters.[46] While DuMont could get a few of its programs
on stations across the country, it had trouble lining up primary affiliates
that were likely to air whatever the network offered. Most TV stations
were affiliated with either CBS or NBC, the leading radio operators.
DuMont was the only television network that did not also operate a
radio network, and this lack of broadcast experience was damaging in
the fierce competition for affiliates. More than 80 percent of the pre-
freeze TV station owners also had AM radio stations in the same markets. As they moved into television, these local operators usually retained their AM network affiliations out of a combination of loyalty and
self-interest. The expectation was that radio stars would soon move into
television, and local operators feared that the radio networks would
yank profitable programs, on radio and television, if stations chose a different television affiliate.[47] In a July 1949 report, DuMont executive

Chris Witting warned DuMont Laboratories' top management to "get the FCC to frown upon TV-AM combines."[48] Despite Witting's concerns, DuMont was not in a position to influence the FCC on the matter. The commission did nothing to impede the established radio networks as they extended their control of broadcasting into television.

While many stations chose primary affiliations with one of the radio networks, they also signed affiliate contracts with all four networks, so they had the option of airing the best programs available.[49] Ted Bergmann, who was with DuMont from 1947 to 1955, rising from advertising salesman to managing director of the network, recalled that "even though we had an affiliation agreement with stations, it didn't mean that they would open up time for us. It would depend on the value of the program being offered and the closeness of the affiliation."[50] By the end of 1950, 107 stations were operating nationally, in sixty-two cities. Fifty cities had only one or two stations. These stations carried programing on all four networks, but gave most of their time to CBS and NBC programs. In December 1950, for example, NBC's prime-time programs routinely aired in more than forty markets, and its top shows, like *Texaco Star Theater* with Milton Berle, reached sixty-one markets from coast to coast. CBS also routinely reached at least forty cities with popular programs like *Arthur Godfrey and His Friends*, *Toast of the Town* with Ed Sullivan, and its *Studio One* theater presentations. In contrast, DuMont's most popular program, *Cavalcade of Stars* with Jackie Gleason, aired in only twelve markets at the time, and the program was seen no further west than Chicago. Through the early 1950s, DuMont could rely on outlets in only nine different cities, mostly located in the Midwest and the Northeast, to carry most or all of its programs live. Additional stations from across the country, including San Francisco and Los Angeles, would occasionally telecast DuMont's more popular offerings, but they did not accept everything.[51]

West Coast affiliates aired most DuMont programs as "kinescopes," which were filmed recordings of live programs. Networks and sponsors generally preferred that affiliates carry programs live because it was easier to promote a show nationally if it aired at the same time everywhere. Kinescopes were also of poor technical quality. Nevertheless, all networks and their affiliates commonly used kinescopes before the advent of videotape in 1956. Stations had more flexibility in scheduling the kinescopes, since they could show the films at any time. In some markets, kinescopes also were cheaper and easier to distribute than live shows, which were transmitted from city to city via coaxial cables that were rented from AT&T. Western broadcasters did not even have the option of airing live shows from New York until the coaxial cable that transmitted network programs to California was inaugurated on September 4, 1951.

By the end of 1952, DuMont's nine primary affiliates gave the network access to more than 8.5 million living room, representing about 40 percent of the nation's homes with television.[52] Even though millions of Americans watched DuMont programs, the network did not have the national reach to compete with NBC and CBS. As a last resort, DuMont turned to Washington for help with its affiliate problems. Allen Du Mont and his top executives spent the last three years of the network's life unsuccessfully trying to persuade the FCC, Congress, and even President Eisenhower to adopt a system that would allow more competition and better TV service for the country.[53] Du Mont, who led his company's lobbying efforts, was never very effective in comparison to his counterparts. "NBC and CBS had powerful lobbies in Washington that were intent on keeping the status quo," explained Ted Bergmann, the longtime DuMont executive. "Their head men, David Sarnoff and Frank Stanton, were down there themselves, constantly lobbying to maintain the FCC allocation structure."[54] Sarnoff and Stanton also had skillful people working behind the scenes. Les Arries Jr., general manager of DuMont's Washington, D.C., station, WTTG-TV, remembered the power of Washington lobbyists Frank "Scoop" Russell (NBC) and Earl Gammons (CBS). "They could walk down the halls of Congress and either kill a bill unfavorable to broadcasting or get something passed."[55]

Robert Doyle, a longtime television news producer who had one of his first industry jobs as an assistant to NBC's Russell in the late 1940s, once delivered a packet of cash to an elected official on behalf of his boss. He claimed that Russell "changed the color [television standards] decision all by himself, practically. I'd always accused him of buying off, of bribing, the FCC. He never denied it either."[56] One former FCC chairman dubbed the 1950s "the whorehouse era," because of the agency's reputation for bias and its tendency to show political favoritism and a susceptibility to bribery. As historian Baughman wrote, a pattern emerged of "ex parte contacts: commissioners fraternizing with and accepting gifts and loans from license applicants and their lobbyists."[57] DuMont apparently did not participate in any of these activities.

In comparison with the top management at CBS and NBC, Allen Du Mont was not very smooth. Bergmann remembered a meeting that he and Du Mont had with President Eisenhower in the Oval Office over the UHF standards. "Doc [Du Mont] launched into a dissertation describing in technical terms the difference between UHF and VHF, and how the FCC had screwed up the allocations," Bergmann wrote. "Ike gave him about ten minutes before stating that he didn't understand what Doc was talking about. He said he had people who handled these matters, stood up, and ushered us out of the office."[58] The performance before Eisenhower was not unusual. In many public appearances, including testimony before the FCC and Congress, Du Mont had trouble crafting succinct explanations of technical matters for a general audience. He frequently took his friend Thomas T. Goldsmith, DuMont's head of research, with him to present the company's engineering recommendations. "Tommy Goldsmith was very much an extrovert and Du Mont was very much an introvert," Bergmann said.[59]

Paramount and the "Control" Issue

In dealing with the FCC, DuMont was further handicapped by its relationship with Paramount, a company that had two strikes against it: Paramount was a movie company at a time when the FCC favored established radio broadcasters and Paramount was tainted by its history of antitrust violations.[60] In a decision adopted on February 9, 1953, less than a year after the Sixth Report and Order was released, the FCC dealt another blow to DuMont's network operations by ruling that Paramount "controlled" DuMont. In the FCC's eyes, DuMont and Paramount were a single entity. At the time, the FCC limited companies from owning more than five VHF outlets. Paramount already owned one station in Los Angeles, KTLA, and it was considering applying for others. The 1953 ruling meant that KTLA counted toward DuMont's five-station limit. Since DuMont already owned stations in New York City, Washington, and Pittsburgh, it would be able to apply for, at most, one more license.[61]

The FCC decision cited a history of cooperation between the management of Paramount and DuMont, the voting power of Paramount's stock, and Paramount's authority to appoint directors and officers of DuMont. Even though DuMont was, once again, on the losing end before the FCC, the 1953 decision regarding Paramount was more reasonable than the FCC's Sixth Report and Order, issued the previous year. As Gary Hess noted in his careful but sympathetic study of DuMont, written in 1960 with the cooperation of many former company executives, "Events subsequent to this [1953] decision by the Commission have tended to support [the FCC's] contention . . . Paramount was able to block corporate action on matters which affected the network." The 1953 decision should not have come as a shock to anyone. In December 1948, the FCC had released a "temporary holding" that Paramount controlled DuMont. Nevertheless, neither DuMont nor Paramount addressed the problem directly by severing their relationship or radically reorganizing the company so that there could be no question regarding Paramount's control.[62]

Still, the ruling further hindered DuMont in its all-important quest for program outlets. In a 1953 report to Allen Du Mont, network director Chris Witting recognized a full complement of five stations as "a compelling ingredient in the future success of our broadcast operations."[63] Each DuMont owned-and-operated station provided an important source of revenue and a ready outlet for programing. In addition, DuMont and the other networks sometimes made deals to air particular shows on desirable stations, even though the FCC frowned on the practice because it removed programing power from local broadcasters. DuMont's station in Pittsburgh, WDTV, was especially useful for bartering time because it was the only station in the market. Roy Sharp, who was in network sales and affiliate relations at DuMont, remembered that DuMont's "ace in the hole was that they owned the station in Pittsburgh, so when they wanted clearances in Boston, they could put the arm on NBC or CBS. NBC got one hour in Pittsburgh and DuMont would get maybe six hours on the NBC station in Boston."[64] DuMont's competitors, NBC and ABC, each had five licenses by the start of the 1948 freeze. CBS unsuccessfully gambled on a color system that would have broadcast on the UHF band, and applied only for WCBS (New York) when the freeze began. It scrambled to purchase the full allotment of five stations through the early 1950s.[65]

Financing a Network

In addition to losing the fight for affiliates, DuMont was outstripped financially by its competitors. Prospective network broadcasters had to invest in an infrastructure that included programing, studio facilities, affiliates, and management in order to generate long-term profits in network television. It took an enormous amount of capital to build a television network and compete against CBS and NBC. Companies led by entrepreneurs like Allen Du Mont and Edward J. Noble, the Life Savers candy magnate who owned ABC, were overmatched. DuMont did not have the radio network, cash reserves, experienced management, or luck with the FCC that NBC enjoyed. Nor could it match CBS's assets: a radio network and record business, along with cash reserves of $27 million, to offset initial investments in television.[66] In fact, DuMont may have been spread too thin between network broadcasting, government contracting, and receiver manufacturing. The company had relatively small cash reserves (at most $7 million at the end of 1949), and a credit line that varied from year to year but generally was around $6 million ($45 million in 2003 dollars).[67] DuMont also raised money with additional stock offerings in 1948 ($2.7 million) and 1950 ($5.65 million).[68]

DuMont could have used its cash reserves or available credit to generate additional funds for the network, but such actions would have been risky. The other areas of operation, which had proven to be profitable since the late 1930s, also needed support for research, training, facilities, raw materials, promotion, and distribution. With the country's accelerated defense mobilization in 1950, for example, DuMont had to reconvert plants and conduct new research to support its government contracts while continuing to produce receivers for consumers.[69] DuMont was squeezed in 1950 when receiver sales declined throughout the industry. In 1951, DuMont showed losses of more than $500,000. Rather than having the luxury of using receiver profits to subsidize broadcasting and other areas, DuMont now needed additional funds to retool manufacturing operations and dispose of a large surplus of unsold TV sets.[70] Color television development also represented a multimillion dollar undertaking for DuMont. In fact, the company asked investors to forgo their 1952 stock dividend so that the profits could go into color TV research.[71] "Money would go where it was needed most,"

Ted Bergmann remembered. "Towards the end, manufacturing needed more money. That's why we sold the Pittsburgh station [in January 1955]. To generate more cash for the mother company."[72]

The Battle with ABC

Given DuMont's liabilities—relatively few affiliates and a lack of capital—the primary competitor for survival as the third network was not NBC or CBS. It was ABC, another relative newcomer to broadcasting. ABC was formed in 1943 after the FCC and the Supreme Court forced NBC to sell one of its two networks. NBC retained the more popular "NBC Red Network," allowing Edward J. Noble to purchase the weaker "NBC Blue Network," which Noble re-named ABC in 1946. Like DuMont, ABC had a hard time competing with NBC and CBS on television. Noble's firm did have the major advantage of owning TV stations in five key markets: New York, Detroit, Chicago, San Francisco, and Los Angeles. It secured additional affiliates that were already radio partners; however, equipment shortages and engineering problems stalled the construction of these stations, giving competitors a valuable head start. The key source of programing, WJZ-TV in New York, did not begin operations until August 10, 1948. The other ABC stations followed over the next year. With only a relatively new radio network to draw on, ABC had even less capital and fewer resources than DuMont.[73]

Advertisers and independent producers looking to purchase airtime used ABC or DuMont as a cheap alternative to NBC and CBS. *The Arthur Murray Party; Charlie Wild, Private Detective; The Adventures of Ellery Queen; Tom Corbett, Space Cadet; Johnny Jupiter;* and *The Paul Dixon Show* all appeared on both DuMont and ABC.[74] The two networks offered similar low-budget programing through the early 1950s, and it was hard to separate the contestants for third place, according to the facts and figures that the industry used to measure success: advertising revenue, program ratings, affiliate line-ups, and the number of sponsored programs that were aired weekly. ABC had higher advertising billings than DuMont in 1952 and 1953, but figures in all of the other categories were so comparable that each network could make legitimate arguments for its supremacy.[75] Moving beyond the numbers, however, the salesmen and executives at the two networks thought that DuMont was winning the battle by 1953. "We didn't have a lot of stations, but we had a lot more than ABC did," said Art Elliot, a former DuMont advertising salesman. "If we had been differently financed and differently managed at the top, I don't think that there's any doubt that we would have survived. The only reason ABC survived was that they had been in the radio business and they got [United Paramount Theatres'] backing."[76]

ABC was rescued by United Paramount Theatres (UPT), a new company that was spun off from Paramount in 1950 as part of an antitrust consent decree. Former UPT President Leonard Goldenson remembered that when his company offered to merge with ABC in 1951, DuMont had a slightly better affiliate line-up and provided stations with eight more hours of prime-time programing than ABC. In fact, Goldenson worried that the UPT directors would not approve the merger because of its concerns about DuMont's strength. "In time there would be enough advertising to support three networks," Goldenson wrote. "The trouble was, to most of my board, it was more likely this [third network] would be DuMont."[77] While the proposed merger went through a protracted FCC review process from August 1951 to February 1953, ABC continued to lose money and ground to DuMont. Longtime ABC manager Sterling Quinlan explained his network's situation. "Borrowing power had been extended to the limit . . . Paydays were met at the last minute. If the merger was denied, ABC was clearly facing bankruptcy. Its network would have to close along with some of its invaluable television franchises. DuMont then would [have] become the viable third network because certainly there was not room for four networks."[78] In March 1953, after the ABC-UPT merger was approved, DuMont network president Chris Witting assured Allen B. Du Mont that they had little to fear from ABC. "The last eighteen months have represented a period in which we have been the most serious competitive threat to ABC's existence and have effectively driven them from the position as the third network to that of the fourth in regard to program ratings."[79]

Witting underestimated his competitor. UPT had cash from the sale of movie theaters and was willing to pump a whopping $30 million (more than $200 million in 2003 dollars) into ABC's network operations.[80] In convincing his board to approve the merger, Goldenson correctly gambled that Paramount would not match this figure to bolster DuMont.[81] Under the guidance of Goldenson and network president Robert Kitner,

ABC also made smart programing decisions, including deals to air original productions from two Hollywood studios: Walt Disney and Warner
Bros. In contrast, while DuMont developed many new shows, it had a
spell of bad luck and aired few new critical or commercial successes after
the spring of 1952. DuMont also continued to struggle with Paramount
in a hostile partnership that ultimately contributed to the network's demise and Allen Du Mont's ouster from the company that he built.

The young DuMont production crew, standing in front of the WABD truck that was used to cover remote events, circa 1950.

Source: Courtesy of Arthur Forrest.

3

Who Is in Charge Here?

As the case of ABC demonstrated, strong management and ownership, with ready capital, was crucial in the highly competitive network television business. Instead of United Paramount Theatres or another partner with deep pockets, however, DuMont was saddled with Paramount. Even though DuMont had the opportunity to establish itself as the nation's third network, Paramount was not willing to invest more in DuMont's growth. The studio already owned approximately 25 percent of DuMont's outstanding stock, which it had purchased at a bargain rate, starting with the initial deal in 1938 and subsequently by exercising stock options. By 1950, its investment of approximately $164,000 was worth between $7.5 and $10 million (approximately $75 million in 2003 dollars).[1]

In 1938, DuMont Laboratories issued two classes of stock: Class A and Class B. Paramount was the sole owner of DuMont's Class B stock, which gave the company power the right to appoint three of DuMont's eight directors as well as the treasurer, assistant treasurer, and secretary. The remaining directors and officers were elected by the holders of Class A stock: Allen Du Mont, DuMont's employees, and investors who bought the stock on the over-the-counter market. From 1938 to 1955, the Class A stockholders made Allen Du Mont the president of Du Mont Laboratories and supported his choices for management and the board of directors. Even though the Class A stockholders had the right to appoint the majority of the directors, Paramount had veto power over major actions, such as stock offerings and the sale of assets, which had to be approved by both classes of stock holders.

As DuMont's value rose, Paramount protected its investment by exercising influence over corporate decisions, including financing of DuMont Laboratories and the network.[2] Paul Raibourn was Paramount's chief representative at DuMont. He simultaneously served as Paramount's vice-president in charge of television development and DuMont's treasurer. Paramount president Barney Balaban also served on the DuMont board. "I attended many meetings where Raibourn told Barney [Balaban] how he could save a few hundred dollars here and there at DuMont. Usually the money came out of program budgets," remembered Leonard Goldenson, who was part of the senior management at Paramount from 1938 to 1950 before heading UPT. "Backed by Barney, Raibourn constantly nitpicked and needled [Allen Du Mont] over the smallest expenditures. Du Mont came to the point where, psychologically, he thought he couldn't do anything without Raibourn's approval." Indeed, it was this insider knowledge that UPT could outspend Paramount and DuMont in network television that allowed Goldenson to win the support from his UPT board to merge with ABC.[3]

Allen Du Mont and his managers blamed DuMont's financial troubles on Paramount's frugality: its refusal to invest more in the company, and its attempts to bully network management into cutting costs at a time when DuMont should have spent more money to remain competitive.[4] Furthermore, even though Paramount was one of the country's leading movie studios, the company never shared its films, stars, or production facilities with the television network. As Ted Bergmann later charged, "They [Paramount] would block everything, and we could never figure out why. They didn't want television to develop. They were constantly angry. It was the weirdest syndrome I've ever run into. Every time DuMont went to borrow money to expand the company, the potential lender would call Paramount, and they would inevitably kibosh it."[5] In a 1959 interview, Allen Du Mont questioned Paramount's motives for investing in his company in the first place, suggesting that his partner "got into DuMont [as an] insurance policy more than anything else. They didn't know what television was going to do. If it seriously affected their business, they might have put some real money into it, but I think their real hope was that television wouldn't progress too rapidly and damage their motion picture business."[6]

Given Paramount's range of television investments, the accusation that Paramount was using DuMont to sabotage the new medium seems somewhat overstated, reflecting the intense mistrust and hostility that existed between the leadership of the two companies. Paramount reasonably decided that network television in general, and DuMont in particular, were not worth supporting, given the many difficulties and uncertainties in the industry and concerns about DuMont's management. Paramount could afford to take a "buy and hold" stance in the company, trying to get the most out of DuMont for the least amount of money. As historian Timothy White wrote in his excellent study of Paramount's business strategy regarding television, "Paramount clearly had not been interested in furthering the network ambitions of Allen B. Du Mont; profit was foremost in the studio's television plans."[7] Instead of spending more on network television, Paramount underwrote several experimental ventures, including large-screen television that would have been exhibited in movie theaters, and a pay television apparatus for home sets.[8] It also invested in conventional broadcast television by syndicating made-for-television films and operating a Los Angeles station that was not even a DuMont affiliate.[9]

Despite its strategy to maintain diverse television interests, Paramount would have parted with DuMont if the right deal had come along. However, it had a hard time selling its stake in the company because of DuMont's financial organization and managerial structure. The two classes of DuMont stock provided a set of checks and balances that ultimately limited the authority of all stockholders, board members, and high-level executives. Since Allen Du Mont and his supporters controlled the Class A stock and much of the corporate management, Paramount could not sell its Class B stock to any other company. As Paramount's Paul Raibourn explained, "From time to time we have found people who [were] interested in buying our interest." These deals invariably fell through because investors "were only interested in buying properties in which they could exert their own management efforts and show their management abilities."[10]

Ironically, Paramount's influence in the company, through the Class B stock holdings, probably saved Allen Du Mont's management team for several years because it prevented other investors from trying to take over the company by purchasing blocks of the Class A stock. Owners of Class A stock had their management power checked by Paramount's Class B stock. Between 1939 and 1950, a series of five stock offerings raised funds for DuMont's expanding operations. These sales also diluted Allen Du Mont's stake in the company that bore his name. As of December 31, 1951, Allen Du Mont was the largest single holder of Class A DuMont stock, and he only owned about 54,400 shares, or 3 percent of the outstanding stock. In 1951, DuMont sold for between $14 and $19 a share. For under $1 million ($7.5 million in 2003 dollars), an outside investor could have purchased enough stock to surpass Allen Du Mont as the corporation's leading shareholder.[11]

Because of his relatively weak position, Allen Du Mont rejected proposals that would have converted the Class B holdings into a single class of stock. As he told the FCC, "Companies that would like to take over control, they can't do it if they just have the B. If they have the equivalent amount of A, they definitely could take over control."[12] Du Mont recognized that his strategy forced Paramount to remain invested in the company, but he "certainly preferred to have Paramount in a non-control position [with its Class B stock] rather than having [another] company in a control position" by eliminating the Class B stock.[13] Du Mont faced a difficult choice: retain a partner that did not help with financing, but basically let him run the company as he wanted; or take another partner that might have improved DuMont's operations in network broadcasting and other areas, but also might have pushed Allen Du Mont and his trusted colleagues out of key management positions. Du Mont chose the safe route of retaining Paramount and trying to make the network profitable without outside interference.

This choice was most clear in early 1950. After months of negotiation, DuMont and Paramount reached an agreement that would have ended Paramount's involvement in DuMont. Paramount presented a written proposal to convert DuMont Class B stock to Class A stock. At the time, DuMont Class A stock was traded on the over-the-counter market, but the Class B stock was not traded at all, since Paramount held all outstanding shares. The deal also specified that DuMont's stock would move to the larger and more stable New York Stock Exchange. The Paramount shareholders—mostly small investors, though president Balaban held options for a sizable 40,000 shares of Paramount stock—would finally have been able to cash out their investment in DuMont.[14] As stockholders converted the DuMont shares, Paramount would have relinquished DuMont board members and officers. While these arrangements would have reduced the studio's stake in DuMont, and appearances that Paramount controlled the television company, any arrangement that eliminated the Class B stock left DuMont vulnerable to a takeover, given Allen Du Mont's relatively small holdings in the company.

Representatives from Paramount and DuMont assembled at Paramount's New York offices on the evening of April 5, 1950. Paramount executives expected to sign the agreement that night and ratify it at a company board meeting scheduled for the next day. Instead, Allen Du Mont arrived at the after-hours meeting late and announced that he was rejecting Paramount's offer, apparently without offering a counterproposal or a rationale for his decision. Du Mont irrevocably damaged his already strained relationship with Paramount by rejecting what, in hindsight, seems to have been a fair offer. Paramount's Paul Raibourn remembers his reaction to Du Mont's announcement at their meeting: "I said that I thought he was making a great mistake in that here was something which he had envisioned for some time coming to a consummation . . . I did not see how, with something that he had wanted for so long and had said to me he would do, he could walk away from it that way. He said nevertheless that was his decision, and he was going to stick by it."[15] After the board meeting, Paramount announced to the media that negotiations between the companies were over. In addition, Paramount filled its slots on the DuMont board with senior executives (Edwin Weisel, Balaban, and Raibourn), signaling its intention to keep a tighter rein on the company.[16]

Given his vulnerable position, Du Mont appointed long-term board members and officers whom he knew and trusted, such as his brother Bruce Du Mont and his friend Thomas T. Goldsmith. Several had backgrounds as engineers with little experience, outside of DuMont, in broadcasting, home electronics, or corporate management. Through 1957, the company had only two vice-presidents. The first, Len Cramer, also served as a director of the company and board member from 1942 to 1951 and oversaw the television network during World War II. Cramer, who joined DuMont as the company's sixteenth employee in 1936, made his mark selling oscillographs to engineers during the 1930s and ran the receiver manufacturing operations for many years.[17] Stanley

Patten, the company's other long-term vice-president (1951–1957), joined DuMont in 1947. He was a retired Naval officer who had managed electronic procurement for the Bureau of Ships. Patten was primarily responsible for administrative matters at DuMont's New Jersey plants and he worked with Goldsmith, the director of research, on patent licenses. Goldsmith remembered Patten as a "fine addition" to the company and a "great friend" of Allen Du Mont and his wife Ethel, though Werner Michel, a former executive producer at the network, had a less-favorable impression of Patten. "We had a meeting, and Patten sat next to me, and he told me with a straight face that he had these little boats and he would sit in the bathtub and play with them. You could make a television series out of that group [of DuMont executives]," said Michel.[18] The other three officers were appointed by Paramount.

The End of DuMont Laboratories

Ultimately, Allen Du Mont's weak position forced him to yield control of the network and the company in 1955. DuMont continued to lose money in broadcasting, with no plan for reversing these losses. DuMont's live network offerings dwindled throughout 1954, and it had fallen behind ABC in the competition to win advertisers and affiliates.[19] In January 1955, DuMont sold WDTV in Pittsburgh to Westinghouse Broadcasting for $9.75 million, the highest amount paid for a single station to that time. The sale brought additional capital to DuMont Laboratories but further weakened the network's position. Following the recommendations of a management study by Booz, Allen & Hamilton in early 1955, DuMont decided to cease live network operations. DuMont retained the profitable local stations in New York and Washington. The network stopped soliciting business in the summer of 1955, though it honored the handful of extant contracts with advertisers. That September, identifications for the few remaining programs were changed from the "DuMont Network" to the "DuMont Broadcasting Corporation."[20] Technically the network's final obligation was fulfilled on August 6, 1956, with the telecast of a boxing match from St. Nicholas Arena.[21] The network's equipment and studio facilities became the property of WABD, which continued to produce local programs.

Recognizing the value of DuMont's two remaining stations, Paramount allied with the New York investment firm of Loeb, Rhoades &

Chris Witting (seated, left), now with Westinghouse Broadcasting, finalizes the purchase of WDTV from DuMont Laboratories and Allen Du Mont (seated, right), January 1955. Ted Bergmann, director of the DuMont network, is standing second from the right.

Source: Allen B. Du Mont Collection, Archives Center, National Museum of American History, Smithsonian Institution.

Co., which held 20 percent of DuMont's Class A stock on behalf of many smaller investors. In May 1955, Paramount and Loeb, Rhoades demanded a number of changes, including new management and elimination of the different classes of stock. The shareholders also wanted a clearer separation of DuMont's different activities, proposing that a new company be created for broadcasting, while DuMont Laboratories continued to research, develop, and manufacture equipment.[22] Allen Du Mont was forced to accept these changes because he did not have sufficient stock holdings or support from the board to win a proxy vote.

On October 10, 1955, the DuMont Broadcasting Corporation was officially spun off as a separate entity from DuMont Laboratories. WABD and WTTG formed the foundation of DuMont Broadcasting. The research and manufacturing divisions remained part of DuMont Laboratories. Allen Du Mont was shunted aside in this reorganization. Paramount installed one of its top executives, Bernard Goodwin, as president of the new broadcasting company. David Schultz, a former executive at Raytheon, was appointed president of DuMont Laboratories, though Allen Du Mont remained as chairman of the board of both companies. Ted Bergmann remembered "sitting in Doc's [Du Mont's] study in his house, just the two of us. It was all coming apart at that point. We were having a drink before dinner, and he started to sob and said, 'I can't let them take my company away from me. I can't let them do this.' Then he recovered his composure, but they did take it from him."[23]

In the final insult to Allen Du Mont, on May 12, 1958, the name of the television company was changed from the DuMont Broadcasting Corporation to Metropolitan Broadcasting. According to former Metropolitan officer Robert Dryer, the corporation wanted to change its "aura so as not to be identified with the failure that was associated with DuMont."[24] Allen Du Mont resigned his position as chairman of the board and sold his stock in protest.[25] In 1959, Paramount sold its 21.75 percent interest in Metropolitan Broadcasting to a group headed by an entrepreneur named John Kluge for $4 million. Kluge renamed the company Metromedia in 1961. The former DuMont outlets in Washington and New York were among the six stations that Metromedia sold to Rupert Murdoch, who was building the Fox network, for nearly $2 billion in 1985. Emerson Radio & Phonograph bought Allen Du Mont's prized Receiver Division from DuMont Laboratories in 1958. Two years later, Fairchild Camera & Instrument purchased everything that was left in DuMont, including the instrument and tube businesses with which Allen Du Mont launched his company in the 1930s. Du Mont remained with Fairchild as a consultant until his death in 1965.[26]

Can Anybody Here Run a Network?

Paramount's decision to push Allen Du Mont out of the presidency of DuMont Laboratories in 1955 was the culmination of the studio's many years of frustration over Du Mont's management of the television network. At the top of DuMont Laboratories, Du Mont relied on loyal and trusted officers and directors: Bruce Du Mont, Thomas Goldsmith, Mortimer Loewi, Len Cramer, and Stanley Patten. They deserve credit for helping Allen Du Mont transform DuMont Laboratories from a family business into an influential and successful electronics corporation. Nevertheless, Allen Du Mont was slow to realize that the network television business was very different from the electronics engineering and manufacturing endeavors at which he and his top officers excelled. He and his management team were not equipped to help DuMont compete with established broadcasters like NBC and CBS.

As president of both the network and DuMont Laboratories, Du Mont took primary responsibility for hiring top executives, providing annual budgets for each division of the company, and approving major expenditures for television programing and studio facilities. However, he was not sufficiently involved in the network's daily operations. Du Mont seldom took the train to New York to participate in network management meetings or chat with the television performers and crew members. "I think he came by the office once or twice in the four years I worked there and we all had to line up and kiss the ring," said Irwin Rostin, who worked as a supervising producer in charge of news and public affairs at DuMont. David Hollander, who started at DuMont as a page in 1949 and left Channel Five in 1963, remembered the only time that he ever saw Allen Du Mont. "I was working at 515 Madison [DuMont headquarters] and this little man was walking around. I said, 'I'm sorry. You don't belong here.' Then he asked to be shown around. About five minutes later I get a call at my desk: Dr. Du Mont is in the building and he is walking around." Even one of the network's most popular and loyal actors, Video Ranger Don Hastings, met Du Mont only a few times.[27]

Given his lax management of the television network, Du Mont's selection of broadcasting executives was especially important. Before 1950, many of the standard TV programing and business practices came from radio. Starting with the top position, the network desperately needed managers with experience crafting programs and working with radio talent, advertisers, and affiliates. Seasoned broadcasters were vital because they had personal contacts with the talent and advertising agencies. They could also provide DuMont with intelligence about the other networks and insight regarding the new industry. Rather than hiring advertising or radio veterans, however, Allen Du Mont installed a series of people whose main qualifications were personal loyalty and a long history with DuMont Laboratories. These early network heads didn't fail entirely. Through the late 1940s, they built studios, hired employees, signed affiliates, and devised an administrative structure for operating a television network at a time when nobody knew very much about the new medium. Nevertheless, they did not provide the DuMont network with the sort of coherent, long-range strategy needed to capitalize on its position as a television pioneer. Moreover, the early executives were not effective in helping DuMont recruit advertisers and create successful original programing. By the time a more skillful and stable team took charge in 1950, the network was already in serious trouble.

During the first five years of network operation, DuMont employed three different heads: Leonard Cramer (1945–1947), Lawrence Phillips (1947–1949), and Mortimer Loewi (1949–1951). Cramer and Loewi had grown with DuMont Laboratories since the mid-1930s: Cramer in manufacturing and sales, Loewi as a stockholder and Allen Du Mont's primary financial advisor. In addition to being a longtime DuMont executive, Cramer was Loewi's son-in-law.[28] Lawrence Phillips had a background in manufacturing with a specialty in the paint and graphite industries. In his early fifties when he joined DuMont, Phillips's only previous entertainment job was as executive vice-president of the USO Camp Shows, a company that booked performers for American servicemen around the world.[29] Bergmann remembered that soon after Phillips's appointment, "it became obvious that he knew nothing about broadcasting."[30] While Loewi had always been involved in company decisions as part of Allen Du Mont's inner circle, he took over as head of the network after Phillips left in early 1949. Commander Loewi (he used the title after serving as an officer in the Navy during World War II) was sixty-one years old at the time and had no experience in broadcasting outside of DuMont.

With its management problems and lack of foresight, DuMont squandered many of the competitive advantages that it should have enjoyed from its early television activities. During its first few years, the network produced mostly short-lived, amateurish programs, including many directed by a man named Bob Loewi, the boss's son. The only reason that these shows aired, and sometimes attracted viewers, was that there was a great need to fill airtime. Television was a novelty, and, for the most part, the competition on other networks was not much better. DuMont's main early programing successes were in sports, namely baseball, boxing, and wrestling. It also aired the nation's first daytime television schedule, which started locally on WABD in the fall of 1948 and was offered to affiliates the following year. In contrast, by January 1949, CBS and NBC had each premiered two or three programs that reliably attracted audiences and anchored prime-time schedules for the

DuMont executives and crew members at a Thanksgiving turkey drawing, 1949. Standing next to the camera, from right to left: Carl Gaiti (lighting director), an unidentified person, Millard Dickerson (senior technician), Fred Scott (announcer), Mortimer Loewi (director of the network), and Jim Caddigan (director of programming), kneeling with a rolled-up paper in his hand.

Source: Allen B. Du Mont Collection, Archives Center, National Museum of American History, Smithsonian Institution.

next several years. Of pre-1950 TV stars like Sid Caesar, Ed Sullivan, Milton Berle, and Arthur Godfrey, only Godfrey had been equally popular on radio. Instead of beating CBS and NBC to these performers, or finding others of equal talent and promise, DuMont had nothing. DuMont's programing gradually improved from the summer of 1949 to early 1950, when the network debuted several of its most successful, long-running series: *Captain Video, Cavalcade of Stars, The Magic Cottage, The Plainclothes Man,* and *Rocky King, Detective.* By this time, network head Loewi had an experienced studio production crew and a strong executive staff—including Chris Witting, Ted Bergmann, and James Caddigan—to guide the network for the next five years.

An accountant under Phillips at the USO shows, Chris Witting joined DuMont in 1947 and moved through the network's upper management ranks over the next few years. In July 1951, when Loewi left the network to take a position as special assistant to Allen Du Mont, Witting officially became director of the network. He stayed in charge through the end of 1953, when Westinghouse Broadcasting tapped him to become its president. Bergmann took Witting's place atop DuMont.[31] At the time, he was thirty-three years old, and the youngest man who had ever directed a television network.[32] Bergmann began his DuMont career as an advertising salesman in 1947, and worked with sponsors to develop several popular DuMont shows including *Cavalcade of Stars*. He rose to the position of sales manager in 1951 and general manager of the network the following year. James Caddigan, director of programing at DuMont from 1947 to 1955, was the executive responsible for creating and scheduling shows. It would have taken a combination of extraordinary vision, luck, and wisdom to save the DuMont network after 1950. However, the team of Witting, Bergmann, and Caddigan did a smart and capable job of managing the network despite many obstacles: lack of capital, a weak affiliate line-up, and few major advertising accounts. Throughout the early 1950s, DuMont aired popular and entertaining programs produced on a very low budget.

The Best Buy in Network Television

In a slew of trade journal advertisements and articles starting in mid-1950, DuMont consistently promoted its low-cost programs and flexible rates as the best deal in the industry for sponsors. Rather than targeting the biggest advertising agencies and corporations, who generally had long relationships with CBS and NBC from radio, DuMont tried to attract a number of smaller accounts with lower budgets. It was standard for advertisers on all networks to pay a program's production costs, and additional fees for the network's airtime, based on the time of day that the show aired and the number of affiliates that carried a program. DuMont saved advertisers money in these areas with flexible packages and positioned itself as the voice of wisdom in an industry that was spinning out of control with unreasonable advertising costs. "A large segment of the industry has followed the blind trail of super-extravagance to the point where a single show has cost as much as $70,000," wrote Clarence

Alexander, the director of network operations under Witting, in 1951. "One question comes immediately to mind—how many cakes of soap or packs of cigarettes must be sold to cover such an advertising expenditure?"[33] In contrast, DuMont was the "best buy in network television" because of its reasonable rates, which frequently delivered more viewers per dollar than more lavish productions on other networks.[34]

DuMont was an advertising pioneer, creating innovative formats that have since become standard on commercial television. The company's resourcefulness was borne out of a desperation to court sponsors that were working with a moderate advertising budget. DuMont also wanted to distinguish itself from CBS and NBC. Bergmann explained, "We were the new guys on the block and we were met with a certain amount of skepticism and mistrust. We had to prove to the sponsors that we were worthy of their support."[35] For example, DuMont developed a system for sharing advertising time on select programs with affiliates. The stations then generated extra revenue on DuMont programs by selling spots to local businesses that would not have been able to afford network prime time. DuMont also allowed national advertisers to choose the affiliates on which they wanted to advertise, rather than requiring them to purchase time on all DuMont stations.[36] In its quest to accommodate potential clients, the network brokered deals that allowed two or three sponsors to share the costs of programs, with each sponsor receiving time for one or two ads.[37] When all else failed, DuMont simply debuted an unsponsored program for a short time, hoping that it would eventually attract advertisers. Several commercially successful programs—including *Captain Video*, *The Plainclothes Man*, and Bishop Sheen's *Life Is Worth Living*—began without sponsors.[38]

DuMont's flexible advertising deals gave the network creative control over much of its programing. In contrast, most early CBS and NBC programs were supported by single sponsors that worked through ad agencies. The sponsors "would buy the chunks of time and they would control it," remembered Hal Cooper, who produced and wrote *The Magic Cottage* at DuMont while also directing a daytime soap opera, *Search for Tomorrow*, sponsored by Procter and Gamble on CBS. "Procter and Gamble controlled the show. The network just provided the space and got paid for it. When I was directing the soaps, we would have a live commercial. If the actor wanted to change 'is not' to 'isn't,' we

would have to call Cincinnati. The guy at Procter and Gamble." At Du-
Mont, however, the network owned his show and recruited multiple
sponsors to foot the bill. Cooper was free to do whatever he wanted, as
long as he stayed within the program's tight budget.[39]

Starting with its daytime slate, the first in the country, DuMont beat
the other networks to valuable niches in the program schedule, while
signing many rising television talents. Witting summarized the lessons
from the network's early programing innovations. "Courage pays out—
courage in programing, in personality building, in pioneering new network techniques . . . TV audiences are eager for a type of programing
markedly different from that now seen today—a type that does not ab-
sorb an advertising budget."[40] For example, with *Cavalcade of Stars*, the
network established Saturday night as a family viewing night at a time
when most in the industry thought that people would be out on the
town, not home watching television. The network also furthered the careers of a number of performers, especially comedians like Jackie Gleason, by signing entertainers who were not yet in a position to command
top dollar. DuMont was proud to save advertisers expenses for actors, rehearsal time, and props. "Our philosophy was that we were in the business of selling airtime, not scenery, stages, or talent," Bergmann wrote.[41]

DuMont's mania for cheap programing inspired network personnel to
develop unusual production techniques and premises for programs. *Captain Video* included clips from old westerns in the middle of a live, futuristic dramatic program for kids. *Dark of Night* was one of the first network
dramas to be produced live on location from various factories and other
locations in the New York area, which gave the program an interesting
new backdrop each week at minimal cost. *One Man's Experience* and *One
Woman's Experience* each saved money with bare bones sets and only one
actor. In a pinch, the performer interacted with other imaginary characters who remained off camera. A DuMont press release described an
adaptation of *Hamlet* for *One Man's Experience*, for example, that promised to "make use of the medium's possibilities and utilize all the major
soliloquies."[42] While many strange and exciting shows aired, the novelty
of DuMont's experiments wore off after a few episodes. In fact, a program's long-term aesthetic and commercial success ultimately depended
on how well the DuMont personnel integrated gimmicky techniques
with other program elements, such as characters, narratives, and themes.

As Stan Epstein, assistant director of *Captain Video* and other shows, explained, "Yes, it was low budget, but we were concerned about the shows more than the budgets. We just did what we had to do, but no one was extravagant because we knew that we shouldn't be extravagant."[43]

A Badge of Honor

The creative people working at DuMont had an extraordinary amount of freedom from management oversight. "Once in a while, Caddigan, Witting or Bergmann would just come around and shmooze, but there was never any control," said Don Russell, a DuMont announcer and program host. "I think it was because we all had a healthy respect for the business. They knew that we weren't going to screw up, that we were all eager to succeed in the business, that we had a sense of pride."[44] In addition, the busy executives had no choice but to trust their employees at the perennially understaffed and underfunded network. Caddigan testified before the FCC in early 1952 that he oversaw a staff of ninety-one network employees and he was responsible for managing budgets, program procurement, network policy, contract negotiations, production facilities, and studio design.[45]

DuMont did not have additional supervisors between the network's top two or three executives and the producers and staff working on particular programs. It was different from the other networks because "there was no middle management. Everybody working there had a full plate just doing what they had to do, so they couldn't make work for themselves," according to Howard Rubin, who began his television career in the DuMont mail room in 1949 and then worked as an independent producer for DuMont, NBC, and ABC during the early 1950s.[46] To observe most programs, the busy executives would have had to travel downtown from 515 Madison Avenue, where DuMont maintained offices and a studio. DuMont also leased space in two nearby Broadway theaters, the Adelphi and the Ambassador. However, the primary production facility, with three studios, was located in the converted auditorium of John Wanamaker department store on lower Broadway, more than forty blocks from the network's headquarters. "We never had any executives looking over our shoulder, especially downtown. Nobody ever came down to Wanamaker's," said Epstein, a former assistant director.[47] Production and management facilities were consolidated only in June 1954, when DuMont opened the state-of-the-art DuMont Tele-Centre in a renovated opera house on East 67th Street.

The television directors and crew members responsible for cameras, lighting, props, and set design were almost all under the age of thirty. Supervising producers, writers, and talent varied in age and frequently had experience in radio or Broadway. As Epstein said, "Engineers came off the street. They knew nothing. It was all new and that was the excitement. Everything was new and we were all young."[48] Performers and writers were generally underpaid at DuMont. However, the network offered its engineers competitive wages, due to the union's presence, and retained its production people for many years. Arthur Forrest, who started as a janitor at DuMont in 1948 and worked his way up the studio hierarchy, remembered his salary skyrocketing when he was promoted from page to studio assistant, a union job. "I went from six dollars a week to $41.60. My God, I was a millionaire."[49]

Starting around 1950, DuMont management was quick to promote its young, talented engineers to positions as directors and cameramen, while phasing out some of the older, less skillful people, including Bob Loewi. Several of the crew members in the DuMont studio were recent graduates of college or the military. A few, like David Lowe, Hal Cooper, and Wes Kenney, also had worked in college or professional theater. Frank Bunetta (director) and Barry Shear (cameraman and later director), key members of the Adelphi Theatre production team responsible for DuMont's biggest programs, began their television careers at the Passaic plant during the war, commuting into New York City at night to work at WABD. Others, like Arthur Forrest and Marvin Pakula, joined DuMont shortly after the war. By 1950, the DuMont production crew was as accomplished as any in the television industry. In addition, promising recruits were given the opportunity to spend long hours in the studio and learn from the more experienced engineers. "We were all learning together," said Forrest. "There was nothing that had been established in terms of technology, lighting, camera position and movement, and lenses. We were all discovering television at the same time."[50]

Director Wes Kenney's story about how he was hired by Caddigan in 1950 illustrates how casual DuMont was about hiring and training the people most responsible for delivering its programs. Kenney was a stu-

An early studio production. Barry Shear on camera (center) with Marvin Pakula (left) and an unidentified crew member.

Source: Courtesy of Marvin Pakula.

dent at Carnegie Tech (later Carnegie Mellon) in Pittsburgh when Caddigan first interviewed him. "He asked me, 'So what do you think a television director does?'" Kenney remembered. "I said, 'Well, he's gotta tell people where to stand, and set up camera work and things like that.' I didn't know beans from pieola about television." After the interview, Kenney returned to Pittsburgh to finish college. He graduated and was staying with a friend in New York when Caddigan invited him to 515 Madison Avenue for another brief interview. The two men had the same exchange about the role of the television director. That night, Kenney received an offer to work as a director at DuMont, starting with the daytime programs produced at Madison Avenue. He watched the shows from the control room as they were being produced during his first few weeks on the job. Then he was called to direct. Within two months, Kenney was directing seven shows a day, five days a week, without rehearsals. He remembers taking the place of a former radio director. "It was all too fast for him," Kenney explained. "As a matter of fact, when I took over his shows, they sent him upstairs to management. He was a nice man and they were good about it."[51]

Many former DuMont employees who had successful television careers praised the informal on-the-job training. New engineers were busy producing live programs all day and into the evening. "As soon as one show was over, we had a forty-second break and we were on the air with another show from the other side of the studio. It was fast and furious and great," Epstein said.[52] What's more, the crew members performed a variety of tasks, from writing to directing to set design. "For most of us it was the first job in television and it was a grand opportunity to do things in ways that you could never do within the corporate structures of [other] networks back then," Irwin Rostin said.[53] In contrast to NBC, where engineers were represented by different unions, all DuMont crew members were part of the International Alliance of Theatrical Stage Employees (IATSE). "That doesn't sound like a big deal, but it meant a lot closer working relationship," said Dave Hollander, who started as a page and was later a studio manager.[54]

Some of the more experienced directors and engineers helped the new guys move up. "We were a bunch of silly kids and there was never much of a pecking order. I'd work from nine to five, and then from five to ten at night, I would hang around the control room learning the business, and no one ever bothered me," Howard Rubin said.[55] Since they were all about the same age, working hard in an exciting new industry, the crew members and performers at each studio went out together after the programs were over. "I never went to college, so from age fifteen to twenty-one that [*Captain Video*] was my education in how to behave with adults and how to do my job with discipline," said Don Hastings, who played the Video Ranger from 1949 to 1955. Of course, it wasn't all work. "They taught me how to drink. I never even knew what a martini was," he said with a smile.[56] Dave Hollander had similar memories. "I don't think I ever went home. We were so thrilled and excited and having so much fun that we ended up working all the time," he said. "And when we stopped working, we all hung out together. Married guys went home to their wives, but the rest of us all wound up drinking in a bar or going to a restaurant . . . There were all kinds of personal contacts among the people that worked there. It would be similar to being a cop. The only people that understand your job are other cops."[57]

One of the DuMont network's great contributions to television's subsequent development was as a training ground for talent on both sides of the camera. Of the core group of directors and producers who had their first television jobs at DuMont, several continued to do distinguished work after the network folded. Frank Bunetta produced or directed most of DuMont's Adelphi Theatre variety programs in addition to Bishop Sheen's *Life Is Worth Living*. He later worked with Jackie Gleason at CBS and directed several other NBC and CBS variety shows, including *Caesar's Hour*, starring Sid Caesar. Shear, another ten-year DuMont veteran, directed at NBC in the 1950s before moving to Hollywood, where his credits include many of the top television crime dramas of the late 1960s and early 1970s: *Hawaii Five-O, Starsky and Hutch, Ironside, Streets of San Francisco*. Shear also directed four feature films: *Wild in the Streets* (1968), *The Todd Killings* (1971), *Across 110th Street* (1972), and *The Deadly Trackers* (1973). He died of cancer in 1979 at the age of fifty-six. After heading DuMont's news and public affairs department and directing programs at the network, David Lowe moved to CBS, where he produced *Harvest of Shame* and other classic *CBS Reports* documentaries with Edward R. Murrow.

Hal Cooper directed several well-known comedies of the 1960s and 1970s, including all but the first few episodes of *Maude* along with several other sitcoms produced by Norman Lear. Wes Kenney also directed several Lear sitcoms and was the executive producer and director of popular soap operas including *Days of Our Lives, The Young and the Restless*, and *General Hospital*. Arthur Forrest remained at New York's Channel Five until 1973, directing the syndicated *David Susskind Show* and local fare like *Wonderama*. After leaving the station to direct the *Jerry Lewis MDA Telethon*, he moved to many other network specials, game shows, and series. Forrest has worked on *Rosie, Leeza, Whose Line Is It Anyway?*, and the Thanksgiving Day Parade. He has also continued to produce or direct the annual *MDA* telethon for more than thirty years. Countless others started at DuMont and had successful careers as performers, directors, cameramen, and engineers long after the network folded. DuMont also launched many on the road to executive suites at advertising agencies, other networks, studios, and production companies. In fact, a list of distinguished DuMont alumni would fill many pages. As Norman Baer, an independent producer who placed his first shows on DuMont, explained, "A lot of great people came out of DuMont. It was a fun place. A kind of place that couldn't exist today. It was us against the world, and I think [having worked at] DuMont is almost a badge of honor."[58]

Dennis James works the crowd on *Okay Mother.*

Source: From *Radio-Television Mirror,* August 1951. Courtesy of Library of American Broadcasting, University of Maryland.

4

The DuMont
Daytime Experiment

On November 1, 1948, DuMont inaugurated an experiment that made headlines in *Time, Life, Newsweek,* the *New York Times,* and all of the major trade papers. The firm's flagship station, WABD (New York), began programing shows every day during the daytime hours. At a time when television was primarily an industry of the night, except for an occasional afternoon ball game, the WABD day began at 7 A.M. and lasted through evening prime time. DuMont took its New York experiment national on January 12, 1949, the day after the coaxial cable that connected New York with Midwestern cities was completed. Network affiliates were offered 4½ hours of morning and afternoon programing. As the only television network that did not need to protect radio interests, DuMont was uniquely poised to alter the scope of television broadcasting. Competitors watched DuMont's experiment but did not offer their own daytime slates. *Time* explained that "NBC, CBS, and ABC have hesitated about daytime TV because they are primarily in the radio business and radio profits foot the bill for their TV. If the surveys are right, TV cuts deeply into radio's audience, and the networks cannot yet nerve themselves to kill the goose that has been laying golden eggs for 25 years."[1]

DuMont did not expand WABD's schedule to generate advertising revenue. Instead, with its core business in manufacturing TV sets and station equipment, DuMont was primarily interested in replacing test patterns with live programs. The shows would help its dealers sell receivers during the day, when most people shopped. Along these lines, bargain-conscious consumers now had 9 hours of additional programing each day, so they could feel like they were getting more for their money when they purchased television receivers. DuMont also believed that if its daytime slate attracted sponsors and good trade press, other stations and networks might begin daytime telecasts. DuMont did not mind the competition for advertising dollars if it boosted the sale of television receivers by giving consumers an incentive to purchase their first TV sets.[2]

Although advertisers were not DuMont's foremost target, WABD attracted many eager sponsors as the only regular daytime programer in 1948. Firms ranging from local appliance stores to national food manufacturers such as General Mills took advantage of the rock bottom advertising rates, which started at $25 for a short spot. *Variety* reported that the number of daytime advertisers exceeded even the "optimistic hopes" of the DuMont sales staff. By December, daytime programing was generating between $8,000 and $10,000 a week for the network: a very high figure, especially considering the modest audience and advertising rates compared to prime time. As further evidence of television's viability as a sales medium, DuMont also trumpeted surveys showing that its programs were achieving comparable ratings to more expensive and established afternoon radio shows.[3]

How's the Weather on Madison Avenue?

The programing from dawn to dusk provided DuMont's first showcase for the bare-bones production techniques and bargain advertising rates that defined the network over the next several years. James Caddigan's studio crew aired an astounding 55 hours of live television per week from DuMont's small Madison Avenue studio. The shows were not rehearsed. Most featured spontaneous musical performances, cooking or fashion demonstrations, and talk shows that required only one or two cameras and minimal sets. As soon as one show was over, the crew shuttled to the next set, bringing cameras and other equipment with them. WABD hid the shifting studio from viewers with station identifications, advertisements, and assorted graphics providing the time or weather reports.[4]

Caddigan and his boss, Mortimer Loewi, designed program formats and scheduling practices that have since become standard industry practice. The DuMont day started with news and weather as people prepared for work in and out of the home. One feature that ran a dozen times over the course of the morning, starting at seven o'clock, was called "C-W-T (clock-weather-temperature)." The information usually appeared as a simple graphic; however, in providing the weather, DuMont also inaugurated a technique later refined by the *Today* show, which debuted on NBC in January 1952. Rather than delivering all of the weather reports from the studio, Caddigan came up with the innovative idea of pointing the camera out the Madison Avenue studio window to show viewers the weather outside. "It's one thing to hear or read that the day is cold with rain, and quite a different thing to see pedestrians at 53rd Street and Madison Avenue with coat collars turned up, huddled under umbrellas," Caddigan wrote.[5] The network also took advantage of its prime midtown studio location in its noontime *Man on the Street* interview program. The camera, equipped with a telephoto lens, captured WABD's host (Jack Rayel, later replaced by Dan Peterson) as he interviewed people passing by the busy city corner. Engineers used a walkie-talkie to transmit audio, since the microphone cords did not reach from the street to the studio.[6] The DuMont morning also included an exercise program, periodic news updates, and a 15-minute religious service for people who could not make it to church or synagogue.

The schedule was heavy on news, talk, and music: the kind of programing that viewers could enjoy without having to watch that closely. DuMont executives assumed that people at home during the day were too busy for "leisurely television viewing" before noon. DuMont saved money by repeating programs and using the same studio sets. Still, *Variety* noted that DuMont's schedule was no more monotonous than "the steady diet of disk jockeys and/or soap operas fed daytime radio listeners—and moreover, who will sit glued to a TV receiver for 11 hours a day, five days a week?"[7] DuMont inaugurated a longstanding practice, copied by the *Today* show and other morning television programs, of emphasizing sound over visuals. As Mortimer Loewi explained in a press statement introducing daytime television, "The audio [portion] of the program will give the listener the complete story. When viewing becomes a necessary, as for some outstanding event, an audio signal will cue the listener to watch the screen."[8] The shows were not driven by dramatic plots and narratives, so if a viewer had to leave the room for a few minutes, or tune in during the middle of an episode, she could still get the essence of the program.[9]

By the afternoon, WABD featured shows with more exciting visuals: fashion, house-hunting tips, music-variety, human interest stories, and discussion with guests ranging from designers to musicians to members of civic clubs.[10] The programs were designed to help women manage their housework more efficiently. "Show me how to fix something tasty and different for supper; teach me how to refurbish my tired old living room for little money and I shall be eternally grateful," wrote Adelaide Hawley, reflecting her own preferences and the common industry wisdom about what women wanted from television. Hawley covered women's television for the New York *TV Guide* and hosted *Fashions on Parade* (WABD).[11] Nevertheless, at DuMont, the rules were seldom hard and fast. Two of the programs that made the most effective use of television visuals, *Your Television Babysitter* and *Your Television Shopper*, aired before noon.[12]

Your Television Babysitter (later retitled *DuMont Kindergarten*), hosted by Pat Meikle, was intended for preschool children. It aired from 8:30 to 9, while mothers cleaned the kitchen after breakfast. As Caddigan described the show, "Miss Meikle advises the mother to leave the youngsters 'with me' at the TV set supplied with a pad and pencil . . . As program time comes to an end, Miss Meikle 'calls' to mother in the kitchen, tells her the morning lesson is concluded, and to return to the living room for the youngster."[13] Hal Cooper, married to Meikle at the time, produced *Your Television Babysitter*. He recalled that Caddigan had the general idea for a program that would keep kids busy in the morning, but the program director never offered further guidance after an initial interview. "We went on the air without anybody ever having seen us on camera. We were never auditioned . . . [DuMont executives] would just get something on the air and worry about it afterwards."[14]

Cooper and Meikle created a lively half hour with fairy tales, drawings designed to teach kids the alphabet, craft demonstrations, and sketches illustrating the adventures of a New York City pigeon named Wilmer. "We did a lot of the alphabet stuff that *Sesame Street* later did,

Pat Meikle, the charismatic star of *The Magic Cottage.*

Source: Allen B. Du Mont Collection, Archives Center, National Museum of American History, Smithsonian Institution.

but I didn't have the electronics and the budget that they have," Cooper said. "The concept was to make learning and reading fun."[15] Critics praised Meikle, a friendly and bright screen presence, for not talking down to her audience. *Variety* called her "the answer to a mother's prayers. She's already being touted as a new TV star."[16] Cooper remembered what it meant for his wife to have been a featured performer on DuMont in television's early days. "There was a period when television stars were gods. People would go nuts. 'My god there she is.' If you remember the Beatles, that kind of thing went on with people on television," he said. "If Pat and Milton Berle, for example, would make a personal appearance, the crowds were just as big for Pat as they were for Milton, because Pat was the children's star. We'd get nine or ten thousand pieces of mail a week."[17] In August 1949, Cooper and Meikle adapted the program for slightly older viewers as *The Magic Cottage*, which aired on the network through September 1952. After a one-year hiatus following the network run, it returned locally on WABD every evening until June 1955.[18]

Your Television Shopper epitomized the way DuMont and other early broadcasters exploited television's capacity to demonstrate products for viewers. "As long as people have to wear clothes and eat, [TV executives] figure women will want to know where and how to buy," Hawley wrote.[19] In WABD's early version of the Home Shopping Network, host Kathi Norris mixed guest interviews with a stream of product placements and pitches. The selling started in the opening minute, when Norris invited viewers to join her for a second cup of Aborn Coffee. Viewers purchased items by sending checks to WABD, visiting local stores, or calling sponsors directly. In a 1950 *TV Guide* article, Norris extolled the luxury of shopping by television. "After the children are packed off to school, you leisurely stretch out on the living room couch in your negligee. Tune in a shopping program (mine, I hope!) and relax. All the products are displayed on your screen for your critical appraisal."[20]

The trade press reported amazing success stories from *Your Television Shopper.* Sales of Jane Parker Bread, for example, increased by more than 5,000 loaves a week at New York A&P supermarkets; after a single mention on the show, Jiffy-Stitcher received telephone orders for more than 300 hand-held sewing machines in two days.[21] Even though *Your Television Shopper,* like most other daytime programs, did not earn gaudy ratings, network head Mortimer Loewi used Norris's program to advance the network's philosophy that agencies should value a program's power to sell products over raw audience statistics. He boasted that Norris's program elicited thousands of calls and letters, with checks enclosed, for the products that she was pushing. "The success of our television shopper type of program has been duplicated in all parts of the country . . . Seldom will any of them appear in the 'top ten,' rating-wise, but for actual, accountable results, they stand among the leaders," he concluded.[22]

WABD offered the most complete slate of programs for women that television had seen to date, and the industry carefully watched its experiments throughout 1948 and 1949. However, DuMont's revolutionary daytime programing strategy built on techniques that were established in other media. Several of the shows were modeled on the radio's popular so-called "women's programs," which combined music, discussion, and household advice. Magazines like *Ladies Home Journal,*

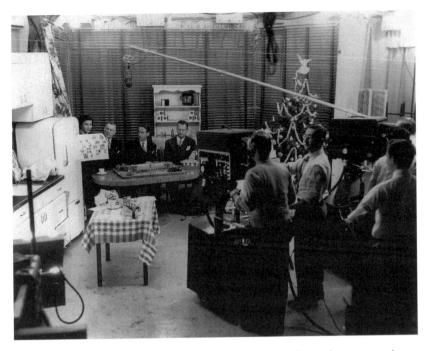

Kathi Norris of *Your Television Shopper* could sell 300 Jiffy-Stitchers in two days.
Source: Courtesy of Marvin Pakula.

Good Housekeeping, and *Collier's* also influenced the presentation of fashion and homemaking ideas. In addition, throughout the 1940s, broadcasting industry magazines promoted TV as a visual medium that was ideal for demonstrating everything from cooking techniques to home decorating tips. A handful of inventive local stations across the country, including WABD, regularly aired fashion, food, and shopping programs on prime time soon after the war ended.[23] DuMont's innovation was to create an entire schedule of programs, with multiple formats and styles, that drew from all of these strategies and ideas about women and popular culture.

Caddigan and Loewi did not buck the conventional wisdom that daytime television should target women and focus on domestic concerns. In fact, contemporary commentators on DuMont's experiment shared the network's excitement that there would be more television that catered to women, rather than criticizing DuMont for expecting that women would primarily be interested in programs about homemaking, parenting, gossip, and the joys of shopping.[24] Like DuMont executives, critics saw themselves as champions of a woman's right to watch daytime TV, scoffing at the popular concern that television would produce a nation of television addicted mothers, watching the tube while the home crumbled from neglect.[25] As Jack Gould of the *New York Times* mockingly mused, "Just what Dr. Du Mont is going to do to our way of life is still uncertain. The idea of a nation of housewives sitting mute before the video machines when they should be tidying up the premises or preparing the formula is not something to be grasped hurriedly. Obviously it is matter fraught with peril of the darkest sort."[26] The New York *TV Guide* greeted fears about daytime television with similar sarcasm. "Monday (November 1) was a momentous day in New York life. Nothing since women's suffrage has been of such a moment, and results of that day will most assuredly resound for many generations . . . That was the day that Mama put down her dust mop, brushed straggly hairs from her brow, and got in touch with Dennis James."[27]

Dennis James and the Strange Origins of *Okay Mother*

James was the charismatic star of the most popular daytime television program *Okay Mother*, thirty minutes devoted to the needs and interests of mothers. James described the show in 1949 as "a happy forum to which mothers of all ages can come for fun and inspiration."[28] *Okay Mother* mixed elements of the talk show and the game show, a genre that was popular on radio and had already moved into television by 1949. It was one of the first programs to incorporate the audience as part of the production. Like later daytime talk hosts, James constantly moved back and forth between a small stage and clusters of fans in the studio. He hosted a poetry contest along with daily "Mothergrams," in which the host asked audience members to identify a famous mother, based on clues. Interview segments featured performers who were not quite big enough to command slots on evening variety shows along with mothers whose only claim to fame was that they had parented a celebrity. Early local and network daytime programs copied *Okay Mother*'s interview-variety format, spotlighting tips for raising children along with heated discussions of issues and problems of interest to women who were home during the day. In promoting Dennis James, DuMont also demonstrated the value of a magnetic host who could pitch products and attract a loyal audience. Recent daytime personalities—Rosie O'Donnell, Oprah Winfrey, Regis Philbin, and Maury Povich—have all included elements of *Okay Mother* in their own programs.

Okay Mother started on WABD's November 1948 schedule and remained popular when it was made available over the network the following year. More than any single program, *Okay Mother* demonstrated that daytime television was commercially viable, and that a daytime television program could draw as many people as a radio show. Within a year of its debut, *Okay Mother* was rated higher than any other afternoon television or radio program in New York. By November 1949, more than 10,000 women had requested membership in James's "Mothers, Inc." club and 2,000 others wrote him letters each week. Sterling Products paid a hefty $200,000 to sponsor the program in four markets: New York, Washington, Baltimore, and Philadelphia.[29] *Okay Mother* remained part of DuMont's schedule through July 1951: a long run at a time when most afternoon programs did not last for more than a season and all of the networks were having a hard time figuring out how to program for daytime.

One of the many strange and ironic twists that defined DuMont and the television industry in the late 1940s was that DuMont's wrestling coverage paved the way for *Okay Mother*. Sports announcer James forged the connection between wrestlers and mothers. A former boxer in college, Dennis Sposa changed his name to Dennis James because he thought that "Sposa" was too Italian sounding for the Jersey City station where he started as a disk jockey in 1938.[30] James appeared on DuMont's wartime telecasts such as *Sports Parade*, one of television's earliest sports interview shows. After serving in the Army, James became DuMont's first star performer when he returned to the network, working with his brother Lou, a director and programing executive at DuMont during the late 1940s. One of their early postwar features was a show called *Cash and Carry*, in which contestants performed stunts for prizes. This early television adaptation of *Truth or Consequences*, the popular radio program, prefigured more recent "reality" programs like *Fear Factor* and *Survivor*. In one *Cash and Carry* episode from 1946, a

Early reality television: Dennis James and a contestant paint a man's bald head on *Cash and Carry.*

Source: The Raster, Summer 1947. Allen B. Du Mont Collection, Archives Center, National Museum of American History, Smithsonian Institution.

woman swam in a large studio bathtub, trying to capture three live carp. In another installment, a contestant allowed his scalp to be used for a demonstration of how to paint faces on a bald man's head.[31] In addition to working on several of television's first game shows, James established himself as one of the most popular early sports announcers. He was the commentator when DuMont increased its wrestling and boxing coverage through 1947 and 1948.

James peppered his wrestling broadcasts with the phrase, "Okay, mother?" ostensibly to be sure that the women in the audience knew what he was talking about, even though his real targets were the men who were too proud to admit that they didn't know all of the wrestling terminology. "If I tried to tell these guys in the bar what a step-over toe hold was, they would resent me and say, 'Who the hell is he?' So I would tell it to 'Mother,'" James explained. "And if Mother was watching, she would say, 'John, is that a hammerlock?' And John would say, 'Of course,' and it would make him into a hero."[32] By the end of 1948, James saw that his technique of "slanting the dialogue to interest the fair sex" was working. "Many wives were showing up at the wrestling ringside with their husbands . . . Sweet matronly ladies were smiling at me in recognition in theaters, restaurants, and on the streets." DuMont and James built on this popularity with women wrestling fans to start the new daytime show.[33]

From Mama's Boy to Bad Boy

Okay Mother revered mothers and motherhood. As James wrote in 1951, "I have always thought of mothers as being the most important member of any family and I wanted them to be an important part of my new show."[34] Publicity materials and contemporary articles on *Okay Mother* portrayed James at ease, smiling as he chatted with mothers, including his own. The program's bouncy theme song further reminded viewers of the show's mission. "Okay, mothers. It's your time of day. Okay, mothers. Time to have your say." After the opening song, James started the show as if he was leading a pep rally for the women and children in the small studio audience. He begins the only extant kinescope of a live *Okay Mother* episode, "Who makes the cooling lemonade?" The crowd answers with a rousing, "Mother!" James continues, "Who's the girl we'll never trade?" Again, the reply, "Mother!" James then eases into the program, "All of you girls at home, take it easy. Relax and settle back. It's warm weather. No work for you to do from one to one-thirty every day. No dishes to do, no lunch to prepare. Just sit back and our entertainers here will entertain you."[35]

James, however, was no mama's boy. He fostered his image as a sensitive "bad boy" by combining a respectful exterior with glimpses of a wanton womanizer. A tongue-in-cheek *Television World* profile, for example, was titled "At Home With a 'Mother's Boy.'" It showed James showering, with the caption, "Dennis proves he's a good, clean American boy." Other photos portrayed him relaxing in his busy, modern apartment, dominated by zebra-print easy chairs. Another magazine spread pictured the star in a nightclub, fixing a cocktail as he entertained two attractive women: a violinist and an actress.[36] In fact, James had been married since 1941, and he had a son in 1947, but "for a long time, his marital status was hushed up," according to a 1953 *TV Digest* profile. When news of his divorce became public in the summer of 1951, "the flood-gates really opened up. Every single girl who was on the Dennis James bandwagon no doubt secretly hoped that she would be the next Mrs. Dennis James."[37]

This combination of a good, devoted son and a restless young man permeates the only remaining kinescope of a live *Okay Mother* episode, from the summer of 1950. Like many early performers, who had not yet learned to modulate their acts for television, James was a ball of energy. Working on live television, where the adrenaline flowed freely and it was impossible to erase mistakes, he managed to be alternately cloying, gregarious, temperamental, and rakish. Early in the program, James loses his temper during a word game segment called "Line and Rhyme." Audience members give James a line, and the host is challenged to throw back a phrase to make a little poem. A young woman asks James to rhyme, "My sister's name is Edna." James explodes, "Oh honey. Every day with that Edna. Let me say one thing here. We haven't had a lecture like this in a long time. The object of 'Line and Rhyme' is to have some fun. I don't care what you stick me with. We ask every day before the show to not use the words that we used yesterday. We can have some fun. You'll get the gifts. We'll have some laughs. But every day I get hit with the same word. It stops me. It stops me dead." Perhaps noticing the slightly confused and sheepish looks on audience members' faces during this brief tirade, James tries to lighten the moment by getting down on one knee, next to the offending mother, and granting her another chance. "You don't want to stop me. Now go ahead." She lets out a nervous squeal then delivers another tough line, "My friend has a Chihuahua." James doesn't even try. Instead, he angrily walks away to the other side of the small audience, instructing his assistant, "Okay, give her a box of Rosedale hosiery," the prize for mothers who could stump James during the segment. "Thanks very much." Such flashes of anger were not unheard of on live television. Stars such as Milton Berle, Jackie Gleason, and Arthur Godfrey were occasionally acerbic; however, performers learned over time that such edginess grated on viewers, and they generally moderated their performances.

Dennis James (standing, left) and Julia Meade (standing, center), circa November 1951, shortly after James and company left DuMont for ABC.
Source: TV Show, November 1951.

James similarly tested the boundaries of television etiquette in his flirtations with co-host Julia Meade, an elegant eighteen-year-old Conover model who was best known for pitching Lincolns and Mercuries on *The Ed Sullivan Show* after she left *Okay Mother.*[38] These moments stood in contrast to the polite and earnest conversation that became standard on early daytime television. In fact, even the more prominent prime-time comedians were learning to subdue their risqué material, and watch their sexual innuendo, so as not to offend viewers. Though James was thirty-two years old at the time and a married father, he alternately acts like a young child and a dirty old man. Throughout the rhyming segment, James leans on Meade suggestively and completes the poems with provocative phrases for the benefit of his co-host. For example, a mother asks, "Have you ever been to Africa?" James's reply, "No, but I'd like to sit on the lap of her," pointing to Meade off-screen. James gives a victorious smile at this clever rhyme, but audience members respond with only polite applause. Meade does not acknowledge James's advances and frequently seems confused and embarrassed by the star.

James was in his glory during the "Problem Playhouse" portion of the show. Each day, Meade and James acted out a problem, and the audience was invited to argue the issue, which covered everything from long engagements before marriage to the amount of a child's allowance.[39] On the kinescope, the "Problem Playhouse" is about "spanking" children, a topic that was of great importance to postwar mothers considering different forms of discipline. James plays a little boy who keeps running through a sprinkler and getting his clothes wet, to the dismay of his mother (Meade). James mugs for the camera and, to the audience's delight, leaps onto Meade's lap at every opportunity, telling her what a bad boy he has been. At one point, Meade tells her "son" to change out of his wet trousers. James breaks character: "In front of all these mothers you want me to take off my trousers. You know, I'm apt to do that." While James laughs at the risqué joke, as do audience members, Meade stays in character as the exasperated mother. The segment ends with a heated discussion between audience members about the merits of spanking.

Giving Mothers Their Due

Like many early daytime shows, *Okay Mother* included a stream of commercial product placements and pitches directed at women. The show was sponsored by Sterling Products, which promoted three items: a toothpaste, an aspirin, and a shampoo. James and Meade performed short live commercials, but the selling did not end there. Each of the contests offered token prizes that advertised other merchandise: a Helbros watch, Rosedale hosiery, a Polaroid camera, and an Evans makeup compact. Along with ads for these "official" sponsors, James also occasionally snuck an unauthorized plug into his program. During the rhyming game, for example, James finds the only two men wearing business suits in the audience. These gregarious fellows, probably in their mid-thirties, are out of place in the audience of mothers, children, and a few older men. Their phrase for James to rhyme: "What is the best bread made?" In typical fashion, James repeats a variation of the line, adding a little spice, "What is the best breast made?" The gaffe elicits a few laughs as James smiles, looking guilty. "I think I said something. I don't know what I said, but I think I said something." He then repeats the question correctly. One of the men mumbles, "Wonder Bread." The second man looks surprised and corrects him, "Bond Bread." The unflappable James continues, "Oh, you got a man from Wonder and a man from Bond?" Audience members laugh. "Well, both of these guys are in the dough." James then prepares his rhyme. "What is the best bread made? I guess I would have a bread if I were being paid." They all laugh at James's clever reference to the game that they are playing. Later, during the closing credits, as he lists the program's sponsors, James includes an improvised reminder to buy the breads.

So-called "free plugs," because the sponsor went directly to the program host or director, rather than making a formal agreement with the network for the advertisement, were an open secret and a frequent source of humor on early live television. Hosts flaunted these independent product placements to show the audience that they had enough cache with companies to be worthy of bribes, and the power to bypass network advertising departments. As *Time* explained in a 1950 cover profile of popular radio and TV host Arthur Godfrey, "So valuable is a Godfrey free plug on the air that manufacturers, on the off chance that he will mention them, deluge him with merchandise ranging from buttermilk to uranium ore to elks."[40]

DuMont Goes Dark During the Daytime

In daytime television, as in other areas, DuMont was a victim of its success. Other broadcasters adapted DuMont's innovations and lured the network's top talent. After working at DuMont for more than a decade, the longest tenure with one network of any early television figure, Dennis James took his afternoon program to ABC in September 1951. The ABC program lasted only six months, though James remained familiar to viewers as the friendly emcee of at least a dozen different game shows, including *Name That Tune* and a prime-time version of *The Price is Right* that ran for four years. Several other popular DuMont daytime figures, including Kathi Norris (NBC), also had moved to other networks by 1951.

Having seen the way DuMont's low-budget programs for women attracted viewers and advertisers, local stations across the country began offering their own daytime schedules. By October 1950, 30 of the country's 107 stations came on the air in the morning, and 89 stations were telecasting before 5:00 P.M.[41] Daytime discussion and demonstration programs for women, along the lines of DuMont shows like *Your Television Shopper* and *Okay Mother*, were especially popular with local station operators. The programs were cheap to produce, yet they enabled stations to build a reputation for community service by providing a discussion forum for local guests and audience members. Moreover, like the first WABD daytime offerings, later women's programs were usually hosted by men and women who were skilled in the delicate art of relentless, but friendly, promotion of sponsor products. Department stores, food brokers, cosmetics companies, supermarkets, and local gas and electric companies eagerly purchased time on the shows.

Local stations also used the inexpensive women's programs to fill gaps that the networks left in the daytime schedule. For example, having accomplished its mission to stimulate the development of daytime television, DuMont cut its volume of morning and afternoon production in half, from 3 hours to 90 minutes, in 1951. However, its stations in New York, Washington, and Pittsburgh produced a full slate of local programing each day. ABC also offered, at most, one or two shows during the day. After the success of WABD, CBS and NBC became more aggressive in courting daytime viewers. The networks aired game shows, talk shows, and music-variety programs, rather than soap operas, so as not to compete with the popular afternoon dramas on radio. Between local productions and network offerings, daytime viewers had many choices by the early 1950s. Almost all of the program genres, along with the production techniques and scheduling strategies, were pioneered by WABD as part of its seminal 1948 daytime experiment.[42]

Captain Video (Al Hodge, right) and his Video Ranger (Don Hastings, left) stand ready to fight the forces of evil.

Source: All uncredited photos are courtesy of the author.

Captain Video

*Protector of the Free World and
the DuMont Network*

aptain Video aired every weeknight at seven o'clock from June 1949 to April 1955. It was DuMont's longest-running program and one of its most consistently popular shows. During *Captain Video*'s first few years, when there was nothing else like it on television, the live space adventure for children was frequently among the top-rated early evening programs, outdrawing shows ranging from *Kukla, Fran, and Ollie* to the nightly news. NBC's *Howdy Doody* was the only daily children's show that was more popular. Even after ratings began to slip and national sponsor Post Cereal pulled out of the program in the fall of 1953, thirty-one stations across the country carried *Captain Video* live or on kinescope.[1] DuMont cut the length of the program back from a half hour to fifteen minutes, but stood by the Captain until 1955, even adding a Saturday morning adventure, *The Secret Files of Captain Video*, which aired for a season from 1953 to 1954. Captain Video rested only on Sunday.

Captain Video boasted an estimated national audience of 3.5 million in the early 1950s.[2] Forty thousand fans typically jammed department stores for an appearance by actor Al Hodge, in character as the children's hero.[3] Video Ranger Don Hastings, the Captain's protégé, was one of television's first teen stars, described in a *TV Digest* profile as a "juvenile heart-throb" and "object of idolatry from the crush age sorority" of girls who joined Hastings fan clubs.[4] The Video

Ranger's commander, Captain Video, was a master of all media, the first television star to spin off into comic books and movie serials. DuMont did what it could to capitalize on the popularity of the show and its stars, licensing a range of official *Captain Video* clothing and toys, from socks to space ships. *Captain Video* gave space-age pizzazz to the prosaic snack foods and cereals promoted by the national sponsors: Powerhouse candy, Skippy peanut butter, and General Foods. In addition, other TV networks and local broadcasters tried to match *Captain Video*'s success, launching a "space opera" fad in early 1950s television and pop culture.[5]

Television's First Program in "Brockenese"

Captain Video was created by program director James Caddigan, along with writers Larry Menkin and M. C. Brock.[6] The show was based on a simple premise, described during each day's opening: "Fighting for law and order, Captain Video operates from a mountain retreat, with secret agents at all points of the globe! Possessing scientific secrets and secret weapons, Captain Video asks no quarter, and gives none to the forces of evil." Captain Video did not have superhuman powers. Nor was it clear in what service or organization he served as "captain," though he wore different military uniforms throughout his television career. According to a 1954 DuMont press release, Captain Video was a "free agent" who worked for the good of a federation of planets called the Solar Council.[7] The Captain usually accomplished his goals through a combination of physical strength, moral rectitude, and mastery of science. He specialized in developing weapons used to thwart evil and was assisted by a corps of loyal assistants, called Video Rangers. Captain Video's main sidekick for the entire program's run was a teenager who, like the Captain, was known only by his title: *the* Video Ranger. Action was usually set in the outer space world of the future, but duty could take Captain Video and the Video Ranger to venues ranging from the Old West to contemporary Shanghai. As reverential announcer Fred Scott reminded viewers, Captain Video was a "master of time and space" and the "guardian of the safety of the world." In fact, the Captain's battleground was anywhere that was more exotic than 1950s Main Street America.

The narratives from *Captain Video*'s first couple of years demonstrated a sophisticated understanding of how to appeal to the imagination of kids with short, energetic sequences and unusual visuals. Each 30-minute episode mixed dramatic scenes, advertising pitches, and fragments from old serials and b-movies. A typical program would start with a live segment showing an evil scientist like the Captain Video's long-time nemesis, Dr. Pauli, building a diabolical weapon to destroy Captain Video and the Video Ranger, along with a random planet or galaxy. The program would then cut to the mountain retreat, as Captain Video either worked to thwart the plans or went about his business with the Video Ranger, tragically unaware of the horrible fate that awaited them. Suddenly the story would be interrupted by an emergency transmission from the sponsor, or a public service announcement about citizenship, unrelated to the day's plot. The action would then shift to a ranch in the American West or an Arabian palace, where the Captain ostensibly checked in on "his agents," as seen in the movie clips that were inserted into the episodes. By the end of the episode, the viewer would see three live sequences, two or three sponsor announcements, and two sections of old films. Since it incorporated so many different segments, each show was jumpy, but it was also action packed. Elementary and middle school kids were not nitpicky about narrative structure and holes in the plot. The live adventures of a space traveling superhero and his teenage assistant were far more exciting than anything else on television after dinner. In fact, *Captain Video* was only slightly less coherent than the enormously popular movie serials that thrilled kids at weekend matinees, and it was available for free, every day of the week except Sunday, through the magic of television and the DuMont network.

Captain Video was notorious for its chintzy costumes and sets.[8] As a 1950 *TV Forecast* article noted, "The entire action takes place primarily in the headquarters of the Video Rangers—a room equipped with flashing bulbs, microphones, panels, dials, telephones which have been given names that come from electronic double talk."[9] Early director Charles Polachek and assistant director Larry White created futuristic weapons by cobbling together different items scavenged from the Wanamaker department store, the building in which DuMont's studio was located. "We created a lot of props out of automobile parts," Polachek remembered.[10] Even *Mad* magazine had trouble accepting some of *Captain Video*'s equipment. In a 1954 parody, the Commissioner is unable to remove Captain Video's cheap head gear. "Furshlungginer prop men buy these kid space helmets at the 5 and 10," exclaims the character. "When's this show gonna get a decent budget?"[11]

It didn't matter that Captain Video's most useful tool, a powerful telescope known as the "opticon scillometer," was little more than a toy gun with an automobile muffler attached to the top of it.[12] The blatantly artificial props only made it easier for kids to inhabit *Captain Video*'s fantasy world of space travel, intergalactic communication, and atomic inventions. Television writer John Javna explained that *Captain Video* "was a vehicle for children's imaginations . . . As they watched *Captain Video*, a whole generation of American children were propelled into the space age."[13] In a 1949 *New York Times* column, critic Jack Gould identified *Captain Video* as the first show of the "electronic era," recognizing an emerging aesthetic of visual excess that had little relation to reality. He noted that the show "boasts enough fancy gadgetry to bewilder the adults and fascinate the youngsters . . . It is in the use of setting, props, and special effects that 'Captain Video' derives its appeal."[14] The young fans carefully studied the spaceships and assorted gizmos on *Captain Video*, using the program to learn about life beyond Earth. In a 1951 article that could have served as a warning to William Shatner and other stars of the cult science fiction shows that followed *Captain Video*, Al Hodge wrote that fans expected him to be "extremely conversant with every new technical marvel of the years to come. It's not unusual for a youngster to approach me after a program to question me about remote carrier patterns, designs for flying saucer rings, radioactivity, time elementation and other terrifyingly complicated mechanisms."[15]

To cut production costs, DuMont hired a journeyman named Maurice Brockhauser, under the moniker M. C. Brock, to script the bulk of *Captain Video*'s daily episodes from 1949 to the middle of 1951.[16] While contemporary articles said that Brock worked on two popular radio detective shows, *Dick Tracy* and *Crimebusters*, old-time radio encyclopedias and books do not credit him (under any name) for these or other shows. As the primary *Captain Video* writer, he was handed the difficult task of filling thirty minutes each day. Brock apparently had trouble with the basics: plot, character development, and plausibility. Gould observed in 1949 that "*Captain Video* is a triumph of carpentry and wiring rather than of writing."[17] Olga Druce, who produced *Captain Video* for General Foods starting in 1951, remembered that even though she had a tight

Richard Coogan, the first Captain Video, aims the atomic rifle, complete with an automobile muffler on top and other props from the Wanamaker department store.

budget, she thought that Brock was so bad that she paid the contracted writer to stay home. Druce used to say that Brock "wrote in 'Brockenese.'" When Druce took over, the feisty producer remembered telling DuMont, "I don't want to see him [Brock]. I don't want to talk to him. I don't want to apologize [for not using him], but he will not do another show."[18] Brock apparently did not write for *Captain Video*, or any other network TV program, after Druce fired him in 1951.

Because it was so difficult to write a fresh half hour of live television each day, Brock and company lightened their workload with a skimpy gimmick. After about ten minutes of live, outer space action, either Captain Video or a colleague at headquarters would announce that it was time to check in on Captain Video's agents via the remote carrier beam. The device would magically show a few random minutes of an old serial or b-movie, with the Captain's agents presumably being the "good guys" in these simple adventures. Westerns were a particular favorite of the *Captain Video* crew. According to Hastings, who was with *Captain Video* from its debut, "The show went on [originally] to show cowboy movies. That was the thrust of it. And all of a sudden people were more interested in us than these antique, and I mean antique, cowboy movies. . . . Sometimes it was ridiculous these films that they showed. We were trying to push science fiction."[19] Producer Olga Druce recalled her frustration over the film clips when sponsor Post Cereal hired her in April 1951. "I was saddled with a show where, plunk in the middle of this futuristic show they had a western . . . Somehow, I had to make some sense out of it." At first, Druce made the best of the situation, writing smoother transitions between the live action and the clips. Over time, DuMont accommodated Druce and the sponsor by reducing the number of b-movie interruptions. DuMont eliminated the clips entirely and cut the show's length from a half hour to fifteen minutes after Post Cereal dropped its sponsorship in the fall of 1953. Druce was on the sponsor's payroll and left the show with Post.[20]

The fragments from old serials did not do much to advance the day's story, and they created some bizarre juxtapositions with the live segments; however, the clips stand as shining examples of DuMont's ingenuity and willingness to experiment with stylistic techniques in order to work within its low budgets. For one thing, the clips reduced the load of everybody working on the program, except for the unfortunate movie projectionist who had to keep these blighted prints running. The gimmick also enabled the dramatic settings to move beyond the primitive space ships where the live drama typically took place. Caddigan explained in a 1950 interview that "the western is there to give us the pace and action that we can't get in a live studio production."[21] What's more, the old westerns provided relief from all of the tense talk of atomic disintegration and intergalactic battle. As one TV writer suggested, "By employing good old-fashioned cowboy movies, all the kids are satisfied and for a few minutes the imagination gets a rest. Baffled adults having cowboy movies thrust upon them in the middle of the 21st century have been known to leave the room muttering to themselves, but the kids take it all in stride."[22] Children had no trouble mastering *Captain Video*'s use of film clips, cheap props, and strange story lines. Thus, critics and parents were forced to acknowledge a generation gap. *Time* skeptically observed that "this atomic-age potboiler appears to make sense to its adolescent audience," though many adult viewers "are soon lost in its trackless, pseudo-technical doubletalk . . . or by the sudden appearance on Captain Video's 'Scanner' of a five-minute stretch of Western movie." [23] After growing up on *Captain Video*—which appealed directly to kids with noise, energy, and chaos—many young people were ready to move on to the teen movies and rock and roll that dominated pop culture with a similar aesthetic by the late 1950s.

Captain Video Is Everywhere

Aimed at a slightly older audience than popular contemporary fare like *Howdy Doody* (NBC) and DuMont's *Magic Cottage, Captain Video* was one of the first television programs to demonstrate the value of the pre-teen market. Nevertheless, it took a little while for advertisers to appreciate DuMont's strange little show. *Captain Video* did not have a sponsor when DuMont introduced it in June 1949. As the network waited for a patron, it simply aired a test pattern with the words "Video Ranger Message" during the time in each episode at which an advertisement would normally appear. In these sixty-second television equivalents of unsold billboards offering space for sale, announcer Fred Scott spoke to viewers at home as if they were part of Captain Video's Video Rangers force. He generally offered the young Video Rangers short civics lessons on anything from prejudice to the meaning of freedom. When Johnson Candy took over sponsorship in January 1950, the company filled some of these public service spots with promotions for special Video Ranger premiums. A 1950 pitch for the Captain Video ring was typical of such segments. The friendly spokesman, dressed in Captain Video military fatigues, looked into the camera and tried to persuade young viewers to enlist as Video Rangers by purchasing the ring. "You'll wear it at all times to show that you're fighting alongside Captain Video as the guardian of the safety of the free world."[24] A cheap-looking show like *Captain Video* was ideal for merchandising: sponsors and licensees could credibly claim that the guns, rings, and uniforms for sale at the local store were the same ones that were used on the set.

Off the screen, DuMont appealed to prospective Video Rangers at home with print ads, radio spots, mail order catalog listings, and attractive product packaging. In addition, the actors who played the Video Ranger (Don Hastings, 1949–1955) and Captain Video (Richard Coogan, 1949–1950, Al Hodge, 1950–1955) scoured the nation's shopping centers, department stores, and summer fairs looking for new recruits. By early 1951, with the Captain's popularity well established, DuMont and merchandisers launched an "all-out merchandising campaign based around the program," according to *Billboard*. DuMont predicted that *Captain Video* products would do more than $50 million worth of business over the next year.[25] Advertisements and articles showed well-equipped kids in Captain Video uniforms, enhanced with everything from a crash helmet to a Video Ranger neck tie to an authentic Atomic Disintegrator Rifle.[26] Department stores established Captain Video Command Posts, which radio ads promised would enable kids "to look like Captain Video . . . They even have official copies of the Atomic weapons the Captain himself uses."[27] Several business commentators recognized television's role in fueling a craze for space toys and apparel. Kids "learn how to operate rocket ships before they're old enough to ride bicycles," wrote Philip Santora in a 1954 *New York Daily News* feature. Outer space had replaced the Old West in the imagination of young people. "For the last two years, toy manufacturers have recognized the fact that most children are no longer as interested in tin soldiers as they are in tin rocket ships and atomic rifles."[28]

Why Does Captain Video Look Different?

Realizing that it had a hot commodity, in December 1950, DuMont hired Al Hodge to replace Richard Coogan, who had played Captain Video since the show's debut eighteen months earlier.[29] Coogan had thirteen years of experience on stage and radio when DuMont chose him as the first Captain Video. He continued to work on Broadway opposite Mae West in *Diamond Lil* while serving as the Captain. "As soon as the show was over, he had to run over to the theater," remembered his co-star, Hastings.[30] Coogan portrayed the television hero with the mildly bemused and detached demeanor of a serious actor, at age thirty-five, paying the bills by dressing up in strange, ill-fitting Army surplus garb every day to play the lead in a poorly written kids' show. Coogan's mode of preparing for each episode helps to explain the minor flubs that marked *Captain Video*'s early years. To keep the role interesting, Coogan refused to read scripts until the day the episode was slated to air. According to the *New York Times*, Coogan also fought off "monotony by occasionally tossing in a line that had not been in the script." Nevertheless, Coogan and the rest of the cast always rehearsed. Coogan explained, "The lines are so corny that we always break up in rehearsal. If it was all new on camera, we couldn't keep a straight face."[31] Coogan usually did not let his irreverent attitude leave the rehearsal studio, but his performance both on camera and in interviews indicated that he was well aware of the program's limitations. In contrast, the man who replaced Coogan was a true believer in Captain Video's mission and the program's power to influence young minds.

Hodge was a Mutual radio network veteran when he took over the role of Captain Video. He started his career as a copywriter and sportscaster at WXYZ in Detroit and was best known nationally as the heroic star of *The Green Hornet* from 1936–1943. In addition, he was an actor and director on other children's adventures produced for Mutual at WXYZ, including *Challenge of the Yukon* and *The Lone Ranger*. Hodge also worked outside the juvenile genre at WXYZ, announcing football games, writing editorials for a local commentary program, and producing ad copy.[32] By the time that he arrived at DuMont, Hodge was equipped to engage in the sorts of activities required of a children's action hero: making personal appearances, contributing to the script, and describing the show's moral mission to reporters. As a bonus, he was also a decent actor.

The initial episodes starring Hodge were not all that different from those with Coogan. Nevertheless, as the new Captain, Hodge provided a gravity and intensity that defined the character over time. "Al was a much straighter guy than Coogan," Hastings remembered. "Al was very much in control. He looked like [someone from] the Joint Chiefs of Staff."[33] Donald F. Glut and Jim Harmon wrote in their appreciative history of early television that Hodge "looked heroic and, even more than Coogan, played Video with total believability."[34] These qualities emerged both on screen and through Hodge's publicity efforts off camera. Whereas Coogan used interviews and personal appearances to advance side projects and establish ironic distance between himself and the role, Hodge stayed in character and amplified values that had been part of the show from its 1949 debut: morality, tolerance, anti-communism, and the need for national strength. In so doing, Hodge helped DuMont define *Captain Video* for kids, parents, and critics. He also provided one of the first examples of the way a TV star's image could be used to promote a program and related merchandise, along with a healthy set of moral ideals.

Unlike Coogan, Hodge felt an immediate kinship with Captain Video, recognizing in a 1951 article that the role required him to merge his identity with that of the Captain even off screen. "No matter what I do," Hodge wrote, "I can't escape being Captain Video. And that goes for twenty-four hours of the day and every day of the week . . . I am hailed in the streets by unknown boys or called up all hours of the day and night. Fans want me to solve all sorts of problems."[35] In these days before frequent flyer programs and easy air travel, Hodge logged an astonishing 50,000 miles a year, mostly via train, making personal appearances while starring on a daily program that seldom went on hiatus.[36] Despite the pressures of being a role model, Hodge treated his position with a grim sense of duty, as any good captain would.

Hodge echoed the beliefs of Allen B. Du Mont and others in fields ranging from broadcasting to the social sciences regarding the power of television to educate viewers. As the actor wrote in 1951, "I have seen first hand how powerfully television influences youngsters . . . I like being Captain Video. I feel the role plays an integral part in instilling fair play, honesty, and integrity in the minds of children."[37] He accepted the responsibilities of a role model on camera and off. Hodge frequently told interviewers about his weekend gig as a Sunday School teacher at a church near his home in Manhasset, New York, where he delivered a short sermon before delving into Bible study. For Hodge, acting in *Captain Video* was a missionary extension of his religious instruction. "We [*Captain Video*] stress the Golden Rule, tolerance, honesty, and personal integrity. We try, during the week, to bring across what we teach on Sundays. In fact, the Scriptures are our inspiration."[38]

Al Hodge: a heroic Captain Video.

The most bizarre product of *Captain Video*'s fusion of pop culture and religion was "Captain Video's Toughest Mission," a short story that Hodge wrote for *Guideposts*, a popular magazine edited by Norman Vincent Peale. Our hero must save Planet City from Callisto, a villain wielding a "hate ray" that destroys churches and synagogues. When the Video Ranger wonders why Callisto is targeting religious sanctuaries, the Captain gravely explains, "They're our greatest strength, Ranger.

Callisto knows it. First he destroys the churches. Then it'll be race against race, planet against planet."[39] Luckily, Captain Video is able to turn the hate ray on Callisto and save the houses of worship. The adventure apparently was not adapted from print for the television series.

General Foods Fuels Blast-Off

A few months after Hodge took over, the casting change began to pay dividends. General Foods agreed to sponsor *Captain Video* nationally, five nights a week. Although exact figures were not released, the agreement was reported as DuMont's largest advertising contract to date. General Foods supported the program from April 1951 through September 1953, when local advertisers took over for the remainder of *Captain Video*'s run.[40] By 1951, DuMont understood that television production techniques, viewers, and sponsors were more sophisticated than they had been even a couple of years earlier. Incomprehensible plots and sets that even a ten-year-old could recognize as inauthentic were no longer acceptable. Together, General Foods and DuMont increased *Captain Video*'s budget and provided a strong creative team. Skillful and ambitious figures like Hodge, producer Olga Druce, and a stable of top writers from radio and science fiction magazines used *Captain Video* to tell complex stories that tackled concepts like freedom, democracy, and scientific ethics.

Producers came and went on *Captain Video* and most other DuMont shows. Some worked for several networks on a freelance basis; others were under contract to DuMont or advertising agencies. Regardless of who cut their paychecks, almost all producers were supervisors who were responsible for several programs. They usually hired writers and approved casting, but had little other direct effect on the program each week. The ones who were most influential, like Hal Cooper on *The Magic Cottage*, created a program and stayed with it for several years.

Nobody took control of an established DuMont show and put a stamp on it the way Olga Druce did. She had the backing of General Foods' influential advertising agency, Benton and Bowles, along with a strong personality and deeply held beliefs about children's television.

Druce drastically changed the tenor of the children's show during her two years at the helm (1951–1953), the longest stint of any producer. Before Druce, the cast and crew recognized and enjoyed *Captain Video*'s sloppiness: cheap sets, flubbed lines, one-dimensional heroes and villains, confusing stories, clichéd writing. In contrast, Druce elevated the show, even though her budget remained low. She remembers her reaction when she took over the program. "I was ready to commit suicide. I had no sense of humor about it. In my maturity, I realize that the guy who was directing it was very clever and he did a good job and he treated it as a big joke, but to me it was an abomination . . . my sense of humor has never extended to child psychology," Druce said.[41]

The forty-year-old Druce was living in London, unemployed, in early 1951. She had never worked in television, but her experience creating radio juvenile programing for Benton and Bowles prompted the agency to call her for *Captain Video*. "I started writing for *Superman* because at that time I had become very interested in child psychology and broadcasting for children," Druce explained in a July 2000 interview. Druce was eighty-nine years old at the time, still active teaching a class in storytelling at the YMCA. In the 1940s, radio "was going through terrific criticism for cruelty and racism and sexism . . . and at the top of the list of radio shows was *Superman*. So I was hired to rescue it."[42] After *Superman*, Druce produced *House of Mystery*, a kids' radio show that told tales of the supernatural, also for Benton and Bowles. Druce built the *House of Mystery* episodes on a foundation of strong stories and scientific accuracy. "Not having a scientific mind, I had to find writers who could supply me with material," she explained. "When you're doing it [children's broadcasting], it becomes like the Bible. It's got to be scientific." A 1951 *Variety* piece noting Druce's arrival on *Captain Video* praised her radio work for integrating "sound educational material into a mysterioso format." The review implied that the new producer would not have an easy time reforming the TV show.[43]

In producing programs that were both instructive and realistic, Druce wanted to paint the Captain and his adversaries as more complex characters. "My emphasis was to create a hero and to show that the hero had faults and weaknesses, and that he had to overcome his doubts to become a hero . . . The emphasis was on making a hero and making

Captain Video producer Olga Druce.
Source: TV Today (Detroit), October 18, 1952.

space really mean something." Prior producers of *Captain Video* were career television people, with additional responsibilities at DuMont, who
apparently did not express missionary zeal for the show's pedagogical
power. In contrast, Druce's production strategy integrated current psy-
chological thinking regarding social learning along with a healthy dose
of 1950s Freudianism. In a manifesto for children's programing that was
published in *Radio-Television Daily,* Druce reminded her colleagues that
"producing a children's show is not child's play. It is serious business."

Like Hodge, she recognized that television figures, especially adventure heroes such as *Captain Video,* served as role models. Their actions contributed to a child's happiness and sense of self-worth. It was important for the producer to "delineate [the hero's] character in the most interesting and admirable way possible . . . When he experiences moments of self-doubt and fear, let him admit it. But make him always a man of faith—honest, persevering and courageous." Implicitly criticizing the old *Captain Video*s, similar children's programs, and movie serials, Druce also urged producers to replace one-dimensional outlaws with more realistic figures. "In life, villains do exist, but they exist as people, seldom as monsters. In portraying the villain, we should strive to show his villainy as compounded rarely of black deeds and deceit alone, but rather as exaggerated expressions of negative drives and desires." Children could then recognize these human traits in themselves and others, and act accordingly.[44]

As was typical, the sponsor paid DuMont for the use of its production crew and facilities. DuMont was reluctant to trim its profits by investing more money in the show. "They fought me every step of the way," Druce later explained with a mischievous smile. "They were the crumbiest network. As far as they were concerned, I was the biggest pain in the neck."[45] Through negotiation and compromise, however, Druce convinced DuMont to boost production values and make the space adventures seem more plausible. Building the slick-looking *Galaxy* space ship for the show in 1952 was one of Druce's greatest achievements. DuMont gave the producer a production budget of $6,500 to cover props, talent, and writers for five shows a week. In comparison, NBC's *Howdy Doody,* a far less technically ambitious show, spent between $1,500 and $2,500 per episode.[46] Druce saved a bit each week until she had enough for the *Galaxy,* which cost $12,000 ($80,000 in 2003 dollars). Her friend, science-fiction writer Arthur C. Clarke, aided Druce with the design and construction of the *Galaxy.* "With Arthur's help, and the young painters and sculptors who worked with me, we built the first [television] space ship . . . It was Arthur's biggest joke, but when he did *2001* he called those boys. They were painters. They were artists."[47]

Starting in 1952, TV critics began to take *Captain Video* seriously, analyzing the program's presentation of science, politics, violence, and interpersonal relationships. The pioneering DuMont show was accorded a respectful position in numerous articles about the "space opera" craze in early 1950s popular culture.[48] *Captain Video*'s world seemed less unusual as kids and their parents became accustomed to juvenile comics, short stories, movies, radio adventures, and TV programs set in outer space. In addition, *Captain Video* had matured stylistically. The plots became easier to follow, while the treatment of science and space travel became more plausible. As TV critic Jack Cluett recognized, "James L. Caddigan, DuMont's Director of Programing and Production, plus Druce and a large chunk of sponsor cash put an end to this jumbled mess, shoved the Captain into a rocket ship, and sent him skyward, where he rightfully belonged."[49]

Those Guys Wrote for *Captain Video?*

Druce hired acclaimed writers from science fiction magazines to create programs that were scientifically accurate and morally instructive. The producer demanded stories that would help the young viewer "take his place as a responsible citizen of his community, his country, and the world."[50] The list of contributors to *Captain Video* during Druce's reign includes many important figures from the so-called Golden Age of Science Fiction: Jack Vance, Damon Knight, C. M. Kornbluth, Robert Sheckley, James Blish, and Walter M. Miller. "They were very happy to be on TV and to learn the form," Druce said. "They all worked very hard and very seriously. For all of them it was the first time they had written for television. But they wrote for *Galaxy* and *Astounding* [*Science-Fiction*]."[51]

No kinescopes of the *Captain Video* episodes by these talented authors remain, but a set of scripts written by Jack Vance exemplify the way Vance provided riveting outer space action while incorporating current psychology, sociology, and a dash of Cold War politics. In the series, circa May 1953, Captain Video returns to the aptly named Black Planet, a totalitarian society. His mission: to help young Prince Spartak begin a Video Ranger Academy which will train warriors in "the principles of humanity and democracy."[52] From the first program of the ten episode series, Vance powerfully communicates Druce's themes regarding the need for heroes to confront their fears.

Captain Video has bad memories of his last visit to Black Planet, where an entity called the "Voice of Ultimate Authority" injured him using a "gravitic ray." Showing more self-doubt than he would have pre-Druce, Captain Video reminds the Video Ranger that "Black Planet's a queer place. I hope we're not in for anything more like that."[53] Still, Captain Video answers Spartak's call and places himself in a number of precarious situations over the next two weeks. Early in the first episode, for example, a villain named Komar challenges Captain Video to a dangerous game of "space jousting." Initially, the hero does not want to play. "What's the matter, Captain? Afraid?" asks Komar, in the manner of a schoolyard bully. Captain Video is strong enough to admit his fear. "I certainly am. I'm afraid that one of us might get hurt." Nevertheless, when pushed to confront this fear and fight Komar, Captain Video is successful.[54]

In a subsequent episode, Spartak is humiliated because he loses a boxing match to a Black Planet adversary. Spartak and Captain Video believe that the fight was rigged, but they cannot prove it. The loss triggers an identity crisis: as one of the Captain's Video Rangers, Spartak knows that defeat in a fixed fight is no disgrace, but his Black Planet countrymen insist on labeling him a failure. Spartak struggles to explain his feelings to the Video Ranger in the sort of fractured, frustrated language guaranteed to strike a chord with the teenage and pre-teen viewer. "I've been brought up a Black Planet noble. Failing—does something to me. It's emotional . . . I know better—but I can't help it."[55] In a later episode, Captain Video explains, "You're suffering from what a psychologist would call 'suggestion,' Spartak." The tormented young man wonders how he can shed the shameful anguish of defeat. The Video Ranger suggests that "it's a matter of getting your confidence back." Captain Video adds helpfully, "That comes from inside yourself."[56]

Beyond offering models for overcoming labels and social stigmas, the story of Captain Video's mission to open the Ranger Academy reinforces the show's pro-democracy message. A series of climactic duels, "broadcast all over the planet," serves as the forum by which Captain Video and Spartak must prove their mettle and demonstrate a model combination of military strength, maximum effort, and a sense of fair play.[57] Even though the overmatched Captain loses these battles, his noble efforts are not wasted on the Black Planet television audience. The oppressed workers are inspired by Captain Video to "leave their collective farm." One rebel explains, "If failure didn't discourage Captain Video, it's not going to discourage me."[58] Writing about a similar sequence of Black Planet episodes, a *TV Digest* praised *Captain Video* for instructing kids about the value of the American way. "Spartak's realization that the ways of democracy are an improvement over the only kind of government he has ever known is an excellent example to the small fry and teaches them, better than any amount of lecturing, the lessons of personal freedom and the privileges of a free world."[59]

Mommy, What's an Atom Bomb?

Vance's scripts featured all sorts of tense and violent scenarios, from nuclear ray fights to the Video Ranger falling through a bottomless mine shaft. A sense of terror had always lurked within *Captain Video*'s stories. Mad scientists invented all sorts of devices, many with atomic-sounding names, to destroy civilizations. In a 1950 kinescope, a scientist known as the Sparrow, with a vaguely German accent, unleashes a weapon that levels a large area. According to one of the Captain's men, "The heat of flames was so intense that even stones were burned to a powder." Nevertheless, the Sparrow promises that this initial blast was only a demonstration of the new weapon's devastating capabilities. He warns that "my next experiment will really astound the world. My next experiment. Fire, flames, smoke will cover the sky like an unbroken cloud and extend far into the universe. Destruction by fire. Ha ha ha."[60] During this 1949–1950 period, when it was clear that the Russians had the atom bomb and the United States pushed forward with its own hydrogen bomb program, parents may not have found the Sparrow's gleeful destruction all that funny. They were attempting to navigate the very real ethical and practical implications of living on the brink of nuclear annihilation.

Captain Video was rebuked because of its violence by the individuals and groups that monitored children's television. One of the show's staunchest critics was the National Association for Better Radio and Television (NAFBRAT), the most prominent early 1950s watchdog.[61] Headed by Clara Logan, the Los Angeles-based association's diverse board included communications professor Dallas Smythe (University of Illinois), education professor Paul Witty (Northwestern University), critic and former CBS executive Gilbert Seldes, and psychologist Frederic Wertham, whose *Seduction of the Innocent* (1954) stimulated intense public debate about the effects of mass media on children.[62] In its annual surveys, NAFBRAT evaluated particular shows according to three criteria: (1) portrayal of "the moral and social ideals of American life"; (2) influence on the "emotional and intellectual development of a child"; (3) "standards of showmanship, i.e., good writing, acting, and directing." As NAFBRAT explained, in criticizing several westerns, "crime is never acceptable as the theme of a children's program." Nor did the organization condone programs that placed "undue stress upon fear and aggression."[63] Of fifty-one programs rated in the 1954 survey, *Captain Video* was one of the five shows that NAFBRAT placed in the "most objectionable" category, its lowest classification. In its brief notation, the organization faulted *Captain Video* for airing "crime themes of the most frightening varieties [and] suspense endings."[64]

Olga Druce was originally hired to bring *Captain Video* in line with the standards of good television established by organizations like NAFBRAT. "General Foods was presented with a very cheap buy and they wanted someone to clean it up," she said. "I was the sanitation department."[65] Druce's agenda gave the parents' groups some of what they wanted. The producer demanded good stories, with strong doses of science education and moral instruction. Druce and Al Hodge constantly promoted these qualities in their publicity for the show. Still, *Captain Video* was undeniably violent. In 1954, after Druce left the show, the Senate Subcommittee to Investigate Juvenile Delinquency called upon Hodge to discuss *Captain Video*. In a courteous exchange with the senators and committee council, Hodge emphasized that DuMont vetted scripts to make sure that the show conformed with the National Association of Radio and Television Broadcasters (NARTB) Code created by the television industry. Still, he explained, "of necessity, we have to have violence. Otherwise, there is no excuse for a heroic character existing. He has to go after somebody." Much of Hodge's testimony emphasized the show's "good taste" and moral responsibility regarding the presentation of violence. For example, Hodge noted that "these villains are never hung. They are never subject to capital punishment." In fact, Captain Video tried not to kill anybody. "We use a gun we call a blaster or a stungun. We have been very careful to point out that this gun does not kill anybody. This gun merely immobilizes

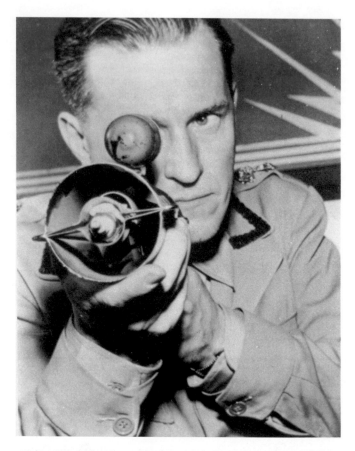

Captain Video (Al Hodge) searches for evil-doers with the help of the opticon scillometer, an x-ray device that allowed Captain Video to see virtually anything. Though Captain Video struck a fearsome pose, Hodge insisted that any violence was in good taste.

an adversary to the point that we can take whatever lethal weapon he may have away from him."[66] The congressional questioners seemed satisfied with Hodge's explanation of these weapons, apparently accepting the right of TV superheroes to temporarily paralyze rivals.

Without explicitly condemning the show, most television critics described Captain Video's brutal arsenal more accurately. "The cosmic ray vibrator, for instance, shakes a victim into submission and the atomic rifle pelts him with atomic energy," explained Murray Robinson in *Collier's*. "The thermal ejector can douse him with enough thermal waves to roast a small heifer . . . The nucleamatic pistol, a paralyzing ray gun, can give a man a hard time, too. Hard, but not fatal."[67] Every day for nearly six years, *Captain Video* gave children thrills by showing them a universe, in as much graphic detail as 1950s standards would allow, filled with nefarious and crazy outlaws of all types: from brilliant scientists bent on destroying the world, to cool dictators who ban religion and enslave the masses. Despite the show's reassuring messages about American physical, moral, and technological superiority, *Captain Video*'s world was not very safe. *Captain Video* was one of the first TV programs, for kids or adults, to dramatize, and occasionally exploit, the perilous world situation. Kids saw a thrilling and scary future fraught with dangers beyond the control of even *Captain Video*. The hero could only act as an itinerant freedom fighter, traveling to horribly troubled spots throughout the universe, hoping to contain damage until viewers tuned in the next day. Still, as children pondered their own daily battles with dangers ranging from schoolyard bullies to communists at home and abroad, Captain Video provided a model of moral rectitude, tolerance, and ingenuity. His weapons—cool gadgets, a loyal squadron of Video Rangers, and the ability to land a mean left hook when absolutely necessary—could be deployed from outer space to Levittown.

Captain Video Returns to Earth

Even the great Captain Video, however, could not save DuMont. On April 1, 1955, Captain Video ended his last adventure, a casualty of DuMont's weakening position and the show's diminishing ratings after nearly six years and approximately twelve hundred episodes. Video Ranger Don Hastings used *Captain Video* as a springboard to a successful television acting career, including a long stint as Dr. Bob Hughes on *As the World Turns* (CBS). Al Hodge returned as Captain Video on local station WABD, hosting more conventional children's programs. In the first spinoff, a Sunday afternoon show that premiered in July 1955, Hodge introduced a mixture of educational films and serials. The Captain then emceed a daily cartoon program, *Captain Video and His Cartoon Rangers*, from March 1956 to August 1957. From there, he had a couple of short-lived programs on Newark, New Jersey's WNTA-TV (*Super Serial Show*) and New York's WOR-TV (*Al Hodge's Space Explorers*). His final stint as Captain Video ended in 1961.[68]

One of the first victims of television's power to pigeonhole actors, Hodge migrated to Hollywood in search of work after *Captain Video*. He found little there "because of his typecast image, and soon returned to the New York area," according to his 1979 *Variety* obituary. In New York, Hodge "dropped reluctantly from the business—doing odd jobs that included real estate, bank guard, and store clerk." Even years after the show ended, when Hodge was back in civilian life, working as a security guard and doing occasional commercial work, strangers stopped him on the street. Hodge remembered that one wise guy, echoing the opening to *Captain Video*, asked if Hodge was on his way to his "secret mountain headquarters on planet Earth to rally men of good will and lead them against the forces of evil everywhere." In telling the story, Hodge joked that he was relieved that this man did not recite the entire opening. Still, the encounter illustrates the extent to which DuMont's space opera defined Hodge's life and career.[69]

Morey Amsterdam.

6

What'd He Say?

Morey Amsterdam Meets Norman Rockwell

Television was cutting-edge, futuristic entertainment after World War II. Ironically, however, DuMont and other broadcasters filled airtime by looking back to vaudeville variety and silent-movie comedy: two related forms of entertainment that had been dead for nearly twenty years. This nostalgic programing quickly became the most popular TV genre in the late 1940s and early 1950s. The stand-up comedians who held the programs together became national celebrities within weeks of their television debuts. Milton Berle, Sid Caesar, Jack Carter, Morey Amsterdam, Jackie Gleason, and the team of Dean Martin and Jerry Lewis were not exactly show business novices. They honed their acts in nightclubs and resorts over many years, but were not household names. Most had tried radio or film, without a great deal of critical or commercial success, before finding a home on television. Consumers decided to buy TV sets so that they could watch the comedians host variety shows filled with singers, dancers, and oddball acts in weekly live performances from New York studios and theaters. Arthur Godfrey and Ted Mack brought their amateur talent shows to television in 1948, but most of the biggest radio names—Fred Allen, Jack Benny, Burns and Allen, and Eddie Cantor—remained in Hollywood, watching their TV screens and the ratings books to see what kinds of performances worked before plunging into the new medium.

With television producers looking for new acts in nightclubs and stage shows, DuMont was primed to compete with the other networks. Even as radio's stars moved to TV in the early 1950s, DuMont producers found a wealth of young and affordable talent in the nightclubs and theaters of Broadway, a few blocks from their offices at 515 Madison Avenue. The network aired a whopping forty different live music or variety series from 1949 to 1954. Like much on DuMont, most of these programs and their stars lasted only a season or two before moving to another network or, more commonly, back to the streets of New York. Nevertheless, the astonishing conglomeration of live acts offered early viewers the pleasure and novelty of seeing New York entertainment for free in the comfort of their living rooms. DuMont made variety shows the centerpiece of its corporate strategy for popularizing the medium. The company's Receiver Division technically operated independently from the Broadcasting unit, but it sponsored several variety programs on the network, including *School House*, *Window on the World*, and *The Morey Amsterdam Show* (also known as *The Silver Swan Café*). In its print ads and the shows that it sponsored, the Receiver Division tried to portray television as a wondrous and classy new medium that could transport viewers to exciting, distant locales. Unfortunately, DuMont's early variety programing was not always able to support the lofty claims, and hopes, of the advertising department.

Milton Berle and the Return of Vaudeville

The figure who provided a model for early television variety on DuMont and everywhere else was based at NBC. Milton Berle is synonymous with the Golden Age of Television: the single figure most credited (or blamed) for sending Americans to the local appliance stores, where they placed down payments on their first television receivers. Berle and the army of comics who followed him to the small screen were seen as revolutionaries in 1948. Berle showed particular audacity in recovering an entertainment form, the vaudeville production, that had been dormant for nearly twenty years. In an enthusiastic review of Berle's June 8, 1948, pilot, sponsored by Texaco gasoline, *Variety* magazine critic Joe Cohen voiced surprise and sentimental approval over the reappearance of vaudeville. "The *Texaco*

Star Theater projects a new kind of show business—a revival of an era that had its greatest showcasing at the old Palace Theatre before the days of air conditioning."[1]

The Berle show adopted a vaudeville format, with multiple acts, and brought back stock characters, such as Sid Stone's fast-talking pitchman, whose "tell ya what I'm gonna do" line became one of the first phrases popularized by TV. Berle's *Texaco Star Theater* (NBC) and other variety shows introduced America to rising talents and gave established stars a chance to promote their latest film, play, or recording. Television variety also resurrected the careers of old, and largely forgotten, vaudevillians. After all, who knew the style better than they did? For example, when the Berle show premiered as a regular series on September 21, 1948, following the success of the summer pilot, the guests included the old comedy team of Smith and Dale, who became ubiquitous on early variety shows. Smith and Dale were also known to later audiences as models for the title characters in *The Sunshine Boys,* the 1972 Neil Simon play that was adapted for film in 1975.

Berle was not alone in bringing vaudeville back to America, via television, in the summer of 1948. On June 20, a little over a week after Berle's pilot telecast, CBS debuted Ed Sullivan's *Toast of the Town,* which was essential Sunday night viewing through 1971. In addition, ABC's flagship station in New York, WJZ-TV, rented the Palace, the old theater that symbolized vaudeville's heyday, for its inaugural broadcast, on August 10. The 5-hour variety show featured a dog act, singers, dancers, acrobats, and comedians. At a time when a New York TV station opening was worthy of national attention, *Time* waxed nostalgic about the night's entertainment, leading its review of the telecast with the news that "vaudeville, long pronounced dead, has never looked more alive."[2] By the end of the pivotal summer of 1948, so-called "vaudeo" (vaudeville on video) was all over the television dial.[3] During the 1949–1950 season, when national Nielsen ratings were first available, Berle and Sullivan helmed television's two highest-rated shows.[4] Networks scoured New York's nightclubs and talent agencies for performers to fill slots on variety programs. The most sought after figures were emcees, especially comedians, who could energize a production, make an audience laugh, and build a loyal following for a program and its sponsors.

Early DuMont Variety: *School House* and *Window on the World*

In January 1949, six months after the Berle and Sullivan shows debuted, DuMont premiered two comedy-variety shows: *School House* and *Window on the World*. Each ran through the summer of 1949. Examples of DuMont's early success in lining up national affiliates to carry some of its more high-profile programs, *School House* and *Window on the World* aired live in sixteen of the thirty cities that had television in early 1949. Another five stations aired kinescopes of each program. In comparison, the *Texaco Star Theater* secured live clearances in fourteen markets (an additional eight stations aired the show on kinescope) and Sullivan's *Toast of the Town* was seen live in seven markets, while two stations aired it on kinescope. The only program with wider live coverage than DuMont's variety shows was the *Admiral Broadway Revue*, starring Sid Caesar, which aired for a little over four months on twenty-one NBC stations and seventeen additional DuMont affiliates.[5]

DuMont failed to take advantage of its success in clearing stations. *School House* and *Window on the World* were not expensive, high-quality programs likely to deliver blockbuster ratings and major sponsors. Both programs employed gimmicky framing devices, perhaps to compensate for deficiencies in writing and production values. *School House* was modeled on the "School Days" vaudeville shows that used classroom sets as showcases for "student" performers. The program serves as a reminder to historians that all variety programs from television's early age were not golden; however, the novelty of television was so great before 1950 that even these erratic shows aired on national networks and found audiences.

Most of the *School House* cast members were skillful actors, musicians, dancers, and comics. The students included Wally Cox as a pedantic pupil and Arnold Stang, who was starting to attract attention as a radio actor on *The Goldbergs* and *The Henry Morgan Show*. Stang played an awkward class clown on *School House*. Both actors later found more appropriate showcases for their skills on other television networks: Cox graduated to star on NBC's *Mr. Peepers* and Stang worked as a character actor on a number of programs, including *The Buick-Berle Show*, Berle's successor to *Texaco Star Theater*. The *School House* instructor was Kenny Delmar, also well known to audiences from *The Fred Allen Show*, *The Henry*

Morgan Show, and other radio programs. *Variety* magazine wrote in its review of the debut episode that *School House* "came up with top talent and dissipated its opportunities . . . Two major weaknesses were the absence of a suitable script and the faulty direction."[6] Performers sang and danced in front of a single, immobile camera. *School House*'s bare visual style, awkward pacing, and stiff writing was standard pre-1950 fare, but it was a cut below the top shows on other networks.

Like *School House*, *Window on the World* was sponsored by DuMont's Receiver Division in the hopes of moving TV sets. Taking its title from the company's slogan at the time, *Window on the World* illustrates the combination of wild optimism and mild frustration with which DuMont and others in the TV industry regarded television in early 1949. TV manufacturers and broadcasters were excited about the almost magical potential of television, but they were also bemused by the restraints under which they operated. Using a more experimental format than *School House*, the series aimed to take viewers on a virtual world tour each week. Unfortunately, DuMont and the other networks had neither the production budgets nor the technological capacity to telecast each week from multiple locations. Instead, director George Justin created the illusion of world travel from the DuMont studios and control room. *Window on the World* mixed live music and comedy performances staged on exotic studio sets along with very old stock footage of foreign cities. An off-screen narrator functioned as both a pilot and tour guide, explaining where the show was taking viewers. Each episode also included a series of short narrative sketches in which a fictional couple, the Halls, praised their new DuMont TV receiver.

The TV set is front and center from the start of the single surviving episode of *Window on the World*.[7] A teenage babysitter named Betty arrives for work at the comfortable Hall family home. The Halls are about to attend a neighbor's party celebrating the purchase of a new television. Although Betty usually requires lots of notice, she is happy to take the job at the last minute because the Halls own a DuMont set. "I'd break almost any date to sit for you now," Betty explains to Mrs. Hall. The model family on *Window on the World* is upgrading to a new DuMont from an old receiver, manufactured by another company. Young Betty notices the difference as she stands next to the new DuMont table-top model. "This set has such a big, bright screen and the pictures are so steady and it's direct view." She then stops her reverie. "Oh my goodness. It's time for the DuMont show."

After this short prologue, the camera pans to the TV set. The shot of a TV screen in the living room dissolves to the show's title, as the premise of *Window on the World* is described by a friendly narrator named Leslie Litamy. "Stay right where you are. You don't have to move. Television brings everything to you. Just keep your eyes on the window on the world." In early 1949, when it was an achievement to connect New York and Chicago via coaxial cables, television could not yet fulfill this grandiose promise of being an omnipotent window on the world. It took a tremendous amount of planning for telecasters to transmit occasional live sporting events, political conventions, and presidential speeches from remote locations. Network entertainment, for the most part, originated in New York studios. *Window on the World* spoofs television's limited technical capacity and DuMont's proclivity to run shoddy films as filler by presenting the world as a series of grainy, blighted travelogues with wry commentary. In the first segment, for example, the show starts in Acapulco with a dance routine. The cheery announcer starts with a bad pun about television transmission. "A lot of people travel by air to Acapulco. We bring Acapulco by air to you." He overlooks the poor quality footage of beaches and old buildings. "There's some mighty fine scenery down in old Mexico. What would you say to a boat ride?" The old films yield to a better quality live segment from the DuMont studio starring a dancer named Estelle Sloan, who does a nice Irish jig but makes no attempt to follow the Mexico theme.

The live performances are accorded respect in that they are presented without the comments that accompany the travelogues, or the blatant commercialism of the Hall family segments. The most esteemed slot in the program is reserved for the headliners that close the show: the old comedy team of Smith and Dale doing their Eskimo National Savings Bank routine. The actors employ thick Yiddish accents and construct their humor from silly words and well-timed puns. For example, the banker tries to sell a patron insurance. "If you should die, what would your wife bury you with?" The customer replies, "With pleasure." Joe Smith breaks character after one unsuccessful punch line to tell viewers that they are watching "advanced vaudeville." With its slow pace and dated humor, the closing vaudeville act from *Window on the World* is too long for television and seems incongruous on a program devoted to high-lighting the medium's promise as a window on the world of 1949; how-ever, like many early variety programs, *Window on the World* relied on the comforts of the past as it moved viewers into the future.

Ladies and Gentlemen: Morey Amsterdam

Searching for stars to match figures like Berle (NBC), Caesar (NBC), and Sullivan (CBS), in April 1949 DuMont replaced *School House* and *Window on the World* with programs that served as vehicles for popular entertainers. *The Ted Steele Show* featured the New York disk jockey and band leader who, by mid-1949, was a television veteran, having hosted music variety shows on NBC, CBS, and DuMont. The Tuesday evening Steele program competed against NBC's popular *Fireside Theatre*, which had Berle as a lead-in at eight o'clock. Steele lasted only through the end of the summer, though he returned the next year as a host of DuMont's *Cavalcade of Bands* variety show.[8]

Comedian Morey Amsterdam had more luck with a program that replaced *Window on the World* on Thursday evenings. At a time when there were only about one hundred stations operating nationally, Amsterdam's show aired live on fourteen stations, and via kinescope on another seventeen. It was seen in more markets than any 1949–1950 DuMont program.[9] Amsterdam was one of several performers who served an important role in popularizing television through the mid-1950s. A handful of new television comedians (Martin and Lewis, Milton Berle, Sid Caesar, Jackie Gleason) and older film and radio stars (Bob Hope, Eddie Cantor, Jimmy Durante, Red Skelton, Abbott and Costello) stood atop the comedy-variety pantheon. These figures had long, successful careers in show business and are still revered in nostalgic television specials and books about the medium's Golden Age. However, comedians like Amsterdam, Jack Carter, and Jerry Lester, though not as well known today, were also very busy in the early 1950s. They moved from one network to another, giving people additional reasons to purchase their first TV sets or to upgrade older models. Most of these energetic comedians had honed their acts in front of demanding audiences in nightclubs, banquet halls, Jewish "Borscht Belt" resorts, and traveling vaudeville shows before coming to television. They knew how to grab and hold people's attention with a large repertoire of stories, jokes, improvised one-liners, clever puns, occasional slap stick, and a little song and dance. In addition, they used the public recognition from early variety shows to launch long careers as featured performers in nightclubs and on television.

Like many others who emerged as stars on early television, Amsterdam paid his dues as a joke writer, nightclub comedian, and supporting player on radio. Amsterdam's show business career began on vaudeville stages in the late 1920s when the fifteen-year-old cello player and his older brother formed a musical comedy act that toured West Coast theaters. After his brother quit the act, Amsterdam left San Francisco for Chicago, where he trained as a comic and emcee before some pretty tough customers, including Al Capone. Amsterdam later returned to the Bay Area. He was most successful writing novelty songs and jokes for Fanny Brice, Will Rogers, Jimmy Durante, and other radio stars. Amsterdam's best-known song, the calypso-flavored "Rum and Coca Cola," sold seven million copies after it was recorded by the Andrews Sisters in 1944. In 1948, Amsterdam finally had his own hit recording, a novelty song called "Yuk-a-Puk." Performed solo on cello, "Yuk-a-Puk" became Amsterdam's theme song. Over the years, the comedian brought new lyrics and jokes to the tune when he played it on live television. The success of "Yuk-a-Puk" opened broadcasting opportunities to the show business veteran. Producer Irving Mansfield signed Amsterdam to headline a radio program on CBS in July 1948. The network added a television series similar to the radio show in December. After four months, it failed to find a sponsor and CBS lost its patience. Amsterdam moved to DuMont.[10]

Amsterdam was a natural for early television variety. He was warm, funny, and always ready with a joke or a quick retort. A versatile and unselfish comedian, Amsterdam could play the role of star or straight man. What's more, unlike contemporaries like Berle and Gleason, Amsterdam projected confidence and irreverence without directing sharp barbs and insults at others on the stage. At a time when live television programs needed performers who could think fast on their feet, Amsterdam was in demand. Through the early 1950s, he hosted a number of quiz and variety shows on CBS and NBC, including a stint alternating nights with Jerry Lester on NBC's pioneering late-night talk pro-

Amsterdam with Jacqueline Susann at the Golden Goose Café, the CBS precursor to DuMont's Silver Swan Café.

gram, *Broadway Open House*. He was also a reliable guest on most major variety shows.[11]

Amsterdam was the biggest name on DuMont after the network picked up the show from CBS in April 1949. Sponsored by the DuMont Receiver Division, *The Morey Amsterdam Show* lasted eighteen months and became the primary vehicle with which DuMont promoted the company's brand name for network broadcasting and TV manufacturing. In addition to shilling for DuMont on screen, Amsterdam made himself available to DuMont dealers and distributors for personal appearances and store openings.[12]

The Amsterdam show was set in a faux nightclub, the Silver Swan Café. A few lucky audience members sat at tables near Amsterdam, but most watched from farther back, in the Adelphi Theatre seats. Amsterdam played to his strength, stand-up comedy, offering an opening monologue and one or two additional routines in a typical half-hour program. Each episode usually included a dance number by the team of Freddie Blair and Dottie Dean, a guest singer, and a skit that broadly parodied a movie or theater genre. DuMont staff announcer Don Russell, wearing a fashionable white tuxedo, kept the show on track and introduced the live commercials. Amsterdam—who served as the show's producer, co-writer, and star—assembled an impressive group of talent for the program, including several people with whom he had worked at CBS. Jacqueline Susann, CBS producer Mansfield's wife, played Lola, described by Susann's biographer as "the wide-eyed cigarette girl, a klutzy/sexy sidekick and foil who wore the shortest of skirts and lowest of necklines." The Amsterdam show traveled to DuMont without producer Mansfield, and Susann appeared only in the debut episode on the new network. Susann's on-air performance probably was not the cause of her departure. The vaudeville routines between Susann and Amsterdam were funny and racy. Years before *Valley of the Dolls* (1966) made her into a popular literature superstar and TV talk show staple, Susann projected openness and sensuality while demonstrating good comedic timing as a "Dumb Dora."[13] Susann resurfaced on DuMont for six weeks as the host of a celebrity talk and advice program, *Jacqueline Susann's Open Door*, in May 1951.

Amsterdam's house orchestra was led by Johnny Guarnieri, a well-known jazz pianist who had recorded as part of the Benny Goodman and Artie Shaw bands, and in smaller groups with Louie Armstrong, Ben Webster, Coleman Hawkins, and Lester Young.[14] Looking dapper in matching double-breasted suits, Guarnieri's band contributed to the Silver Swan Café's swanky and urbane atmosphere by playing the show's swinging opening theme, adding music and sound effects to the weekly skits, and occasionally bantering with Amsterdam. For example, in the final episode of the series, Guarnieri complains that the theme is corny and old-fashioned. Amsterdam wonders what has happened to his band leader, asking, "Have you been hanging around Birdland?" Apparently, Guarnieri has, indeed, been spending time in the hip New York jazz club that opened the previous year. Like a little kid, he replies, "I wanna play the theme in bop. I wanna live." His band launches into a speedy and exciting be-bop version of the theme song, including an improvised saxophone solo and a happy shriek by the band leader to signal the end of the song.[15]

The Amsterdam show's most valuable asset was an emerging comedian named Art Carney, who played Newton the Waiter in a weekly routine with Amsterdam. Throughout the 1940s, Carney worked as a nightclub comic and supporting player on several radio programs, most notably *The Henry Morgan Show*, where he honed a talent for impressions and creating different characters. Carney also performed on Amsterdam's CBS show, playing the role of Charlie the Doorman. CBS's intellectual property lawyers forced Amsterdam and Carney to change Charlie into Newton when the program moved to DuMont. The character remained the same, except for the addition of a wide mustache, dark eyebrows, and a towel draped over his right arm. The new props gave Newton the cartoonish and antiquated look of a waiter who was fifty years behind the current fashions. Newton shared a similar name, attitude, and set of mannerisms with Carney's more famous creation, Norton from *The Honeymooners*. As Audrey Meadows, who played Alice on the CBS version of *The Honeymooners*, noted, "Art had put Norton together over the years in radio parts and on *The Morey Amsterdam Show*."[16]

In their skits together, Carney flaunted his skill at creating characters and performing physical comedy. Amsterdam played the jovial straight man. The two men seemed to have fun together and they brought the audience in on the jokes by imitating each other, commenting on the silliness, or exchanging compliments in the middle of the act. The energetic Newton, looking like a cross between Norton and *Seinfeld*'s Kramer, typically announced his presence by stumbling onto stage, lifting his lanky leg and giving a high kick to greet Amsterdam. Much of the vaudeville-style humor derived from Carney's weird outfits, surreal images, silly puns, and edgy banter. In a typical Newton moment, for example, the waiter starts throwing wads of dollar bills at the audience, proclaiming "haircuts for everybody," after he thinks that oil has been discovered on his property.[17]

Amsterdam specialized in funny stories about everyday life in the city. Like most live television comedians, he played the part of the hip, irreverent, wise guy. Amsterdam never joked about children or suburbia, the major sources of television humor in the sitcoms that grew to dominate television. Instead, he took the viewer into his urban world of

Art Carney (left), as Newton the Waiter, performs with Amsterdam.

Source: The Raster, July 1949. Allen B. Du Mont Collection, Archives Center, National Museum of American History, Smithsonian Institution.

glamorous nightclubs, fast women, hip jazz, and ethnic (especially Jewish) culture. In a typically rapid gag, Amsterdam opens a fancy gift box to find a pen with a ball the size of a marshmallow stuck on the end of it. "This is the Manischewitz Matzo Ball Point Pen," he announces. "The only pen that writes under chicken soup."[18]

Amsterdam was one of many Jewish comics on early television who assumed the persona of a fast-talking and experienced outsider. They owed a debt to the previous generation of performers who came from New York and perfected their craft in national theater and nightclub tours. As historian Michael Alexander pointed out, Jazz Age comedians like Al Jolson, Fanny Brice, and Eddie Cantor created "the impression that show people were somehow in the know—carriers of a privileged cultural knowledge, usually sinful in nature . . . entertainers were worldly, and much of their art was to make the audience to believe it was worldly as well."[19] Amsterdam and other comics occasionally spiced their routines with Jewish and Yiddish phrases for a little novelty and as a litmus test of the audience's comfort with urban ethnicity and sophistication. Those audience members who caught the references would bond with each other and the comedian, enjoying a comfortable, insider knowledge. You didn't have to be Jewish to understand the punch lines about matzo balls, but it didn't hurt if you were. Still, the talk of exotic foods in a strange accent may have gone over the heads of some viewers. Amsterdam recognized that his act was not for everybody. In one of his standard bits, he would suddenly start talking very rapidly, until his words sounded like gibberish. He would then stop, tilt his head slightly, and take on the persona of a viewer, pointing with a confused look at an imaginary comedian as he asked, "What'd he say?"

While radio and television sponsors sometimes used the star to pitch commercial product, DuMont's Receiver Division jettisoned Amsterdam each week for a slicker 3-minute skit about the wonders of a DuMont set. Amsterdam's urban, occasionally lowbrow style seemed to contradict the corporate image that DuMont was trying to project for its network and its receivers. DuMont took its new slogan, "First With the Finest in Television," seriously and was proud of its status as one of the industry's pioneers, with a reputation for building America's best TV sets. Though the network later became a repository for defiantly lowbrow and low-budget entertainment, early programs like *Champagne and Orchids* (1948–1949) and *Fashions on Parade* (1948–1949) featured high society, well-dressed models, singers, and actresses sharing their fabulous lives with television viewers. Along these lines, the company frequently created musical numbers for the Silver Swan Café commercials that were showcases for dapper young couples or glamorous models dancing to big band swing tunes in their fabulous living rooms. The handsome new DuMont console was always a central prop in these numbers. As narrator Don Russell promised viewers at the end of one commercial, "The new 19-inch DuMont Mount Vernon [model] is a magic carpet to whisk you into a fabulous, exciting world."[20]

Other DuMont advertisements, in print and over the air, illustrated how a television set could enhance the lives of the typical middle-class family, gathered around the "electronic fireplace." As historian Lynn Spigel has noted, "These kinds of advertisements almost always showed the product in the center of the family group . . . The product-as-center motif not only suggested the familial qualities of the set, but also implied a mode of use: the ads suggested television be watched by a family audience."[21] DuMont even hired popular illustrator Norman Rockwell to draw magazine ads featuring all-American parents, children and little pets, contentedly watching DuMont TV sets.

The Rockwell family (a boy, a girl, and two parents) came to life one week in the portion of the Amsterdam show devoted to a live DuMont promotional skit. The piece starts with a tight shot of the magazine ad, which then dissolves to a live action family, resembling the models in print, laughing and enjoying television together. The next shot reveals the source of their pleasure: a singing quartet, on the TV screen, extolling the "treasure of pleasure that's far beyond measure with DuMont." From there, the spot goes to an upper-middle-class living room. A model fawns over the latest DuMont television set while announcer Don Russell describes the machine's "clear, sharp pictures" and "magnificent tones." The advertisement ends as it began: with a tight shot of the happy Rockwell family watching TV.[22]

Amsterdam was a likable program host, but he wasn't the type of comic who could slide into a Norman Rockwell ad. The fact that Amsterdam's Thursday night show became DuMont's showcase program for promoting its receivers to the nation is one of many examples of DuMont's difficulties in crafting a strategy for using talent and selling receivers. In a February 1950 DuMont management meeting, the head of the Receiver Division reported that his dealers and distributors "complained that the Morey Amsterdam show is very poor." Allen Du Mont's response was that "Amsterdam's contract should be renewed for thirteen weeks, but some effort should be made to pep up the show." However, neither Du Mont nor his lieutenants had any concrete program ideas, and there were even questions raised at the meeting over whether DuMont and its advertising agency had the contractual right to make changes on the Amsterdam program.[23] Despite the apparent dissatisfaction from the sponsor, the Amsterdam program remained on DuMont, unchanged, for another eight months. It survived more from inertia, and DuMont's unwillingness to invest in another program with a star of Amsterdam's stature, than from the company's enthusiasm for the show. Nevertheless, Amsterdam ultimately lost his battle against Norman Rockwell. In October 1950, the network closed down the Sil-

The 1950 magazine advertisement by Norman Rockwell that came to life on *The Morey Amsterdam Show*.

ver Swan Café, replacing it with *The Adventures of Ellery Queen*. At the time of its cancellation, Amsterdam's show was DuMont's longest-running prime-time entertainment program, having debuted eighteen months earlier.[24]

The End of Shtick

By the end of 1950, ratings were declining on many variety shows that were early hits. Berle, for example, still had the top-rated show during the 1950–1951 season, but his numbers were down from the 1949 high, and they continued to slip until he was out of the top ten by 1954–1955.[25] Television historians attribute this decline in the popularity of variety shows to the growing national audience. They suggest that rural and suburban viewers did not like, or even understand, the New York Jewish style practiced by performers like Berle and Amsterdam.[26] Even before 1950, writers for industry magazines noted that comics needed to avoid being too obscure, vulgar, and racy for the growing audience. As the New York edition of *TV Guide* suggested, "Local jokes, insult routines, Broadway humor, off-color material, all the sure fire stuff in the nightclubs, is not going over too well in the hinterlands . . . Video must now be treated as a family product, a product being sold to living room groups of different age levels."[27] These regional differences in taste are an important part of the explanation for why Berle did not "play in Peoria," or DuMont's national dealers did not prefer Amsterdam; however, throughout the early 1950s, support for many comedians who relied on ethnic humor and vaudevillian routines gradually declined in big, East Coast cities like New York and Washington, not just in smaller, less ethnic markets. Even viewers who understood this brand of humor apparently grew tired of the old routines and familiar style that many comics offered weekly.

Instead, audiences were starting to show a preference for entertainment driven by funny stories and situations. Networks tried to develop programing that spoke to an increasingly affluent, suburban audience that still wanted to remain connected to the older urban, ethnic culture. After 1950, figures like Amsterdam and Berle continued to perform as variety show guests and hosts, along with other comedians who trained in big city nightclubs. They still used the occasional Yiddish phrase or a reference to lively New York clubs and ethnic neighborhoods. But routines that relied on a quick wit, Jewish humor, and a zippy monologue were no longer enough. Shtick was yielding to skit, and nightclub "comics" were being replaced by more artistic "comedians." Each week, the most successful TV variety performers required a fresh monologue and running characters, portrayed by the star and a supporting cast, who would appear in original sketches. Old performers such as Berle retooooled their acts while new stars ascended to fill this order. In fact, as Amsterdam's Silver Swan Café was preparing to serve its final martini, Jackie Gleason of DuMont's *Cavalcade of Stars* was developing a stable of characters and sketches that attracted national attention and top ten ratings.

Jackie Gleason.

1

And Away He Went . . .

Jackie Gleason and the Cavalcade of Stars

avalcade of Stars debuted in June 1949. From the beginning, it booked an incredible mix of performers each week. On a given program, viewers might find athletes, singers, actors, comedians, and novelty acts such as magicians, jugglers, and trampoline artists. Jackie Robinson, Roy Campanella, Peter Lorre, John Garfield, Henny Youngman, Paul Winchell, Dizzy Gillespie, and Cab Calloway all appeared on *Cavalcade of Stars* during the show's first season (1949–1950), when Jack Carter and Jerry Lester hosted. After Jackie Gleason took over for the show's final two years, 1950–1952, the program still hosted singers like Vivian Blaine, Georgia Gibbs, and Pearl Bailey, along with the June Taylor Dancers, and occasional comedy and novelty acts. In addition, Frank Sinatra made his only DuMont appearance on *Cavalcade of Stars*, surprising his friend Gleason at the end of a pie-throwing melee in October 1951. However, as Gleason's confidence increased from 1950 to 1952, the program tended to book fewer performers and relied more on Gleason's growing repertoire of characters and skits to keep the audience happy.

When *Cavalcade of Stars* debuted, CBS and NBC had the lion's share of network advertising revenue.[1] The two large networks usually pitched to the big agencies and sponsors, who were already business partners from radio. The list of CBS and NBC sponsors from 1949 reads like a who's who of corporate

America: Chevrolet, Ford, Gulf Oil, Texaco, General Foods, General Electric, Westinghouse, Procter and Gamble. Next to this distinguished roster, the sponsor of *Cavalcade of Stars*, an association of regional drug store chains called the Drug Stores of America, looks out of place. As part of its limited television activity, Drug Store Television Productions later sponsored two other DuMont programs: a short-lived dramatic show, *Cosmopolitan Theatre*, and a musical variety companion to *Cavalcade of Stars* called *Cavalcade of Bands*. *Cavalcade of Stars* illustrates the combination of innovation and desperation with which DuMont approached program sales. In fact, without this resourcefulness, *Cavalcade of Stars* and other programs probably would not have made it to prime time on DuMont or any other network. Ironically, DuMont became a victim of its own success: three different hosts cemented their reputations as popular entertainers on *Cavalcade of Stars* before leaving for slots on NBC or CBS, making DuMont and its sponsor look like small-time outfits.

Cavalcade of Stars was one of DuMont's most expensive and lucrative productions. It generated $800,000 in advertising billings a year (approximately $6 million in 2003 dollars) and $3,300 per week in profit for DuMont in 1950.[2] The show's budget was approximately $15,000 per episode for the cost of production (including studio expenses, crew, and talent). In addition, Drug Store Television paid DuMont for the network's airtime. *Cavalcade* was more expensive than many other TV programs, including the NBC Friday night boxing telecast that was *Cavalcade*'s main competition from 1950–1952. However, variety shows were costly to mount and DuMont offered a bargain compared to similar shows on CBS and NBC, like Sullivan's *Toast of the Town* ($29,500), *Your Show of Shows* with Sid Caesar ($25,000), the *Texaco Star Theater* with Berle ($45,000), and *Colgate Comedy Hour* ($40,000), which employed a rotating cast of stars.[3] While the writing, production crew, talent, and guests on *Cavalcade* were top drawer, DuMont and its sponsor cut corners by featuring comedy and music routines that could be mounted on simple sets without a lot of fancy props or extra performers. The economical measures did not fool anybody. Before he left *Cavalcade* for a more elaborate NBC showcase, emcee Jack Carter joked about the sparse props. During a sketch in which he hangs his coat on a cardboard coat rack, he explains to the audience, "This is all DuMont can afford this week."[4]

Cavalcade of Stars was a true bargain for the Drug Stores of America: the program did not cost the sponsor anything. DuMont and its sponsor adapted an innovative means of selling time that had been pioneered locally on DuMont's WABD. Drug Stores of America technically sponsored *Cavalcade of Stars*, but the sponsor sold short segments of time to individual manufacturers of shampoos, cosmetics, deodorants, and other products. "Six manufacturers each took one minute of commercial time at one-sixth of the entire time and talent cost, giving us a big-name variety show paid for by multiple sponsors," explained Ted Bergmann, the DuMont advertising salesman who packaged *Cavalcade*. The drug stores rewarded their partners with merchandise displays in their shops.

On every program, *Cavalcade* viewers endured the whopping six commercial interruptions: a mixture of live pitches by announcer Don Russell, dressed as a druggist, and filmed commercials supplied by advertisers. At the time, most big-budget shows had only a single sponsor. Advertisers tended to seamlessly insert product plugs within the programs and limit the number of outright commercial interruptions because of fears that they would lose viewers and incur the wrath of the FCC. As Bergmann remembered, the multiple-sponsor format was "a new way of advertising television." The success of *Cavalcade*, he explained, proved that "individual network programs could be sponsored by more than one manufacturer." Furthermore, DuMont had already used this format of inserting multiple product pitches in both its daytime programing and its local evening programs, allowing several advertisers to share program production costs. The format eventually became standard on all of television. By the 1952–1953 season, other variety shows such as *Your Show of Shows* (NBC), *All Star Revue* (NBC), and *The Jackie Gleason Show* (CBS) had adapted variations of this sponsorship technique.[5]

DuMont's sale of multiple, short advertising spots provoked some of the earliest criticisms of television commercials. *Variety* magazine noted in a review of *Cavalcade of Stars* that "the oft-heard complaint of the frequent and unimaginative commercials are sufficient to knock any show off its keel. The filmed plugs too often break up the mood and the program's personnel must get started again. Under sensible standards of commercials, this show would have hit the upper rungs of audience acceptance."[6] Even with constant interruptions, during its first nine months on the air, *Cavalcade* was usually the highest-rated program in the fourteen cities that aired the show on Saturday night at nine o'clock and it was the only DuMont program to crack the national Nielsen top ten. It accomplished that feat during the 1949–1950 season, which started with Jack Carter as host and concluded with Jerry Lester filling the role.[7]

Jack Carter and Jerry Lester

The twenty-five-year-old Jack Carter was already a veteran of night-clubs, Broadway, and variety television when he hosted *Cavalcade of Stars* for the premiere on Saturday night, June 4, 1949. Like many em-cees, the versatile Carter could sing and dance, and he excelled at the opening monologue and the quick one-liner. Though Carter was some-times too hot and hyper for the small screen, he was successful enough that NBC snapped him up after eight months on *Cavalcade*. Carter was the lead in for Sid Caesar on *Saturday Night Revue*, NBC's new, big-budget variety rival for *Cavalcade*'s Saturday night viewers. While Carter never attained superstar status, he was one of many entertainers who parlayed the success and audience recognition achieved during televi-sion's early days into a long entertainment career. After NBC cancelled his variety show in 1951, he continued to appear as a guest on variety shows and TV movies. Carter also worked the casino circuit and starred in regional musicals during a career that lasted more than fifty years.

Jerry Lester, Carter's successor, hosted *Cavalcade* from February to July 1950. He was not the most original comedian on early television; however, in a pinch, Lester was able to draw on his experience as a tap dancer and music hall entertainer. Lester had a nice run from 1950 to 1953, starring on every network except for CBS, because he had an es-sential skill: he could keep a program moving. Lester seldom ran out of things to say or do for a laugh and he seemed comfortable whether jug-gling bowling pins or portraying a sick boy's father in a more serious sketch with baseball player Jackie Robinson. In an early episode of *Cavalcade*, for example, Lester runs onto the stage in a clown outfit, shakes his rear end at the camera, and launches into a circus routine. Lester was a skillful jester, and the introduction is entertaining and en-

Jerry Lester.

ergetic, but the site of the forty-year-old program host as a clown is also juvenile and cloying.[8]

Lester was not especially handsome, funny, or creative, but network executives hired him because he knew how to entertain a live audience while performing in front of an intimidating bank of TV lights, microphones, and cameras. *Newsweek*, for example, reported on Lester's surprising popularity hosting NBC's *Broadway Open House* after the star left *Cavalcade*. "Lester, with years of show [business] experience behind him, still had very little success to recommend him. His best qualities were a sure knowledge of the trade's tricks, a mug's face as pliable as chewing gum, and a professional pixiness that belies his 40 years."[9] *TV*

Guide similarly described his personality as a "pixyish blend of the brash and the abashed."[10]

Lester was thrilled to be on television, working as hard as he could to desperately make the audience like him. In a 1950 interview, he recognized that a person could succeed on television without great looks or talent, as long as the public liked him. "If they like you, you don't have to worry about whether every gag goes over big or if every sketch is the best thing they've ever seen," he explained.[11] Lester elicited enough audience empathy and appreciation during his tenure on *Cavalcade* to earn an NBC contract at the end of the DuMont program's first season in June 1950. He achieved the height of his stardom as the part-time host of *Broadway Open House*. Lester left the late-night program in May 1951, after losing a well-publicized battle for top billing with a co-star named Dagmar, who was tall, blond, voluptuous, and ultimately of greater value to NBC than Lester was. Like many TV entertainers whose luck and fame faded in the early 1950s, Lester had a long career in local television and touring theatrical shows, along with occasional parts in movies and network shows. In the meantime, *Cavalcade* continued after the initial 1949–1950 season with a new host and a new night, Friday, where the competition for national affiliates and viewers was not as fierce.

Gleason Gets His Big Break

On July 8, 1950, Jackie Gleason replaced Lester on *Cavalcade of Stars*. Gleason's two years at DuMont were thrilling for viewers and crucial to his artistic development. Gleason came to DuMont in 1950 a virtual unknown, having had limited success despite more than a decade of effort in nightclubs, radio, Broadway theaters, and Hollywood movies. He had failed in his only turn on television: a short stint as the title character in *The Life of Riley*, a domestic sitcom that was filmed in Hollywood for NBC. The network pulled *The Life of Riley* in March 1950, after only six months, although the program had a more successful run starting in 1953. William Bendix, who had played Riley on radio since 1944, pleased TV viewers as the perennially frustrated, but devoted, family man and factory worker. "The psychic makeup of Riley was ultimately too passive for Gleason to be at his most effective," observed William

A. Henry III in his perceptive biography of Gleason.[12] On *Cavalcade*, Gleason learned to articulate the joys and frustrations of life in America as a fat, working-class man who dreams of fame and fortune. As Karen Adir wrote in her history of television comedy, "In the 1950s, Jackie Gleason was the personification of the American dream come true. From the lowly origins of the streets of Brooklyn to the zenith of conspicuous consumption, he tantalized the average American with the fanciful possibility of what could be."[13] Gleason's rags-to-riches persona had credibility because people saw him live this fairy tale through his two-year stint on the DuMont Television Network.

When *Cavalcade* producer Milton Douglas called on Gleason, the thirty-four-year-old comedian was working at Slapsie Maxie's, a comedy club in Los Angeles to which he had frequently returned over the years when he needed a pay check. At a time when a top comedian could earn $5,000 a week performing live, Gleason was making around $325.[14] Gleason began his run at Slapsie Maxie's "with the feeling that he had tried, and failed, at television as well as motion pictures. He had a hopeless feeling that he was going to go through life miscast," according to Jim Bishop, who published an authorized biography of Gleason in 1956.[15] Gleason was not even producer Douglas's first choice. After experienced radio comedian Peter Donald turned down the job, the Drug Stores of America signed Gleason to a short, four-week contract at $750 a week. The modest trial offer was still better money than Gleason could make elsewhere. The fact that Gleason was willing to journey across the country via train for a one-month stint on DuMont is a testament to the comedian's ambition to try television and the paucity of other show business opportunities available to him. The initial four-week engagement on DuMont lasted two years.[16]

Gleason was tentative and nervous during his first few months as a variety show emcee. Perhaps he felt pressure because *Cavalcade of Stars* was an important opportunity and his previous experience on live television was limited to a handful of guest appearances on other programs. Although the *Cavalcade* format required Gleason to deliver an opening monologue, throughout his career he was never a great stand-up comic. In his early days as a nightclub emcee, Gleason's "biggest laughs came when he traded insults with customers" wrote Bishop, Gleason's biographer.[17] The genteel *Cavalcade* audience that assembled at DuMont's

Adelphi Theatre, located in the heart of New York's theater district, did not offer Gleason opportunities for the edgy banter on which he thrived. Moreover, by 1950, performers and network executives were well aware that variety acts had to avoid "blue" humor so as not to offend viewers. For Gleason, this meant cleaning up his nightclub language and expunging the racy stories from his act.

Before Gleason crafted his distinct TV persona, his initial impulse on *Cavalcade of Stars* was to imitate other successful, vaudeville-inspired comics. His opening monologues were short and predictable. Gleason occasionally supplemented the jokes with mediocre impressions of old performers from the 1920s like Joe Penner and Ted Lewis. Perhaps sensing that Gleason needed help, Douglas brought popular vaudeville and 1930s movie comedian Bert Wheeler onto *Cavalcade* as a co-host for a few of the early episodes. The presence of the more experienced Wheeler thrust Gleason into the awkward role of straight man in the routines that they did together. In addition to performing the vaudevillian skits, Gleason and company presented genre parodies and costume pieces that went on for too long.

Gleason also may have appeared awkward because the show's writing was so weak. In four different reviews of *Cavalcade* episodes during Gleason's first few months at the helm, *Variety* magazine faulted the scripts while praising the star's performances. The review of his July 8 debut perceptively noted that "Gleason was considerably better than his material, indicating that his comedy resources are larger than what was revealed."[18] In fact, Gleason's talent for physical comedy and improvisation occasionally broke through the stale routines. In one skit from September 1950, for example, Gleason plays Ali Ben Shishkebob, an Arab prince visiting Monte Carlo. Gleason struts through the casino wearing a fake moustache and a ridiculous military outfit: high socks, black shorts, a button down shirt with fringes on the shoulders and extra padding in the stomach, making the hefty Gleason look like a tree stump. A fez and walking stick complete the ensemble. The beautiful Vivian Blaine, in a strapless evening dress, must choose between two suitors: Gleason and a dapper Frenchman named Alfonse. As she looks at the two men and announces her obvious decision, Gleason's stomach padding starts to slip, and his shorts slowly slide to the ground, along with the fake belly. Gleason responds to this miscue by pulling the shirt down so that it practically reaches the floor, and doing a little jig around the stage.[19] The inspired moment is the highlight of an otherwise clichéd sketch and reminds viewers that, even under padding, the big comedian could be surprisingly graceful.[20]

By the end of the first season,1950–1951, Gleason and his writing team had found the star's forte: bringing a set of characters to life in a series of weekly skits. All of the figures synonymous with Gleason— including the Poor Soul, the Bachelor, Fenwick Babbitt, Joe the Bartender, Rudy the Repairman, Reggie Van Gleason, Charlie Bratton the Loudmouth, and Ralph Kramden—originated during the DuMont years. All except for Kramden were invented by the *Cavalcade* writers, Coleman Jacoby and Arnie Rosen, during Gleason's first season. A new team of writers, Joe Bigelow and Harry Crane, replaced Jacoby and Rosen and created "The Honeymooners" with Gleason during *Cavalcade*'s second season.[21] "They had a lot of trouble in the beginning with Gleason. They didn't know what do with him, so Arnie and I started inventing," remembered writer Jacoby. "Almost everything Jackie did, even the way he crossed his legs, I invented."[22]

The character sketches made life easier for Gleason and his writers because it gave them a well of material from which to draw. "I think a comedian has to develop characterizations to keep going in television," Gleason told the *New York Times* in a 1951 interview. "I don't care how strong a personality he might have, if he tries to be just himself for 1 hour every week, his popularity is bound to fall off. The most important asset a television comedian can have is a writer who can do sketches."[23] As Gleason biographer William Henry pointed out, the idea of using recurring skits on TV was "not absolutely unprecedented. Both Milton Berle and Sid Caesar were in the process of developing the same idea. But no other early TV comic took the idea as far as Gleason did."[24] Following the success of early TV performers like Jackie Gleason, Sid Caesar, and Red Skelton, running characters became a staple of comedy variety, remaining popular with television writers and fans of shows ranging from *The Carol Burnett Show* to *Saturday Night Live* to *Late Night with David Letterman*.

The ability to portray a range of characters established Gleason as a serious and sensitive actor at a time when many other variety hosts were seen as shoddy and crass. Gleason contributed to this image of an artist by placing himself in a tradition of silent movie comedians whose work was in vogue with audiences and critics following the publication of an influential 1949 *Life* magazine cover story by James Agee. In fact, Gleason told *TV Guide* readers that he considered silent movies "the highest development in the art of comedy."[25] Gleason named Charlie Chaplin as the "greatest show business personality of our day." His favorite movie actor was Jack Oakie, even though both Chaplin and Oakie were more popular in the 1930s, when Gleason was a teenager, than they were in 1951. The article noted that "Gleason says he has deliberately set out to resurrect the type of comedy that made immortals of people like Chaplin, Harold Lloyd [and other silent comedians]," *TV Guide* wrote. "Their kind of humor disappeared with the rise of radio and talking pictures. Jackie wants to bring them back."[26] To his credit, Gleason created characters who elicited a broad range of emotions, in contrast to the many TV variety comedians who parodied silent movies for quick laughs. In a typically grandiose statement, Gleason once told interviewer Dick Cavett, "No comedian is great unless he can also move you to tears."[27]

The Gleason Persona

Many writers and fellow comedians have suggested that, even at the height of his popularity in the mid-1950s, Jackie Gleason was never the funniest man on television. Woody Allen, for example, didn't like Gleason's variety show. "I thought it was bad, a consistently bad show," he said in a 1968 interview. "He could do one bad show after another and everyone [would] love him and find him funny because there's something in him we respond to."[28] Through trial and error, Gleason was both lucky and smart enough to have created a persona that resonated with viewers. He played the part of an average guy who made it big on television, and enjoyed every minute of his fame, but had not forgotten his humble roots. In one of the most perceptive contemporary articles on the Gleason phenomenon, a generally flattering 1953 portrait of the star in *Coronet* magazine, author Sam Boal records Gleason's many deficiencies. For example, Gleason "isn't very funny. He doesn't feed out straight gags, like Bob Hope . . . He is neither handsome nor ugly, extremes which often are valuable to television comedians." Boal then

quotes popular sports columnist Jimmy Cannon's assessment of Gleason's particular talent, "The thing about Gleason is that he is everybody. He is the fellow next door that you like and he is also the man
across the street that you don't like."[29]

Of course, for most viewers, the guy across the street was probably
not a 250-pound (give or take a few steaks) entertainer, living in a New
York City penthouse palace that included everything from a television
set implanted in the ceiling above a giant bed to a huge pool table that
dominated the living room. The suite also served as headquarters for
the production company that Gleason established when he moved from
DuMont to CBS in 1952.[30] However, the reality of Gleason's life only
added to his mystique and appeal. Without seeming pretentious or pa-
tronizing, Gleason had a knack for portraying a superstar who somehow
understood the hopes and frustrations of the less-favored men and
women watching at home. As David Marc argued in his witty and insightful study of television in American culture, *Demographic Vistas*,
"Gleason was a uniquely American comic original. In both life and art
he projected the persona of the Depression-bred blue-collar ethnic
who demanded the right to live like a king."[31] Ralph Kramden, Reggie
Van Gleason, the Poor Soul, and the other characters contributed to the
making of a star who could convince viewers at home that he was one
of them.

The Birth of Sketch

On *Cavalcade*, Gleason introduced several sad characters, liberally borrowing from the work of silent film comedians. The big man showed
his sensitivity to the problems and suffering of the lonely in a series of
affectionate vignettes that were different from any other continuing
bits on television at the time. The gentle sketches balanced the more
raucous aspects of *Cavalcade*. In addition to Fenwick Babbitt, the meek
clerk, Gleason portrayed two similar figures who appeared in pan-
tomime skits: the Bachelor and the Poor Soul. Accompanied only by a
lugubrious instrumental version of George Gershwin's "Somebody
Loves Me," Gleason's Bachelor walked through everyday situations
that went awry for these hapless men. The star was open about the way
he crafted the Bachelor to court mass appeal: The character "seemed a

natural for the Keystone comedy-type routines I like to do," he explained in 1951. "You know—a bachelor whom the ladies will love the way they would a helpless, clumsy puppy and the kind of bedeviled character the males can sympathize with."[32]

These pieces could be sentimental and predictable, but Gleason used the skits to showcase his acting skill and make the most of the flawed material. His facial expressions and body language allowed viewers to discern the characters' combination of hope and ultimate resignation. Biographer Henry observed that the Bachelor's appeal "was his sad loneliness, tempered by his pesky determination to cope."[33] In "The Bachelor Does His Laundry," for example, one of the first character sketches on *Cavalcade of Stars*, Gleason putters around a small and messy apartment, walking with a slight hunch, dressed in unflatteringly tight long underwear and an apron. He sets up a series of physical gags. The Bachelor knocks over everything on a table as he tries to smoothly remove a tablecloth without clearing the dishes first. Later, he punctures the soft music with two mighty yells after the Bachelor burns his rear end on a hot iron, then tries to cool himself in a tub of steaming, soapy water, before he finally finds relief by sitting in the refrigerator, eyes bulging in shock and pain. As the skit continues, it takes a more wistful turn. The Bachelor puts his laundry out to dry on a clothesline outside his window. When he reels the clothes back in, he finds a woman's garments. After looking at the clothes with wonder, the Bachelor sniffs a dress with a smile and hangs it upright on the indoor clothesline. He enjoys an imaginary date, first talking over dinner, then taking the dress for a dance around the apartment, with the orchestra still playing in the background. Suddenly, the fantasy is interrupted by a knock on the door. The funny and sad payoff: rather than finding a pretty young lady in his doorway, the Bachelor finds a scrawny actor named Leo Guarnieri dressed as a woman. The son of the band leader on the *Morey Amsterdam Show*, Guarnieri made the rounds at DuMont as an unbilled character actor when the scene called for a wacky guest who could get a laugh by crossing his eyes or affecting stereotypically homosexual mannerisms. As the neighbor, Guarnieri indignantly picks up "her" clothes, slaps Gleason, and leaves the Bachelor alone in his sloppy apartment. In the last shot Gleason can only look into the camera, pout like a guilty little kid, and shrug.[34]

Gleason was sometimes the victim of funny-looking guys in drag, but he could also be an arrogant bully, quick to insult or tease others on the air and to revel in his access to life's pleasures. In fact, part of Gleason's appeal on *Cavalcade* was that he played the part of an unrestrained hedonist with the wit, bankroll, and television platform to say and do whatever he wanted. This harsh, flamboyant side surfaced in *Cavalcade* characters Rudy the Repairman and Charlie Bratton, also known as The Loudmouth. As *Washington Post* critic Tom Shales noted in a 1988 review of a Gleason retrospective, these characters were attractive because of their brash self-confidence. "The Loud Mouth, Charlie Bratton, is an obnoxious boor, but even he seems to be getting more out of life than the constipated milquetoast Clem Finch (Art Carney) he regularly terrorizes at the diner."[35] Gleason's grandest character in this vein was Reginald Van Gleason III, a wealthy, but crude, playboy. Dressed in a tuxedo, which Gleason wore along with a cape, walking stick, and a brush moustache, the fabulously rich Reggie always had a drink nearby, a party on his agenda, and a disdainful comment for anyone who stood in the way of his fun. Reggie's genteel parents were his most frequent target. In a 1951 sketch, Reggie greets his parents at a charity bazaar held at the family estate: "Hello, dad. Hello, mother. My, but you're getting fat." He proceeds to a kissing booth, where he grabs a young woman and gives her a long smooch. The object of his affection faints, as smoke fills the space where she was standing. "Burnt to a crisp," Reggie notes with satisfaction. The skit goes downhill from there, as Gleason insults a frumpy guest and then barks orders to a motley collection of musicians, including Guarnieri, hired to perform at the party.[36]

The Honeymoon Begins

The characters from the first DuMont season laid the foundation for Gleason's greatest role. Ralph Kramden and "The Honeymooners" combined the sentimental pathos of figures like the Bachelor with the bluster and ego of the Loudmouth and Reggie Van Gleason. "The Honeymooners" debuted as a segment of *Cavalcade of Stars* on October 5, 1951. While accounts differ over exactly who first thought of the idea for the skit, it is safe to say that Gleason, assistant producer Joe Cates, and the writing team of Harry Crane and Joe Bigelow were all in a room together

Jackie Gleason as Reginald Van Gleason III in a CBS promotional photo, circa 1958.

when the sketch was born. Crane later wrote for Gleason at CBS, as did others who started on *Cavalcade*, including Snag Werris, Marvin Marx, and Walter Stone.[37] Perhaps because many of the writers and cast members also moved with Gleason from DuMont to CBS, it is striking how similar the earliest DuMont "Honeymooners" are to the more familiar episodes that aired on CBS for one season (1955–1956) and have continued on local and cable ever since. In fact, even though he was working for CBS, Gleason filmed these thirty-nine episodes at DuMont's Adelphi Theatre, using many crew members who worked on *Cavalcade of Stars*.

That great 1950s American icon, the Kramdens' kitchen, was developed on *Cavalcade*. It was a product of DuMont's stingy operations along with Gleason's vision of realism. Cates was under instructions from Gleason to build an apartment that would replicate the scruffy Brooklyn tenement dwelling in which Gleason grew up twenty years earlier.[38] Given DuMont's limited budget for set design, the assistant producer relied on a New Jersey props company and the goodwill of a man named Skippy, who worked at the Adelphi Theatre. The bare bones set contributed to a mise-en-scene of urban claustrophobia and poverty that, as television historian David Marc observed, "eternally bore the mark of the thirties."[39] Perhaps imagining a life for himself as Ralph Kramden if show business hadn't lifted him to stardom, Gleason housed the fictional Kramdens at 358 Chauncey Street in Brooklyn: the actual address of Gleason's childhood home. Marc explained that "the compelling pathos of Ralph Kramden, Gleason's greatest mask, derives in large part from the painful spectacle of a Jackie Gleason rendered impotent from lack of money."[40]

Gleason's co-star was veteran actress Pert Kelton, who was unable to continue the role on CBS due to heart troubles, "aggravated, no doubt, by attempts to blacklist her as an erstwhile leftist, which the apolitical Gleason had nobly resisted," while at DuMont, according to Henry.[41] In 1950, Kelton was listed in *Red Channels*, a book put out by the influential editors of the *Counterattack* newsletter. *Red Channels* named 151 actors purported to be communists or communist sympathizers.[42] A listing in *Red Channels* usually made an actor unemployable; however, Kelton remained on *Cavalcade of Stars* through its final season, 1951–1952. Kelton was not the only accused communist who worked at DuMont. The network did not go out of its way to hire writers and actors who were tainted for alleged communist sympathies; however, it was more hospitable than the other networks were to these people. DuMont's relatively lax management, desperation for an edge in recruiting talent, and independence from the pressures of big sponsors and advertising agencies gave producers and network executives a little bit of leeway. Former DuMont producer Hal Cooper remembered having to clear names of actors with the network brass before hiring talent for his program, *The Magic Cottage*. He was still able to hire friends who were blacklisted by making last-minute changes to the scripts and adding actors before there was time to clear them.[43] In his autobiographical account of his years at DuMont, former executive Bergmann related only one case of interference by the advertising agencies and independent watchdog organizations that monitored the television industry and enforced the blacklist. This lone incident was a result of mistaken identity. "By and large, we had no political problems. We carried what we wanted when we wanted to carry it," Bergmann said in a later interview.[44]

A casualty of Gleason's post-DuMont upward mobility, Kelton's departure when the show moved to CBS was a significant loss. Kelton portrayed Alice as a tough-talking broad with a high-pitched voice and a harsh Brooklyn accent. As Henry wrote, her "appearance suggested that she really had been through the marital wars and had given as good as she got."[45] Kelton was a perfect match for Gleason's rough and boisterous Ralph Kramden. Critic J. Hoberman believed that the early "Honeymooners" sketches on *Cavalcade* may have been the most perfect ones, due to the charged rapport between Gleason and Kelton. "Careworn yet ethereal, Kelton seems better suited to Ralph than do subsequent Alices—her premature drabness complements his passé pompadour," Hoberman wrote. "You can even sense the sexual attraction that binds her deprived and faded hausfrau to his gone-to-seed poolroom Lothario."[46]

From the beginning, Gleason and his writers used sentimental endings to soften the edges that Ralph and Alice displayed during their nasty fights. In one early sketch, for example, the Kramdens appear on a radio quiz show together. The episode begins with Ralph angry at Alice for missing an important question. After Alice has had enough of Ralph, and seeks refuge in the bedroom, Norton and Trixie visit. Next, a crew from the radio station arrives, including the program host, the cereal company mogul who sponsors the radio show, and a team of engineers. Upon further review, Alice's answer was correct, and the Kramdens have another opportunity to strike it rich. Without any help from anyone, Ralph must answer the jackpot question: What did Marconi invent? After a long, panicky pause, he can only mumble the first thing that pops into his head: "marcaroni." Following Ralph's incorrect response, everybody quickly rushes out of the apartment, without even deigning to inform the hapless man of the correct answer. The sponsor is especially condescending, taking a parting shot at Ralph, "Too bad you're not as smart as your wife."

As the sketch ends, the apartment feels empty. Ralph and Alice are alone. They sit in silence, unable to look at each other. The camera pans from a tense Alice, sitting at the bare kitchen table, to Ralph, who paces around the small space in back of her, looking guilty. Violin music plays as Ralph gives a shrug and offers an explanation that serves as a good summary of his relationship with Alice. "Every chance I get, I try to take advantage of you, sweetheart. I try to make you look dumb. That doesn't work out either. I try to make everything your fault. That doesn't turn out. There's something I just can't understand. Of all the things I've done to you, of all the embarrassment I've caused you, why do you stick with me? Why?" Alice offers a predictable but tender response to close the skit: "I'll tell you why I stick with you. I love you."[47]

By the time "The Honeymooners" debuted at DuMont, Carney had been Gleason's partner in other *Cavalcade* skits for more than a year. Producer Milton Douglas signed Carney following the recommendation of the show's writers and DuMont crew members, who were impressed with the comedian's work on *The Morey Amsterdam Show*.[48] Carney was the regular scapegoat of two other Gleason characters, The Loudmouth and Reginald Van Gleason, so it probably was not surprising to regular *Cavalcade* viewers that he showed up in the first "Honeymooners" sketch covered with flour. Carney played a policeman, not Norton, who happened to walk by the window of 358 Chauncey Street as Ralph hurled a tin of flour out the window during an argument with Alice. Later in the season, Carney was recast as the more familiar sewer worker and neighbor for several sketches, but the character was not as prominent on DuMont as he later became on CBS. Instead he provided comic relief as Ralph's dim-witted sidekick and sounding board when things became too intense with Alice. In their informative and appreciative history of "The Honeymooners," Donna McCrohan and Peter Crescenti described Norton in the show's early years as "looking and sounding like a lobotomized version of his later self."[49] In fact, one of Norton's striking traits in the DuMont episodes is a strange, slow speech pattern with slurred words, choppy phrases, and a Southern accent. In the quiz show sketch, for example, Norton tries to console Ralph after it appeared that Alice missed the question: "Ah tell ya,

Art Carney (left), an unidentified actor, and Gleason are center stage at the Adelphi Theatre for *Cavalcade of Stars*.

Source: Allen B. Du Mont Collection, Archives Center, National Museum of American History, Smithsonian Institution.

Ralph. Ah was on a quiz show once. Ah can understand why people get nervous. Ah was nervous. On a quiz show. They asked me my first question. Ah didn't know what the answer was."

Ralph asks, naturally, what the question was.

Norton's reply is more pathetic than it is funny: "What was my first name?"[50]

Jackie, Frank, and Toots

By the start of Gleason's second season, 1951–1952, *Cavalcade of Stars* was the most commercially successful program on DuMont, airing in twenty-five cities (fourteen live and eleven via kinescope) from New York to Los Angeles.[51] What's more, *Cavalcade* was winning the ratings battle against tough competition from NBC's Friday night fights and a CBS talent show called *Live Like a Millionaire* from ten to eleven o'clock. The week of October 1, 1951, for example, *Cavalcade* earned a rating of

30 in New York, a higher figure than all of the other programs combined.[52] For national viewers, perhaps the best evidence that Gleason was now big time was that he was either a guest host or featured performer on the two most prestigious network comedy programs: *Colgate Comedy Hour* (NBC) and *Toast of the Town* (CBS).[53] Gleason was also a frequent visitor on *The Frank Sinatra Show* (CBS), appearing alongside his old friend in skits and serving as a ready substitute in case Sinatra was late making the commute from Los Angeles to New York for the program.[54]

To illustrate his growing confidence, sophistication, and stature in the entertainment world by the second season, Gleason regularly used his *Cavalcade of Stars* monologues to poke fun at his orbit of show business friends. At one end of the spectrum was Sammy Spear, in what has become the expected role for the variety show band leader as sycophant and good-natured straight man to the host. On the other end was Sinatra, a frequent target for being small and scrawny next to Gleason and other "real men." Gleason started a November 1951 monologue referring to a well-publicized story about Sinatra's largesse. "Frank Sinatra gave me a Cadillac, a beautiful car, and every day we go riding in it together. I like to take him on long trips because he is very valuable to me," Gleason pauses. "I stick him in the gasoline tank to find out how much gasoline I have left." After another joke about Sinatra's size, the comedian moved to a more sensitive topic: Sinatra's scandalous affair with movie star Ava Gardner. Sinatra "took me to a party last night," Gleason continues. "A whole mob of people. All celebrities. I was dancing with all the movie stars," he then hesitates. "Poor Frank. He was stuck with Ava." Gleason then gives one of his trademark expressions, the bulging eyes, though it is not clear whether the star is excited over Gardner or his own nerve at joking about his friend's lurid situation. The *Cavalcade* episode aired on November 2, 1951, the day after Sinatra married Gardner and two days after Sinatra was legally divorced from his previous wife, Nancy. For more than a year, the Sinatra-Gardner affair had been regular fodder for the showbiz gossip columns and scandal sheets, but not prime time monologues. Typically, variety show performers teased each other about looks or abilities, such as a bad singing voice or a repertoire of stolen jokes, but illicit love affairs were off limits to all except for Gleason. After Gleason's joke, the surprised crowd is silent for a little longer than usual before erupting in laughter.[55]

Gleason was also a fixture at Toots Shor's in New York, the most famous bar in the country. In the New York City of the 1940s and 1950s, "everybody went to Shor's, to eat, to drink, above all to see and be seen," wrote Henry in his biography of Gleason. "[Shor's] was not for the café society of tuxedoed gentlemen and gilded debutantes. Rather, Shor's was for saloon society, the self-confident men of attainment in sports, journalism and entertainment, plus their hangers-on, admirers and gawkers." Tourists knew that if they didn't mind waiting in line for a while, they could find themselves drinking with Mickey Mantle, Joe Dimaggio, Frank Sinatra, or Jackie Gleason.[56] In his opening monologue, Gleason included insider anecdotes about the bar and its charismatic proprietor. He relished bringing his national television viewers into Toots's world of late-night drinkers, raconteurs, celebrities, hustlers, and assorted Broadway guys and dolls. What's more, the stories showed Gleason to be a tough boozer, comfortable in the city at night.

Gleason added to this macho image by employing the June Taylor Dancers to open each show, starting within a few weeks of his DuMont debut. The dance troupe featured athletic men and women performing energetic, elaborate, sexy routines. Gleason sometimes joined the dancers as a lead in to the monologue. While the June Taylor Dancers attracted press notice for their artistic performances, Gleason described their contributions in lowbrow terms, claiming that he wanted to give viewers "pretty girls who could hoof," rather than fancy choreography. "The folks in Utah don't know from entrechats!" he explained emphatically.[57] These dancers made an important contribution to the program and Gleason's image, lending "an aura of nightclub conviviality and sex appeal to his homey hour of sketches," Henry wrote. "And it provided an opportunity for [Gleason] to flirt, on camera at least, with lots of leggy young women, enhancing the devil-may-care playboy image of both Gleasons, Reggie and Jackie."[58]

Gleason occasionally mentioned his wife and children during interviews; however, his playboy image overwhelmed any signs that Gleason was a family man. In fact, the star had been living apart from his wife Genevieve since well before his *Cavalcade* debut, though the couple made periodic efforts at reconciliations until 1951. Their Catholic beliefs precluded the couple from securing an annulment or a divorce until 1970.[59] In the meantime, Gleason was very happy to enjoy the attention of the pretty singers and actresses who were guests on *Caval-cade of Stars*. In one racy routine from November 1951, cabaret singer and actress Julie Wilson appeared on the program. Introduced as "a big hit in London and all the smart supper clubs across the country," Wilson takes the stage in a tight, low cut, black dress and a seductive wrap around her neck, performing a jazzy medley with a New Orleans flavor. From "Sadie Green (The Vamp of New Orleans)," Wilson segues to "Ballin' the Jack," a Dixieland classic filled with sexual double entendres. Wilson glides through the dance moves described in the first verse of the song. She then stops singing and teases the audience, "You know, I'm sorta lonely. I think I need somebody to help me do 'Ballin' the Jack.'" On cue, Gleason walks by as Wilson brightens up. "Why Jack!" she exclaims happily. They banter until Wilson makes her move. "Have you ever done 'Ballin' the Jack'?" she asks. Gleason replies eagerly, "No, but if you're ready, I am." The routine concludes with Wilson walking the dapper host through the simple dance steps and brassy lyrics. Bringing it to a big finish, Wilson belts out, "Ballin'" Gleason answers with a big smile, "Yeah, baby. Ballin'." Then together: "That's what we call 'Ballin' the Jack.'"[60]

For Gleason, seduction did not end on the TV screen. In 1953, after he left DuMont, he began to compose and release a popular series of orchestral jazz recordings whose titles epitomized the moods that they were intended to evoke. The first one was *Music for Lovers Only*. A follow-up from 1954: *Music, Martinis, Memories*. Over the years, Gleason released a total of forty albums that collectively sold more than 120 million copies.[61] Popular entertainment was changing. Rather than drawing inspiration from urban life and ethnic culture, many of the performers most popular with critics and chic audiences now celebrated adult pleasures that were accessible to a broad middle class. All it took was a little bit of money and resourcefulness to plug into a new world of cool jazz, dry martinis, stylish clothes, spectacular entertainment, and sexual freedom. TV production houses located in Hollywood continued to churn out a range of popular entertainment, including the family-oriented sitcoms, Westerns, and crime dramas that dominated television by the late 1950s. New York still had Broadway, the visual arts, the nation's great daily newspapers and weekly magazines, and a Greenwich Village avant garde that fostered jazz and poetry.[62] But within a few years, the national capital of sophisticated, stylish, slightly risqué, middle-class entertainment shifted to Las Vegas: a mythical setting for movies and newspaper gossip about Rat Pack celebrities. It also emerged as the stylish vacation destination for adult singles and couples who wanted to escape everyday routine and live like a Sinatra or a Gleason for a weekend.

It is no coincidence that in 1953, Gleason's first full year at CBS, Hugh Hefner launched *Playboy* magazine from Chicago. The magazine came to define "the modern man as tasteful, knowledgeable, cultured, urbane, well dressed and coiffed, open about his sexuality," wrote Richard A. Schwartz in his encyclopedia of Cold War culture.[63] From the statement of purpose published in the first *Playboy* issue, Hefner spoke to, and for, his readers across the country: "We like our apartment. We enjoy mixing up cocktails and an hors d'oeuvre or two, putting a little mood music on the phonograph, and inviting in a female for a quiet discussion on Picasso, Nietzsche, jazz, sex."[64] Gleason could probably have done without the Picasso and Nietzsche, and he would have had more than a couple of hors d'oeuvres; nevertheless, for the most part, he shared this aesthetic and helped to sell it to the country through his television programs. Gleason was a New Yorker and he was old friends with several of the Jewish comedians who dominated early television variety programing. Nevertheless, he had more in common with Hefner, a self-made Midwesterner who appreciated all of the worldly delights that America confers upon its celebrities, than he did with the Borscht Belt comedians who commanded early variety stages with the nervous energy and irreverent attitude of outsiders who were not quite sure what to make of American culture and their place in it.

Gleason Moves to CBS

Gleason secretly signed a contract to move from DuMont to CBS in October 1951, with the understanding that he would continue working on *Cavalcade of Stars* until his Drug Stores of America agreement expired at the end of May of 1952. He expected to clear a minimum of $400,000 annually from the CBS deal: a significant increase over the $1,500 a show that he was earning on DuMont's *Cavalcade of Stars*. Gleason's decision was motivated by more than money. CBS had a reputation for quality

Gleason hits the big time on CBS.
Source: Library of American Broadcasting, University of Maryland.

production, operated from fancy corporate offices in midtown Manhattan, featured programs with other big-name talent, and treated Gleason like a star from the time that negotiations commenced. According to Bishop, his authorized biographer, Gleason remembered having an awkward moment at DuMont shortly after signing with CBS. *Cavalcade* producer Milton Douglas approached the star, asking what kind of a deal the star expected in his contract extension. "He [Gleason] could not say, 'I'm signed. I'm going to be one of the biggest entertainers in the world. For the next three years I'm going to be on top, moneywise, prestige-wise, showwise. DuMont is too little and too late.' He could not say any of that," Bishop wrote. Instead, Gleason made an unreasonable offer ($10,000 a week and the privilege of producing the show from Los Angeles) and forced DuMont and Drug Stores of America to reject him.[65]

Part of DuMont's difficulty in matching CBS's offer was financial: the corporate strategy favored programs with modest production costs. DuMont did not have sufficient affiliates or support from major advertisers to risk matching CBS's offer; nor was it willing to lose money in exchange for the prestige of retaining a talent like Gleason. Ultimately, in its programing and handling of personnel, DuMont rejected the star system. Furthermore, as Henry suggested, the more modest style of Allen B. Du Mont and his company, based in the hinterlands of Passaic, New Jersey, represented the minor leagues to Gleason. Allen Du Mont and his managers, at both the network and corporate level, did not court Gleason with gifts or displays of friendship. "The absence of a personal bond between tycoon and star might not seem important," Henry wrote. "But it contributed to Gleason's ultimate itchiness to leave *Cavalcade of Stars* . . . Du Mont and his network made Gleason the star he had always dreamed of being. But in his mind they did not treat him like one."[66]

Gleason left DuMont in the summer of 1952. The network was already reeling from the FCC's Sixth Report and Order, released in April, which instituted a system of assigning stations that was unfavorable to the network. Gleason's departure made DuMont appear to be even less of a player in network television. Ted Bergmann, director of sales for the network at the time, remembered that Gleason's leaving had a "very bad effect" on DuMont. "He was probably the brightest star that we had. When CBS lured him away, we looked pretty bad. It didn't take long for *Cavalcade* to fold after that."[67] In fact, *Cavalcade of Stars* ran for only three more months with Larry Storch filling in as the host. DuMont subsequently aired only a handful of typically low budget, weekly variety shows (*Stars on Parade, Guide Right*). The network was never able to replace Gleason or match the prime-time success of *Cavalcade of Stars*.

DUMONT

Roscoe Karns as Rocky King.

Source: Photofest.

Law and Order, DuMont Style

fter World War II, threats to the American way of life posed by two different sources, criminals and communists, gripped law-abiding citizens across the country. An alarmed public looked to popular culture for enlightenment about Frank Costello, Joseph Stalin, and the minions who did their bidding. Television producers responded to the public's concerns about security by creating a range of dramas. Lawmen occasionally encountered political subversives, but they spent most of their time fighting urban crime. In April 1952, there were twenty-nine different weekly crime shows on television.[1] From 1949 to 1955, DuMont alone aired at least twenty crime series and a few additional international spy adventures. The programs featured a range of heroes: newspapermen, lawyers, writers, private detectives, and a quirky, reformed con man named Colonel Humphrey Flack. DuMont found its niche, however, with its first two police procedurals: *The Plainclothes Man* (1949–1954) and *Rocky King, Detective* (1950–1954).

The long-running programs moved around the network's schedule until the summer of 1951, when DuMont programed them on Sunday night to offer national viewers a powerful and popular hour of police drama. DuMont's gritty, urban detective shows aired in approximately twenty cities (live or on kinescope) and achieved good ratings as alternatives to more expensive and polished competition: live drama on NBC and Fred Waring's musical variety show on CBS.[2] Like other programs on DuMont, *The Plainclothes Man* and *Rocky King* incorporated creative production gimmicks that helped them stand out. Perhaps drawing inspiration from Robert Montgomery's production of Raymond Chandler's *Lady in the Lake* (1946), a Hollywood experiment from a few years earlier, *The Plainclothes Man* presented its weekly crime stories primarily through the eyes of the main character: an urban detective, never seen on the screen, known only as the "lieutenant." *Rocky King* also creatively employed an unseen character. Every episode started and ended with a conversation between the detective and his wife, Mabel. For the entire series, however, Mabel did not appear on camera. Instead, viewers could only imagine what she looked like when she conducted her end of the witty banter from just beyond the screen. *Rocky King* and *The Plainclothes Man* offered enduring models of television detectives: the policeman as the typical, hard-working guy next door with an interesting and healthy life outside of the office; and the cop as an urban superhero, calloused by the everyday violence of his job, and obsessed with the minutia of police work to the exclusion of family and friends. Despite his stony moniker, Rocky King tracked criminals with a sharp mind and a gentle smile, though he could be tough on an uncooperative witness when he had to be. In contrast, *The Plainclothes Man* was a prototype for *Dragnet* and the many subsequent hard-boiled police shows focused on the process of detection. Each episode included dead bodies, unfriendly witnesses, nasty criminals, and spartan, one-dimensional lead detectives (the lieutenant and Sergeant Brady) who relentlessly pursued justice, but were not big on small talk about life outside the office.

You Are *The Plainclothes Man*

The Plainclothes Man was network television's first police drama and one of the most popular and creative early detective programs, airing for nearly five years, starting in October 1949. It was produced by DuMont in association with an independent company, Transamerican. *The Plainclothes Man*'s popularity was remarkable considering the show's challenging visual style. The jumpy, subjective camera showed viewers crime scenes exactly as the lieutenant surveyed them. Tough-talking criminals and equally rough cops looked directly into the camera when they answered to the lieutenant, sometimes appearing in dangerously tight close-ups. The noirish atmosphere was frequently enhanced by cigarette smoke courtesy of the primary sponsor, Edgeworth Tobacco, proud makers of Holiday Cigarettes, Holiday Pipe Mixture ("looks good, smokes good"), and Edgeworth Pipe Tobacco, "America's finest."

The Plainclothes Man made every effort to maintain the illusion that viewers were seeing the world through the lieutenant's eyes. Ken Lynch, the former radio actor who played the lieutenant, asked plenty of questions, but did not appear before the camera. The only actor who received significant screen time each week was a journeyman named Jack Orrison, who portrayed Sergeant Brady, the title character's dogged deputy. The subjective camera was the star of the program and the most compelling reason to tune in each week. *The Plainclothes Man* provided an opportunity for DuMont staff director William Marceau and his production crew to flaunt their skills while searching for new ways of presenting detective stories. "I loved *The Plainclothes Man* because of the challenges. We didn't look to hold back in those days," said Arthur Forrest, a cameraman on the program. "We looked to go forward, to be challenged with new things and ideas because we felt that this was more [interesting] than being a shipping clerk or something." Forrest's camera was mounted on a bulky pedestal known as the "Fearless" because of its manufacturer, the Fearless Camera Corporation. The Fearless was difficult to control but was valuable because it included a small vertical crane, so the camera could simulate the lieutenant's field of vision. Forrest maintained focus while following the character's gaze down to the tiny typewritten letters on a coroner's report or the end of a carefully packed pipe dangling from the unseen detective's lips.[3]

Though suspects generally did not pick fights with the law, occasional scraps warranted "sensational camera effect(s)," according to a *TV Guide* article. "When the lieutenant once got a black eye, the audience saw a huge fist smash into the lens. Another time, the lieutenant was knocked unconscious, and the audience saw a beautiful, swirling kaleidoscope before he blacked out."[4] The camera absorbed the blows, while actor Lynch remained out of harm's way. Still, using the camera as his stand-in had its drawbacks, since Lynch held papers, pipes, weapons, and other items before the camera while reading his lines. "Ken has to be a contortionist and acrobat to avoid the camera, and to

As the eyes of the lieutenant, DuMont cameraman Arthur Forrest focuses on a piece of paper. Brady (Jack Orrison) looks on from across the desk.
Source: Photofest.

hop from set to set without really being on the set at all. He has climbed on all sides of the camera, knelt for long stretches underneath it; [and] lain prone on the floor."[5] For audio, the DuMont crew fashioned a hook around Lynch's neck that held a microphone the size of an eight-ball, so the actor's hands were free and he could maneuver near the camera.[6]

Each episode departed from this subjective style in a series of more conventional flashbacks through which suspects and witnesses told the lieutenant their stories. In addition, the opening crime scene was usually shot in a familiar, objective style, though the criminal's identity was carefully concealed. The shifting perspectives could be jarring. *Variety* noted that "just when the viewer is oriented to watching the show through the eyes of one person, the camera switches over to [its] standard objective role, thereby creating more than a mild sense of confusion."[7] In fact, director Marceau and his crew even took liberties in these "objective" scenes, bringing the style of film noir to live television through shadowy lighting and unorthodox camera angles that hid more than they revealed. The anxious visual style suited the weekly adventures of honest detectives struggling for supremacy in an urban battlefield.

The Plainclothes Man was the first television program to take viewers for a ride alongside the cops. As Marceau explained, "The unusual 'Plainclothes Man' format is built directly around the fact that there is in all lovers of the detective story the subconscious desire to be a detective and actively share in the unraveling of clues. By subjective use of the camera . . . the illusion is indelibly created in the mind of the viewer that he is living the role of his favorite detective—himself!"[8] The idea that readers or viewers enjoy solving crimes has long been a foundation of detective fiction. On radio, *The Adventures of Ellery Queen* exploited the "whodunit's" appeal by stopping the action and inviting celebrity "armchair experts" to guess the solution.[9] *The Plainclothes Man* encouraged a similar level of audience engagement but it did not demand that viewers possess the skills in observation and deduction of Sherlock Holmes. *TV Digest* noted that compared to a typical detective program, *The Plainclothes Man* plots were more "down to earth," involving simple, albeit brutal, cases of urban murder, theft, and extortion. The lieutenant and Brady "are old-fashioned enough to look for fingerprints and footprints; listen to ballistics experts, chemical analysts, and police surgeons; and expect such old-fashioned motives as greed when a murder's been committed."[10] The viewer received information as the lieutenant did and probably shared the conclusions of Brady and his boss. Brady helped the lieutenant (and the viewer) by sharing reports from the police lab, summarizing the evidence, and suggesting ways to move the investigation forward. Brady's observations, directed at the camera, positioned the viewer as part of the force.

Birth of the Police Procedural

The *Plainclothes Man* set the stage for later police procedurals like *Dragnet*, which premiered on NBC in 1952 after a three-year run on radio. DuMont's detectives showed viewers the way big-city officers worked with each other and went about solving crimes. Contemporary articles

commented on the show's realism, with one noting that "the staff pho-
tographers of a big city tabloid, who have covered crime at its goriest,
have voted the show 'the most authentic mystery on television.' The
police department of another city uses kinescopes of the show as a
training feature."[11] In an article from the DuMont publicity department
published under Sergeant Brady's byline, the character scorned other
crime shows on the air. "Television mysteries are in a rut," he declared.
"Private detectives, newspaper men, flower fanciers, and old maid
aunts may do the sleuthing on TV, but not in real life. Hunches always
work on TV, but they're million to one shots in real life. The plain truth
is that detective work has become so scientific and painstaking that an
untrained person hasn't a chance of cracking a case."[12] These notions
of the way "real" police worked often came to television writers and directors via prominent law enforcement figures like J. Edgar Hoover;
William Parker, chief of Los Angeles police; and O. W. Wilson, an influential professor at the University of California who later served as
chief of the Chicago police force. They extolled the training, expertise, technological sophistication, and bureaucratic efficiency of the
powerful, modern crime-fighting force.[13]

The highlight of a *Plainclothes Man* episode was the first investiga-
tive sequence after the initial crime. The scene could last five minutes,
all in a single take. Viewers followed the lieutenant's gaze, examining
bullet fragments, open windows, or picked locks. The segment required virtuoso command of the massive cameras and crude focusing
knobs, as the lieutenant darted around the crime scene and focused on
different clues. In one episode, the camera pans a room while the lieutenant assesses the trajectory of a bullet and the location of a shooter.
Suddenly, the camera stops on a close-up of a tiny bullet hole in the
wall. The lieutenant digs at the hole with a pocket knife and produces
a bullet in the palm of his beefy hand. The tense and exciting sequence
showcases both the lieutenant's technical proficiency in finding evidence and the DuMont production crew's skill at designing and exe-
cuting a difficult live scene.[14] This flashy technique of moving from
sweeping shots to microscopic camera detail was one of the signature
devices of *The Plainclothes Man*. The dazzling camera work and direction allowed the home viewer to experience modern modes of police
investigation.

Dead Men and Femme Fatales

The lieutenant and Brady frequently used their evidence from crime scenes and labs to trap the witnesses and suspects interviewed over the course of an investigation. *The Plainclothes Man*'s visual style provided a vivid illustration of the importance of physical evidence and the unreliability of people. When other characters told the lieutenant their stories, *The Plainclothes Man* switched from the subjective camera to voiceovers and flashbacks that were shot from the more traditional, objective style. However, like the detectives, viewers could find out that a witness was lying, and a dramatic scene that had appeared earlier in the episode was a fabrication. These lies were never really a surprise to the lieutenant. The investigator searched for the truth in a world of femme fatales, small-time hoodlums, racketeers, thieves, and killers who looked like they would sooner pull a gun on the lieutenant than provide straight answers to his questions. While none of the early TV shows romanticized crime or criminals, *The Plainclothes Man*'s subjective camera was especially effective at showing the amoral denizens of the urban night. The suspects and witnesses were scary, ugly, and desperate when they directly addressed the camera, squirming before the law. In one episode, for example, an aging burlesque dancer, played by veteran actress Eileen Ryan, is on the hot seat after her husband of only two weeks is murdered. Under questioning, she attempts to use her charms, moving toward the camera with a sincere pout, "Look, lieutenant. I'm the type of girl that likes to have everything out in the open. If I knew more I wouldn't hold back on ya. Ya get what I mean, lieutenant." Brady puts an end to the desperate and pathetic flirtation, stepping in from the side. "Get what he means? You can go now."[15]

The cops in the *Plainclothes Man* were tough guys in a world that was surprisingly brutal and graphic, compared to the most popular TV shows of the time: *Martin Kane* (NBC), *Man Against Crime* (CBS, DuMont, NBC), *Racket Squad* (CBS), *Dragnet* (NBC), and *Rocky King* (DuMont). The stark *Plainclothes Man* stories and images were more like TV versions of the popular material in pulp detective magazines, big-city tabloid newspapers, and dark police films like *The Naked City* (1948) and *The Big Heat* (1953). In its unflinching focus on police work, *The Plainclothes Man* regularly showed corpses on screen, covered by thin sheets,

A Plainclothes Man interrogation. Ken Lynch stands in the foreground, off camera, asking questions. The witnesses, or suspects, answer directly to the camera. Sergeant Brady (standing, right) keeps everybody honest.

Source: TV Showtime (Omaha, Nebraska), August 2, 1950.

rather than following the more common practice of providing verbal reports or suggesting a murder with a gun shot without actually showing the body. In a typical episode, a man named Freeman lies shot, crumpled in the fetal position with his back to the lieutenant (and the camera). Rather than calling an ambulance and administering emergency care, the investigator looks down on the dying man as he and Brady conduct the investigation.

LIEUTENANT: "Who shot you, Mr. Freeman?"
FREEMAN: "I don't know. They ran out back."
LIEUTENANT: "Why were you shot?"
FREEMAN (sounding weaker with every question): "Robbery."
LIEUTENANT: "Where's your wife?"
FREEMAN: "Away."
LIEUTENANT: "We better get tough with her."
FREEMAN: "Leave her out of it. She didn't have anything to do with it."

The camera pans from the man, now dead, to the hard, unflappable Brady, sitting on a chair above the body. "You say they ran out back," he continues, then pauses mid-sentence, reluctantly acknowledging that all good interrogations must come to an end at some point. He deadpans, "Well, I guess I'll have to leave my question unanswered." The lieutenant is similarly unfazed, as his attention shifts back to the dead body and he speculates on the identity of the murderer, based on the dead man's final words. Brady realizes that the dying man was lying to the police because the back door was chained from the inside. The lieutenant responds to Brady's observation by rifling through the corpse's pockets, and removing the dead man's wallet. Viewers may feel voyeuristic excitement, power, and guilt as they share the lieutenant's perspective during the questioning.[16] In some ways, these scenes stretch credibility: Would the police really be so insensitive? But the program also communicates a higher reality about the gritty life of homicide detectives, in which corpses are a fact of life. Hardened investigators must remain detached, despite the death and danger that surround them, to serve justice and maintain order.

In its continuing quest for action, *The Plainclothes Man* sometimes employed an innovative technique, also used on DuMont's *Not for Publication* series, of shooting complicated scenes on film before the telecast and then inserting the film into the live program. Whereas most climactic fist fights and gun battles on live television looked artificial, these film inserts allowed *The Plainclothes Man* to achieve a heightened intensity. The program moved outdoors and used cinematic photography and editing. In one film insert, a woman named Leddie, the suspect, slips out the back door and heads up the fire escape toward the roof. Brady chases her. The camera cuts between the two people running up the stairs, firing gun shots at each other. Suddenly, on the roof, Leddie is cornered against a flimsy railing. She backs up; director Marceau cuts to a close-up of the railing breaking, then Lettie's terrified face, and a final high angle shot from the roof when she falls to her death. The scene involved lots of movement, outdoor scenes, tricky editing between the two characters during the chase, audio effects like gun shots and screams, and a dummy to be substituted for the actress before she takes the plunge. Such tricks would have been extremely difficult to execute in a strictly live program.[17]

Ultimately, the combination of subjective camera techniques and film inserts invited viewers to appreciate warriors like the lieutenant and Brady for their bravery in navigating a dangerous world. While viewers were invited to share the lieutenant's perspective and try to solve the crimes, *The Plainclothes Man* offered constant reminders that policemen were different from the typical armchair detectives at home. Indeed, the life of the detective appeared to be a lonely one. Like *Dragnet*'s Joe Friday and many other TV lawmen, the main characters in *The Plainclothes Man* were unencumbered by family obligations as they went about the job. The show's opening tells us all we need to know about the lieutenant, while establishing the subjective visual style. It starts with a tight overhead shot of a desk with a gun and a badge, as an anonymous detective prepares for another day on the job. The man takes the gun, methodically examines it, and places it into his holster. He then slowly picks up the badge, shows it to the camera, and puts it down. Jazzy, atmospheric horns, punctuated by gunshots, play in the background. An authoritative announcer sets the tone: "Hero without uniform. Unknown, unsung, but always on guard, protecting you against crime. Now see another criminal brought to justice through the eyes of the plainclothes man."[18] The tools of police work, the gun and the badge, symbolized the lieutenant's official authority and absolute moral certainty regarding his social role as a guardian of law and order. These qualities distinguished the lieutenant and the television policemen who followed him from the many amateur sleuths and private detectives who populated early television.

Rocky King: Nice Guy, But Where's Mabel?

Realizing that a full hour of tough talk, body bags, and swirling, subjective cameras would be too much for most viewers, DuMont tempered the lieutenant with a gentler detective as a Sunday night lead-in to *The Plainclothes Man*. Rocky King was a rarity amidst the sea of pop culture detectives, circa 1950, who went home to little more than a bottle of booze at the end of the day. Equally devoted to his family and his position as an unspecified city's chief of homicide, Rocky King rivaled *Martin Kane* (NBC) as the most popular TV detective before *Dragnet*'s Joe Friday started working his Los Angeles crime beat in

1952. A typically supportive contemporary critic explained that "Rocky stresses the believable and human in police work, rather than the horrible. Sure he carries a gun and uses it, but for the most part Rocky is a warm, kindly-intentioned Chief Inspector in a big city detective bureau."[19] With *Rocky King*, DuMont offered the television industry an early example of the way a strong lead character on a police show could charm viewers, despite mediocre stories and a visual style that was proficient but unremarkable. In fact, DuMont specialized in these quirky, character-driven crime shows, featuring sweet protagonists who were tough only when they had to be. They quietly restored justice and protected the underdog with a weary smile and an appreciation for the strange and ironic twists of fate that defined life in the big city.[20]

Rocky King was co-produced by DuMont and Stark-Layton, one of several independent production companies hired by DuMont to lighten the work load for its small team of staff producers. The outside producers hired writers and talent, while the network was still responsible for most other tasks: providing a production crew and facilities, setting budgets, selling advertising, and securing distribution. By the time *Rocky King* went on the air in January 1950, Wilbur Stark and Jerry Layton were already television veterans. Stark-Layton had produced nearly eight hundred episodes of network programs, including DuMont's daytime *Your Television Shopper*, which was hosted by Stark's wife, Kathi Norris.[21] Wes Kenney was the director for most of *Rocky King*'s run, but Dick Sandwick and Lee Polk also directed some episodes. Roscoe Karns had appeared in more than 150 movies when he took over the role of Inspector King at the age of 57, happy to have the starring role on television as his career wound down. Film roles were drying up for the character actor who, according to *TV Digest*, "had been typed as the 'light comic,' portraying newspapermen, salesmen, and press agents with just enough of the whimsical touch to garner giggles."[22]

Rocky dressed in the rumpled trench coat and fedora that were de-rigueur for any 1950s detective, but Karns was older, shorter, and less intimidating than his media gumshoe counterparts. He approached the world more like the solid, hard-working, beleaguered father in a 1950s sitcom or a period movie like *Father of the Bride* (1950). "As played by Karns, King is neither fearless nor especially tough," wrote one commentator. "He's just an average guy working at a tougher-than-average job."[23] Rocky King and his assistants were not flawless detectives. Rocky got his man, but sometimes he made dumb mistakes, failing to recognize obvious clues or arrest suspects in a timely manner. This fallibility was part of the show's charm and enhanced its credibility. *Rocky King* earned high marks in a 1953 *TV Guide* feature that asked a real New York detective to rate the TV cops. The expert thought that *Dragnet* supercop Joe Friday was unbelievably efficient. "That know-it-all wouldn't last a week on the New York force," he said. In contrast, he liked Rocky King because the DuMont detective sometimes blundered. "When Rocky pulls a rock, I right away start pulling for Rocky."[24]

Rocky King found a skillful and sophisticated balance between the dramatic segments demonstrating police procedures and lighter portions featuring witty banter between Rocky and his wife Mabel (Grace Carney). Similar to the routines of George Burns and Gracie Allen, these exchanges enhanced Rocky's image as a typical family man and provided a welcome respite from the murder investigations. Like many 1950s TV wives, Mabel occasionally hatched kooky schemes, spent a little too much money, and nagged her husband about chores or the latest adventures of their son. "Various reasons have been given for Rocky's superefficiency [solving crimes], but it seems that the best one is that his home life isn't all that it should be and as a result he can put his heart into his work," suggested one TV magazine. "The grimace on Rocky's face whenever she's speaking to him is strong evidence that he may be picked up for homicide himself some day . . . It's not hard to guess that Rocky would rather deal with criminals that with his wife."[25] Still, Mabel had a good heart, a quick sense of humor, and warm chemistry with her husband.

In a sequence from a typical episode, Rocky reads through the family check book while Mabel defends her unusual spending habits:

ROCKY: "The next check. Father's surprise. Fifty dollars. Now look, Mabel. I don't want you spending that kind of money on me on Christmas. I've got everything I need."

MABEL (laughing): "Oh ho ho. That isn't for you. I meant that you'd be surprised if you found out what it was for."

ROCKY: "Well, what is it for?"

MABEL: "I can't tell you until I have a conference with a very shrewd businessman tomorrow."

Rocky King, shot live on location at DuMont's Engineering Department shop in Long Island City, New York. One of the show's early directors, Dick Sandwick (at left, wearing cap), supervises Karns (wearing the black hat) and Earl Hammond, who played Sergeant Lane.

Source: The Raster, December 1950. Allen B. Du Mont Collection, Archives Center, National Museum of American History, Smithsonian Institution.

ROCKY (pointing angrily): "Well I'm a shrewd businessman and I want to know what you're spending fifty dollars of my money for."

MABEL (unruffled, in a cheerful voice): "Your money. I like that. Don't we make a joint income report?"

ROCKY: "Sure, but what's that got to do with it?"

MABEL: "It makes me just as important as you are, even if I am just the power behind the throne."

ROCKY: "Is that so? Well, don't take this argument into foreign countries; we can settle it right here."

The discussion would have probably continued for hours if Rocky had not received a phone call from Sergeant Lane (Earl Hammond), the cue to shift gears from light comedy to the evening's murder investigation. The eternally chipper Mabel calls Rocky at work later in the episode to tell him about her plans to invest the fifty dollars in the rental of an empty lot that could be used to sell Christmas trees.[26]

Dialogue on a page does not fully convey the playful, and strange, characteristics of Rocky's interactions with his invisible wife. Mabel was always available for conversation, but she never appeared on the air. Instead, Rocky would talk to Mabel as if she was positioned to the right of the camera. In typical DuMont fashion, Mabel's birth was a happy accident. The debut episode was running short and Karns was desperate to kill time. He enlisted the help of actress Carney, but she had to remain off screen, since she was already slated to play a different role on camera. Mabel became a regular for the entire run of the series, her identity a constant source of playful speculation by commentators. As on radio, the voice without an accompanying image allowed viewers to use their imagination. Karns explained the appeal of Mabel and Junior, their son, who was a constant presence in Mabel's stories, but was also beyond the reach of the DuMont cameras. "For many months now, my home life with my 'wife' Mabel and my 'son,' Junior has overshadowed, at least from the standpoint of fan mail, my work as a police inspector in *Rocky King, Detective*," Karns said. "The two characters have probably aroused much more interest by remaining off-stage than they ever would by being seen. Viewers form their own ideas of what Mabel and Junior look like."[27]

Aside from the scenes with Mabel, the writing on *Rocky King* was undistinguished. A typical critic recognized that "as a detective thriller, the show is no great shakes, but it still makes more sense than most of the crime shows on TV."[28] A *Rocky King* investigation usually included multiple suspects, all with a motive for murder. Rocky solved the case by following an obscure lead or, when all else failed, setting a trap for the killer: leaving the murder weapon or a blackmail note at the murder scene while he waited to see who would recognize and retrieve the incriminating evidence. Many episodes climaxed with Rocky gathering the suspects in a room and solving the crime. Unfortunately, the inspector usually forgot to disarm these dangerous figures before exposing the guilty party. Realizing that the law had caught up with him, the murderer would pull a gun, take a shot at Rocky, then run. However, with the limited production budget for sets and props, he usually did not get very far before he was cornered by Rocky and his backup, Sergeant Lane.[29]

Overworked DuMont staff writers like Larry Menkin occasionally churned out *Rocky King* scripts. For most episodes, however, DuMont and producer Stark-Layton brought in low-paid freelance scribes who submitted the clichéd mystery stories. As on the many other DuMont programs that employed a rotating staff of writers, the performers and network production crews were valuable sources of stability and continuity. *Rocky King*'s star, Karns, contributed additional dialogue, including the conversations with Mabel. Director Kenney also helped with the writing and controlled all aspects of the visual style from cinematography to set design. "We had one guy in charge of art direction for all of the shows," explained Kenney. "I got to the point where I knew all the scenery they had. If [the director] didn't say anything, they would just throw up schlocky sets. So I would go down to this guy with a floor plan, knowing their pieces. They would grumble, but inevitably I got what I wanted."[30] Kenney's search for authentic set pieces did not end at the Wanamaker's studio. In a city transfixed by television's mystique, all of New York served as Kenney's prop department. For example, the director remembered preparing for a *Rocky King* episode that took place at a print shop. "I found this little shop [in downtown New York City], and they had all of the equipment that I would have needed. So I went to the owner and said, 'I'd like to use some of your equipment. It's during a weekend so it'll be back and we'll pay you a fee for the rental and everything.'"

"He said, 'Is this live television?'"

"I said, 'Yes.'"

"He said, 'Can I come down and watch the show?'"

"And I said, 'Of course.' Those were the kinds of things you could do in those days with no money because it was so new."[31]

Kenney, Karns, and the others had fun working within DuMont's low-budget parameters. More than the popular detective shows on other networks, *Rocky King* invited viewers to share the adrenaline rush of producing a live detective program. Led by Karns, the actors on *Rocky King* made little attempt to hide the many flubbed lines. Karns would frequently botch a character's name or simply turn to his assistant, Lane, and ask to be reminded where he was supposed to go next. What's more, the cast and crew openly peppered episodes with sly, self-reflexive comments. In one episode, for example, King and his assis-

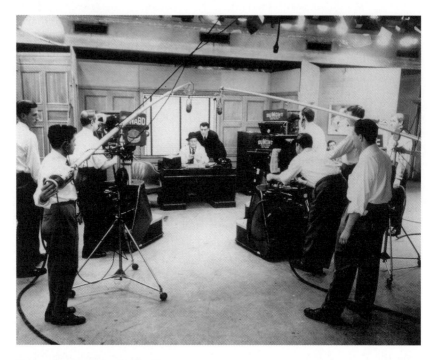

The studio setup for *Rocky King*.
Source: Courtesy of Marvin Pakula.

tant, Detective Hart (Todd Karns, Roscoe's son), investigate the murder of a mystery writer:

> HART: "You know, I kind of go in for those mystery stories."
> KING: "Hey, you got a television set?"
> HART: "Yeah. Do you look at them once in a while?"
> KING: "Sure."
> HART: "Who's your favorite?"
> KING: "Well, I'd rather not say. It's kind of personal."[32]

Such funny, honest, lightly self-deprecating moments enhanced the
title character's appeal and the show's credibility by openly acknowledging that *Rocky King* was a TV show, rather than an unmediated window on life. Yet King's success at closing cases showed that he was no
bumbling Keystone Cop. This friendly and capable inspector provided
a nice balance to the adventures of the tougher lieutenant who followed

Rocky King on Sunday nights. With both Rocky King and the lieutenant on the job, viewers could start the work week knowing that detectives were fighting crime with an impressive arsenal: experience, training, devoted colleagues, an efficient police lab, a sense of humor, and a .45 tucked away for when things got rough. What's more, DuMont used style and panache to deliver its conventional and reassuring message about law and order.

Bishop Fulton J. Sheen.

9

A Bishop for Berle Fans

uMont's last hit program was also its least likely success story. *Life Is Worth Living* starred Fulton J. Sheen, a fifty-seven-year-old Catholic bishop who delivered weekly, half-hour lectures about life and how to live it in Cold War America. Bishop Sheen's commercial success stood as an example of the nation's growing religious tolerance and a popular hunger for spiritual guidance in how to deal with a changing world. Sometimes Sheen spoke about the home, proscribing behavior toward spouses, parents, children, and neighbors. Other sermons counseled viewers about the global Soviet threat or the morality of atomic weapons. Regardless of the topic, Sheen spoke directly to the camera with conviction, intelligence, comfort, and charm. Sheen distinguished himself as a skillful social and political commentator for an audience that was raised on radio and appreciated nimble wordsmiths. His only peer was CBS's Edward R. Murrow. Sheen remains the only figure ever to captivate a broad television audience with a weekly sermon. His achievement was still acknowledged by industry veterans like Roger Ailes, the chairman and C.E.O. of Fox News, more than fifty years after the debut of *Life Is Worth Living.* In a 2003 *New Yorker* profile, Ailes criticized Chris Matthews, a commentator on the rival MSNBC, for performing monologues rather than conducting interviews. "The last guy to do a good monologue on TV was Fulton J. Sheen," he said. In a further tribute, Ailes and another Fox News executive then repeated an old joke about Sheen. "And he had a good writer," the executive said. Ailes replied, "Yeah—God!"[1]

Sheen debuted on February 12, 1952, in one of the roughest time slots on television: Tuesday at eight o'clock, opposite Milton Berle's *Texaco Star Theater* (NBC) and *The Frank Sinatra Show* (CBS). Berle's program, the second-most popular show on the air behind *Arthur Godfrey's Talent Scouts* (CBS), was synonymous with Tuesday night television.[2] DuMont executives did not expect Sheen to pull an audience. Instead, they thought that the bishop's program might fill air time, appeal to Sheen's core followers, and help the network satisfy FCC requirements for public service.[3] The previous DuMont program in the time slot was a quiz show called *What's the Story?* in which newspaper columnists answered questions about world events. According to the ratings books, it had one viewer for every twenty who tuned in to Berle. Before that, a political discussion program, *The Georgetown University Forum*, was even less popular.[4] Whereas DuMont's other Tuesday night offerings lasted only a few months before moving to oblivion, or at least a softer time slot, Sheen owned the spot until April 1955. After DuMont ceased network operations, Sheen moved to ABC for two seasons.

Within a few weeks of Sheen's February 1952 debut, it was clear that DuMont had stumbled onto a brilliant counter-programing strategy against Berle. Rather than airing another variety show, as CBS did with Sinatra, DuMont appealed to the audience's desire for self-improvement. Commentators watched with glee as the Catholic priest battled the Jewish comedian for ratings and respectability. *Life* proclaimed that "the DuMont network put on a program that violated almost all of television's precepts . . . It had no orchestra, no script, no supporting cast, almost no props. All it had was Roman Catholic Bishop Fulton J. Sheen standing before the camera talking." Yet, the magazine reported, Sheen was stunning the television industry with his popularity. In less than two months, *Life Is Worth Living* had jumped from three stations to fifteen. What's more, its ratings in the key markets of New York, Washington, and Chicago had risen to 11.1, while the audiences for Sinatra and Berle each dropped in those cities.[5] By April 1, 1952, Sinatra's show was off the air. Sheen may have dealt the Sinatra program its final blow, but the series was already in trouble after Sinatra's affair with Gardner, his series of subpar records, and the weekly competition from Berle. For his part, Berle took the bishop's popularity in stride. "If I'm going to be eased off the top by anyone, it's better that I lose to the One for whom Bishop Sheen is speaking," Berle said.[6]

While Sheen never surpassed Berle in the ratings, his program was the most widely viewed religious series in the history of television and the only such show to find a large prime-time audience on network television.[7] Sheen used his DuMont pulpit to become, in the words of one magazine, "the most famous preacher in the United States."[8] *Life Is Worth Living* received the widest distribution of any weekly television program, on DuMont or any other network. At its height, during the 1953–1954 season, DuMont reported that the show was carried by 169 stations. More than 10 million people watched Sheen each week.[9] The bishop's loyal viewers showered him with letters, donations, and requests for free tickets to the live program. Critics saw Sheen's popularity as proof that viewers would tune in for substantial television and they praised DuMont for its public service. The nation's broadcast writers and editors honored Sheen as its "Man of the Year" in a poll conducted by *Radio-Television Daily* at the end of 1952. That year, Sheen became the only DuMont performer to take home a national Emmy Award, beating out Arthur Godfrey, Edward R. Murrow, Lucille Ball, and three other candidates for the title of "Most Outstanding Personality." Sheen was nominated for consecutive public service Emmys from 1952 to 1954, though he did not win these awards.

Bishop Sheen was a thin, gray-haired man of average height, but he had a regal and authoritative presence on screen and in person. Arthur Forrest, a cameraman at the Adelphi Theatre, recalled the excitement that greeted Sheen's arrival for his first broadcast from the Adelphi. "Here I am, a Jewish boy from the Bronx going to meet the bishop. Most of the crew was Irish and Italian. They couldn't wait. This was like meeting God. So the day comes and we're dressed a little bit better than we normally are, and in he comes. Tall, in his flowing gown, a handsome, handsome man." Like most who encountered Sheen, Forrest was immediately impressed. Fifty years later, he still remembered eyes that "burned two holes in the back of your head. Bishop Sheen was a very intense man. [He had] a lot of power, and you could feel it."[10] Contemporary commentators were equally taken with Sheen's "hypnotic eyes," described by *Time* as "one of the most remarkable pairs of eyes in America, looking out from deep sockets, pupil and iris almost merged in one luminous disk which creates the optical illusion that he not only looks at people, but through them and at everything around them."[11]

Sheen's wardrobe, custom-made by a Fifth Avenue tailor, was of the best quality, from the fine silk zucchetto (skullcap) down. He wore what one biographer described as "full episcopal regalia," including a black cassock with light purple buttons and trimming along with a matching purple ferraiolo (cape).[12] As a final reminder to viewers of his mission, Sheen sported a large gold cross, given to him by Pope Pius XII, that shined when it reflected the stage lights. "He wanted to dress that way," remembered Bishop Edwin Broderick, who produced *Life Is Worth Living* as the head of radio and television activities for the archdiocese of New York. "Some of the priests asked, 'Why doesn't he come out in a regular suit?' He [Sheen] said, 'No.' Anytime he gave a lecture, he used what he called his bishop's uniform. He could be a sensitive guy. And I didn't tell him to give up [the uniform]."[13]

The set, created by Sheen convert Jo Mielziner, Broadway's leading designer at the time, reinforced the program's fusion of Catholic instruction and non-denominational wisdom. It simulated a rector's study, including books, a desk, chairs, and a Renaissance statue of Madonna and Child, on a pedestal, that sometimes seemed to hover over Sheen's shoulder when he spoke. Sheen told a writer for the *Catholic Digest* that the statue symbolized his work on *Life Is Worth Living*: "I am bringing Mary's presence into the homes of millions of Americans who never knew her before," he explained.[14] A blackboard served as both a pedagogical tool and a typically quirky DuMont gimmick. Sheen naturally started his blackboard instruction with the letters JMJ, which many viewers recognized as a representation for Jesus, Mary, and Joseph. Then, after scrawling his lecture outlines or drawing laughably primitive diagrams, Sheen stepped away so that "his angels," the DuMont stage hands, could erase the board off camera.

As a solo performer, Sheen had a difficult job. The live production focused on him alone for approximately 27 minutes. Sheen was up to the challenge. The seasoned speaker knew how to connect with the home viewers and a live audience of a thousand supporters at the Adel-

Bishop Sheen: "One of the most remarkable pairs of eyes in America."

phi Theatre. When talking about the evils of sin and communism, Sheen could sound like the voice of doom, a prototype for the fictional Howard Beale in Paddy Chayefsky's 1976 movie *Network*. Sheen's voice "ranged from tremulous whisper to Old Testament rage," wrote *Time*. "His hands finger the chain of his pectoral cross, or spread outward in supplication, or hammer down a point in the air, or thrust skyward."[15]

Like many smart performers on the cool medium of television, Sheen softened his intense delivery with corny and self-effacing humor, creating running jokes about his poor drawing skills and his competitor, Berle. Critics also loved the bishop's philosophical digressions and detours, which covered everything from Tacitus to Marx's *Communist Manifesto* to Einstein's theory of relativity, all recited from memory. "Bishop Sheen is the embodiment of a theory I have long held (and never before gotten anywhere with) that a man of passionate conviction and a great personality . . . could simply walk out in front of a camera and captivate a large audience without the assistance of dancing girls, trained dogs, or gags," raved John Crosby of the *New York Herald Tribune*.[16] Many people found the intense and intellectual bishop sexy. Writing in the *Reporter*, cultural critic Marya Mannes could not contain her ardor. "The man has magic. He compels you to listen as if the next word were revelation . . . Sometimes there is so much ease and eloquence that one wonders whether truth can be so luxuriously attired. But always there is the Bishop's face itself—a fusion of the spiritual, the intellectual and the sensual with which few living men are endowed."[17] In his memoir, published fifty years after the debut of *Life Is Worth Living*, DuMont executive Ted Bergmann discussed Sheen's "tremendous sex appeal . . . women mobbed him after every show."[18] Sheen's popularity presented a problem for the archdiocese. "We turn down a lot of [ticket] requests that sound as if they might come from girls' schools," a spokesman told *Time*. "We don't want any squealing. First thing you know, he'd turn into a clerical Sinatra."[19]

Sheen reveled in his television success, and, like his viewers, was fascinated by the new medium.[20] He sometimes started programs with production tips and stories from behind the scenes of *Life Is Worth Living*. Away from the show, he was happy to talk about television techniques with magazine interviewers. He told the *Catholic Digest* that television "is enormously more difficult [than radio] for the speaker because of the mechanics, which distract the mind." Sheen's description of the banks of lights, boom microphones, and cameras is a reminder of how cumbersome and alien the television equipment was to early performers trained on stage or in the radio studio. "One of [the cameras] approaching the speaker resembles a huge Cyclops' eye," Sheen said. "Whenever I need most to concentrate on a difficult point or to remember a quotation, the camera comes closing in on me . . . That is why the new medium requires a more complete mastery of the material ahead of time."[21] In fact, part of Sheen's mystique, repeated in numerous profiles, was that he timed his speeches perfectly, delivering the weekly sermons without the aid of notes, cue cards, or a TelePrompTer. Sheen's extemporaneous speaking became such a point of interest that he opened an episode from the first season of *Life Is Worth Living* by theatrically revealing his trick: memorize the conclusion and keep an eye on the clock. When time is running out, go right to the conclusion.[22]

A Haven for Religion

Sheen enjoyed the novelty of television, but he was no stranger to broadcasting or public speaking. For more than twenty years, starting in 1930, he was a regular lecturer on NBC radio's *The Catholic Hour*. The bishop also taught philosophy at Catholic University in Washington, D.C., from 1926 to 1950, having earned a Ph.D. in the subject from the University of Louvain in Belgium. When he wasn't preaching on the air or teaching at the university, Sheen found the time to write more than thirty books, including the best-selling *Peace of Soul* (1949).[23] In his writing, Sheen demonstrated "a gift for reading the discontents of middle-class Catholic Americans and ministering to them," wrote historian Martin E. Marty.[24] Even before he came to television, Sheen was well known for converting a number of public figures to Catholicism. His most prominent converts were Louis Budenz, who had edited the Communist *Daily Worker*, and Clare Booth Luce, the congresswoman, author, and wife of *Time-Life* publisher Henry Luce.[25] In recognition of his work over the years, Sheen was appointed director of the American branch of the Society for the Propagation of the Faith in 1950. The Society "raised the bulk of the millions sent annually to Rome in support of the Church's worldwide missionary activities" explained his biographer, Thomas C. Reeves. Sheen also became one of Cardinal Francis J. Spellman's auxiliary bishops in the archdiocese of New York.[26]

While television was still considered low culture next to literature and even radio, Sheen had no trouble defending his use of the mass medium for serious messages. He told *Look* that Jesus Christ would have used television if it had been around in biblical times. Jesus "used the best means available," Sheen explained.[27] When *TV Guide* called a few months after *Life Is Worth Living* debuted, Sheen was ready with an impressive explanation of his mission. "God has blessed me by putting into my hands the heritage of over 1,900 years of Christian thinking. And just as I would lose my voice unless I used it, and my muscles would atrophy unless I exercised them, so this Truth might be lost unless, like the farmer on his acres, I scattered the seeds on the fertile fields of the airwaves," Sheen wrote, typically sounding grandiose, humble, pious, and philosophical, all within a couple of sentences.[28]

It is not a coincidence that Sheen landed at DuMont. *Life Is Worth*

Living was a reward for DuMont's early and consistent investment in religious programing. DuMont aired the first network program starring an African American minister. From 1947 to 1951, the Reverend Elder Lightfoot Solomon Michaux brought his thirty-five person Happy-Am-I gospel choir to WTTG's Washington studios each week for a local broadcast. The network periodically picked up Michaux's program, which combined music and preaching, in late 1948 and early 1949.[29] DuMont's WABD in New York also created a pioneering daily program, *Morning Chapel,* on which local Jewish, Catholic, and Protestant clergy took turns offering religious services and discussion. One show, for example, featured a Presbyterian minister, the next an Orthodox Jewish rabbi. After debuting as part of WABD's daytime schedule in November 1949, *Morning Chapel* aired every weekday for more than five years. Even as WABD cut back on its daytime programing in the early 1950s, DuMont program director James Caddigan found time for *Morning Chapel.* The DuMont-owned stations in Washington and Pittsburgh also aired versions of the show featuring local clergy. For much of this time, *Morning Chapel* was the only religious program on television during the week.

Broderick offered DuMont *Life Is Worth Living* because he knew Caddigan and fellow DuMont executive Chris Witting from their work with the archdiocese on *Morning Chapel.*[30] Caddigan, a Catholic who later served on the Radio and Television Board of the St. Louis archdiocese, may have had a personal commitment to religious programing, but he also recognized the practical value of slotting the erudite Bishop opposite Berle.[31] Sheen helped the network and its affiliates satisfy the FCC's public service requirements, which called for stations to air religious, news, educational, and discussion shows. The commission did not require a particular number of public service programs per week, but it did compel stations to report their programing on license renewal forms that were submitted every three years. DuMont aired a handful of political discussion programs and educational shows, such as *The Johns Hopkins Science Review* (a Peabody Award winner for outstanding educational program in 1950 and 1952), to balance the more low-budget, commercial shows and live up to its promise of being "First With the Finest in Television."

A good program in science or religion did more than satisfy the FCC.

The Adelphi Theatre setup for Sheen's *Life Is Worth Living*.
Source: Allen B. Du Mont Collection, Archives Center, National Museum of American History, Smithsonian Institution.

It also enhanced a network's image before newspaper critics and the public. With *Life Is Worth Living*, critics commended DuMont for its programing savvy and commitment to public service. In an editorial published shortly after the show debuted, *Advertising Age* proclaimed that *Life Is Worth Living* should "induce those who feel that the public is chiefly interested in light entertainment and meaningless diversion to re-examine their estimate of the television mentality." The trade journal raved that DuMont is "to be congratulated, commended, and generally patted on the back for its decision to put on Fulton J. Sheen . . . Even without sponsorship, it should attract a great deal of attention to DuMont and cause NBC, CBS, and ABC to seem a little less daring."[32]

Jack Gould of the *New York Times*, one of the most influential television critics of the early 1950s, wrote a glowing review of *Life Is Worth Living* when the program was two weeks old and airing in only three markets: Washington, New York, and Chicago. One of the strongest advocates for television that would educate and elevate the masses, Gould wrote of *Life Is Worth Living* as a bold prime-time experiment because of its format: a straight sermon. "Such is the forcefulness of Bishop Sheen's personality and the persuasiveness of his words and philosophy that a viewer, regardless of his individual faith, finds himself not only paying serious attention, but doing some serious thinking as well."[33] More than fifty years after Gould's review appeared, Broderick remembered that the column generated national interest in Sheen's program and enticed additional DuMont affiliates to carry *Life Is Worth Living*.[34] By April, when *Time* put Sheen on its cover as the "Microphone Missionary," seventeen stations were on board and Sheen was drawing the highest ratings of any "inspirational or intellectual show," according to the magazine.[35]

Admiral to the Rescue

Sheen's high ratings and reams of favorable publicity led to something unprecedented after the program's first season: sponsorship for a religious program. Perennially short of funds, DuMont was happy to accept a rival in the receiver business as a sponsor. The Admiral Corporation paid $1 million to support Sheen's twenty-six programs during the 1952–1953 season.[36] The fee included payments to DuMont for its time and affiliates along with a contribution to Mission Humanity, an international charity of which Sheen was executive director. To this day, *Life Is Worth Living* remains the only prime-time network religious program to attract sponsorship from a commercial company. The only other sponsors for religious television in the early 1950s were the handful of (mostly evangelical) religious organizations that purchased television time to spread their messages. These programs usually appeared in unpopular weekend slots, when the time was cheaper and networks could not find more lucrative sponsors. The most successful such program, for example, was Billy Graham's "Hour of Decision," a 15-minute filmed talk that was paid for by the Billy Graham Evangelical Association and aired over ABC on Sunday nights at 10:00 P.M. from September 1951 to February 1954.[37] Most broadcasters and businesses considered religion to be commercial poison. The shows generally did not attract large audiences or lend themselves to seamless product pitches. In addition, any sponsor opened itself to charges that it favored one faith or denomination over the others.

Like much at DuMont, the sponsorship deal was the product of a combination of happenstance and quick thinking, motivated by desperation. Bergmann, the head of DuMont sales at the time, remembered notifying Bishop Broderick and the archdiocese that, despite the popularity of *Life Is Worth Living,* the network would be forced to cancel the show at the end of its first season. DuMont could not afford to reserve a prime-time slot for a program that, it believed, could not generate advertising revenue. "I had never heard of a religious program being commercially sponsored," Bergmann explained. Still, Broderick promised to find a sponsor for the program. A few weeks later, he sent Bergmann to Chicago for a meeting with Ross Siragusa, a prominent Catholic layman and the head of Admiral. At the Chicago meeting, Bergmann recalled, "it was immediately apparent that he [Siragusa] knew nothing about it [the sponsorship] and was shocked to learn that I had been sent to see him by the Archdiocese of New York."

Initially, Siragusa was hesitant to sponsor *Life Is Worth Living.* Like other commercial sponsors, Admiral eschewed religious programs on radio and TV, even those with relatively large audiences. Siragusa said that he did not want to risk alienating his Jewish TV distributors. Bergmann responded by confidently urging Siragusa to telephone the distributors and broach the idea of Admiral's partnership with Sheen and DuMont. The call took place during their meeting. "I could only hear his [Siragusa's] end of the conversations," Bergmann wrote. "But they went something like this: 'I'm thinking of sponsoring Bishop Sheen on television. What do you think? . . . You do? . . . The whole family?. . . Every week?. . . That's great!" After the phone calls, Siragusa was ready to make a deal.[38] In sponsoring *Life Is Worth Living* for five seasons (three on DuMont and two on ABC after DuMont folded), Siragusa supported Sheen while donating to the Catholic charities that the bishop oversaw. Admiral was also associated with a popular and respected figure in 1950s America. In fact, according to a 1956 poll, *Life Is Worth Living* (now on ABC) ranked second to *Arthur Godfrey's Talent Scouts* in "sponsor identification," the proportion of viewers who could identify the program with a particular sponsor.[39]

Newspaper and magazine critics believed that advertising cheapened religious programs, leaving both the sponsor and the television clergyman looking opportunistic and mercenary. Columnists like Gould and Crosby had mixed feelings about Sheen's sponsorship. They recognized that a company with a hefty bankroll represented a religious or educational program's best hope of securing decent airtime and building an audience, but they resented the consumer world's intrusion on Sheen's weekly discourse. "*Life Is Worth Living* was a half-hour oasis that afforded a pause and a moment for individual contemplation free from all the desperately urgent salesmanship so common on TV. It was an invitation to the spiritual plane that allowed a personal reexamination of one's heart and mind. That experience is not something to be made to serve as a cue for a typical, hard-selling commercial," Gould chided.[40]

Anticipating these objections, Sheen limited Admiral to two pitches per half hour: one at the beginning of the show and the second one at the end. He also took every opportunity to remind viewers and critics that all of his proceeds from sponsorship were donated to charity. The first spot was a dignified announcement: the camera dollied in to a desk. On top of the desk sat a leather-bound book titled *Life Is Worth Living*. Rather than selling a TV set or other Admiral product, the announcer simply introduced the program: "Admiral presents his excellency Bishop Fulton J. Sheen in *Life Is Worth Living,* a program devoted to the everyday problems of all of us. The sole beneficiary is Mission Humanity, a nonprofit charitable organization which renders aid to needy peoples in all parts of the world without regard to religion, color, or creed." To further support the show's reverent and dignified tone, *Life Is Worth Living* did not include a sponsor break halfway through the program. Only at the end of the program, after Sheen's talk, did Admiral offer a more conventional advertisement for its products.[41]

Sheen also joked about the sponsorship on the air, as he did about many touchy issues, showing his typical confidence and ease before the camera while poking fun at both himself and the critics who worried that Sheen had compromised his program. For example, in a program about prayer, he discussed the way people fulfill spiritual needs by showing appreciation for others. "At the end of this television program, there is going to be a great burst of applause. And why? Why will there be a great burst of applause?" Sheen asked, as he began to break into the rapid cadences and hyperbolic statements of a stereotypical TV pitchman. "It is because you will have heard something that was transcendentally superior. You will have heard something that was beyond all competition. You will have heard something the likes of which is not given on any other television program. You will have heard something that delights every father in the United States, that thrills every mother, that pleases every child. Namely, a commercial about an Admiral refrigerator."[42] Ironically, such jokes inadvertently called attention to the fact that there were similarities between pitching a product and selling religious contentment on television.

A Bishop for All Americans

Bergmann's story about the courting of Admiral is one of many that drew attention to Sheen's popularity among Jewish viewers.[43] In magazine profiles from the 1950s, Sheen was praised by a range of Jewish figures, from an anonymous California rabbi to a man named Saul Abraham, the manager of the Adelphi Theatre.[44] Articles about Sheen's universal appeal served as subtle markers of the bishop's success at winning over Berle's most loyal viewers. As critic Crosby gushed, the bishop "talked of life and philosophy and God, all pretty large subjects, with such charm and humor and assurance that many people, Catholic and Protestant and Jew alike, began listening to him—Berle or no Berle."[45] Such claims may have been exaggerated. There is not a mountain of evidence from these early days of audience research. However, the best report on the demographics for religious television in the early 1950s, a study of the New Haven, Connecticut market, found that a disproportionate segment of Sheen's audience (about 75 percent) was Catholic. Only 2.2 percent of Sheen's viewers were Jewish, though Jews comprised a little more than 9 percent of the New Haven population. Of the five religious television programs polled, *Life Is Worth Living* had the smallest percentage of Jewish viewers. In short, *Life Is Worth Living* was one of several religious programs that attracted viewers of all faiths.[46]

The articles about Sheen's far-reaching appeal reflected a popular pride that Americans were becoming more religious and more tolerant. As historian Robert S. Ellwood wrote, "In the decade of the Fifties, religion was, and was perceived to be, in a profound upswing. The market was good. Religious institutions were growing substantially year by year in numbers, wealth, and real estate; seminaries and novitiates were full; the influence of religion in people's thoughts and lives was considered to be increasing. Polls said that 99 percent of Americans believed in God."[47] Politicians and social commentators considered one of the country's great strengths to be its respect for the many religions and denominations operating within the "Judeo-Christian" tradition.[48]

Newspaper and magazine writers were not so coarse as to congratulate viewers for making a star out of a Catholic priest, but a subtext to the articles recognizing Sheen's universal appeal was that the country had begun to reverse its history of anti-Catholic prejudice. Sheen's popularity stood as a symbol that Catholics were making progress in a number of areas that were much more restricted before World War II, including housing, education, politics, and the workplace. As biographer Thomas C. Reeves wrote, "Bishop Sheen's phenomenal success on television was a sign that millions of Americans had gone beyond the crude caricatures so familiar in the nation's history and were willing to accept Catholics as Christians and friends."[49] Writing in the Chicago *TV Guide*, Thomas O'Malley articulated Sheen's importance in light of this prejudice more explicitly than many of his colleagues did. "Possibly the happiest note of the unprecedented success of Bishop Sheen on TV is the tolerant acceptance of him by other faiths," he wrote. "It is questionable that he would have been hailed twenty years ago as he is today."[50] The only evidence that Sheen may have struck a nerve with those who did not partake in the era's increasing tolerance was the handful of critical letters to the editors of *Time*, including one from a Protestant minister railing against Sheen as a symbol of "Roman Catholic totalitarianism," after the magazine put Sheen on its cover.[51]

Like other popular religious figures from the time, such as Billy Graham and Norman Vincent Peale, Sheen promised that religion could bring practitioners personal fulfillment and happiness: what he called *Peace of Soul* in the title of his popular 1949 book. Historian Ellwood referred to Peale, Sheen, and Graham as the "big three," because of their success in popularizing religion through their writing, personal appearances, and television programs. "Their faith was characterized by feeling, pragmatism, and attachment to powerful evocative images. Its emphasis was on meeting personal needs, and the message was therefore aimed directly at the individual hearer or reader."[52] A forerunner of later television self-help gurus like Oprah and Dr. Phil, Sheen was a master at using the intimate medium of television to dispense the sort of advice that would help viewers feel better about their lives.[53] The bishop knew that viewers did not want to hear too much about the Bible, church history, theological debates, or Catholic sacraments. Sheen, his publicists at the archdiocese, and DuMont took every opportunity away from the screen to minimize the extent to which Sheen preached specifically Roman Catholic values, teachings, and practices. In a 1953 interview, *Look* magazine asked Sheen about Billy Graham's ABC program. "His [Graham's] type of program isn't the same as mine. I've listened to him with great interest, but his is a specifically religious program," Sheen said. He then denied that his own program was religious. "I am talking as a university lecturer on those programs," he explained. "I was a university professor for twenty-five years, and on television I am discussing subjects in a university sort of way. But I'm bringing them down to the level of the people."[54]

Despite the universal messages in his sermons, Sheen's claims that his program was not intended to promote the views and public image of the Catholic Church, though persuasive, were somewhat disingenuous. From the time that he started each week's program, dressed in his priestly garb with the Madonna statue as his backdrop and symbolic guardian, Sheen was on a Catholic mission. His sermons frequently invoked Biblical passages, parables, and figures. Jesus and Mary were rarely far from Sheen each week, even though, as Christopher Lynch noted in his study of Sheen's rhetoric, the bishop was careful to present Mary in a way that did not alienate his "mixed audience."[55] Sheen was safest, however, when he moved from talk of Mary and Jesus to more general discussion of the joy that viewers would experience through prayer and a recognition of God. For example, Sheen ends one 1952 talk by contrasting those who are "deity blind" with believers in a higher power, "living under the covers of the divine winds above the senses, above reason, in a world of faith and joy and inner peace and happiness that we would not give up for all the world."[56] An episode about prayer from the next season promises that any occupation, from television cameraman to ballplayer, can become meaningful if it is performed in the name of the Lord. "Our own humdrum, routine, workaday lives in the pantry and in the school, in the office and on the farm, in the machine shop can be ennobled, spiritualized and divinized," he explains.[57]

Sheen commands the stage on *Life Is Worth Living.*
Source: Photofest.

The bishop's genius lay in the intelligence and skill with which he balanced the explicit Catholic teachings and references with universal discussion of faith, family, and morality. He used religion as the foundation for advice about everything from child rearing to character building. Sheen's Tuesday night program provided a convenient and welcome dose of spirituality and moral guidance for devout viewers along with the many Americans who drew sustenance from religious ideas but did not commit to weekly church attendance.[58] From the comfort of their living rooms, viewers could vicariously visit church, bask in Sheen's messages, and discuss the bishop's teachings with friends and neighbors.

Anti-Communist Warrior

Sheen seldom missed an opportunity to contrast the strength and superiority of religious belief over the superficial and dangerous alternatives offered by followers of Marx and Lenin. In one program after another, Sheen "analyzed the spiritual source, or rather the spiritual vacuum, that nurtured communism in the lost soul, explained its appeal to the faithless, and depicted the superpower struggle as a cosmic drama with salvific significance," wrote historian Thomas Doherty.[59] Even in an oration on motherhood, for example, Sheen takes a brief detour to explain to viewers why "there is no greater refutation" of communism than the life of a mother. Whereas communists demand conformity and make individuals subservient to the state, any mother, according to Sheen, would defend her child as special and unique. "Every woman in the world arises to proclaim, 'This child of mine . . . may not be submerged in any collectivity or a state or a race or a class,'" he thundered.[60]

While Sheen was a smart and riveting speaker, regardless of the subject, he became most animated and passionate when expounding on communism. In the first season of *Life Is Worth Living*, he devoted two separate programs to a comparison of the Soviet and American constitutions, citing particular articles and sections of each document without the use of notes or a TelePrompTer. He ended one of these talks with a riveting warning. "We want peace. Russia says it wants peace too," he pauses. "The piece that Russia wants is a piece of Poland. A piece of Hungary." The audience laughs at the pun, but Sheen continues. "A piece of China. A piece of the United States." The laughter stops as Sheen becomes portentous. "Beware of any overtures of peace from Russia. There will be a Pearl Harbor immediately after any peace overtures from Russia. Love God, your country, your neighbor. Bye now. God love you."[61] In his most famous and prophetic such sermon, which aired on February 24, 1953, Sheen explained Soviet treachery and godlessness through an elaborate comparison between contemporary Soviet leaders and the characters in Shakespeare's *Julius Caesar*. He ends the program with a funeral oration over Stalin's body.[62] Within nine days of the telecast, the Soviet ruler suffered a stroke and died. "I received telephone calls from newspapers in almost every state of the Union asking me what inside information I had," Sheen recalled in his autobiography. "I told them that I only knew that he was mortal and would have to pay the last penalty of sin, which was death."[63]

Sheen's anti-communist conviction stood out even in a nation that shared his obsession. Unlike other Catholic leaders, including his boss,

Cardinal Spellman, Sheen did not explicitly align himself with Joseph McCarthy, partisan politics, or blacklists. Instead, his attacks were more scholarly, but no less pointed or absolute than those of McCarthy himself. "If Spellman was the political leader of Catholic anti-communism, then its prophet and philosopher was Bishop Fulton J. Sheen," wrote historian Donald Crosby. "For Sheen, as for Spellman, communism was the epitome of both irreligion and un-Americanism. The good Catholic, it followed, was one who gave his unstinting efforts . . . to the destruction of the Communist peril."[64] In his biography of Sheen, Thomas Reeves noted that Sheen laid the foundation for the Red Scare and eased the work of McCarthy and other more overtly political figures. Sheen "was often careless about the targets of his zeal. Sweeping generalities about teachers, professors, and intellectuals, for example, played into the hands of those who wished to destroy academic freedom and condemn all instructors and thinkers on the left as subversives."[65]

Sheen After DuMont

Sheen stayed with DuMont through the 1954–1955 season, then left for ABC after DuMont ceased operations in the summer of 1955. Even though Sheen's program, still sponsored by Admiral, continued to enjoy national distribution on ABC, Sheen no longer commanded the media attention that he had at DuMont. His show ran for two more seasons on ABC. Against competition like *I Love Lucy* and Groucho Marx's *You Bet Your Life*, Sheen was not able to repeat the ratings miracle that he had performed with DuMont. For a television audience that was increasingly turning to sitcoms and game shows for its television entertainment, the site of the lone bishop preaching on stage may have grown stale.[66] Before the 1955–1956 season was over, the trade press reported that Admiral was ready to pull out of its sponsorship due to Sheen's dwindling audience, though the company decided to stay on board through April 1957.[67] The final blow to *Life Is Worth Living*, however, apparently had little to do with ratings. While ABC offered to keep Sheen on the network as a public service, Sheen biographer Reeves suggested that Cardinal Spellman forced Sheen off the air out of anger during a dispute that the two men had over the use of church funds.[68] Sheen formally announced his retirement from television in October

1957, though he has continued to maintain a presence on the airwaves. He returned on a syndicated version of *Life Is Worth Living* that was produced sporadically between 1961 and 1968. Even in 2004, twenty-five years after his death, Sheen continues to inspire the faithful through re-runs of *Life Is Worth Living*. Eternal Word Television Network, a Catholic cable network, airs a mixture of Sheen's DuMont episodes and his later programs three times a week. It is the only original Du-Mont program that still airs regularly.[69]

Ernie Kovacs.

Source: Library of American Broadcasting, University of Maryland.

10

Ernie Kovacs and the DuMont Legacy

ife Is Worth Living was one of a handful of programs—including Captain Video, Rocky King, and The Plainclothes Man—on which DuMont relied as it struggled through 1954, its last full year of operation. At a time when television was booming nationally, DuMont had lost $3.8 million in 1953 and was facing even larger deficits in 1954. Network executives desperately tried to reverse the company's fortunes. Before the year was out, DuMont held merger talks with ABC, found a buyer for its most profitable station (WDTV in Pittsburgh), and commissioned consultants Booz, Allen & Hamilton to conduct a comprehensive study of the network and local stations. The report, released in early 1955, recommended that the network cease operations. DuMont also trimmed the number of programs that it was producing. In the fall of 1953, for example, DuMont aired 20½ hours of network programs a week during prime time. This figure was down to 17 hours a week by the fall of 1954. On December 28, 1954, DuMont announced that it was reorganizing its broadcast operations by further cutting back on the live production and distribution of programs.[1]

Live television was expensive. Viewers expected to see slick shows with high production values. One of DuMont's biggest expenses, however, had nothing to do with studio costs. Between 1950 and 1955, DuMont spent more than $8 million to rent AT&T's coaxial cable lines, which were used to transmit live programs.[2] Generally, each network's affiliates shared these distribution costs with the network; however, Du-Mont's expenses were unusually high because it did not have as many affiliates as its competitors did. AT&T's pricing system further damaged DuMont. Television lines were only offered as a package along with radio lines, so DuMont was forced to pay for radio lines even though it had no use for them. As DuMont network director Ted Bergmann wrote in a May 1954 letter to AT&T, pleading his case for lower rates and more flexible packages, "Our purchase of cable for 1954, undoubtedly, will exceed the two million dollar mark . . . The purchase of cable will represent approximately fifteen percent of our total annual income. I am sure that this is a great deal higher a percentage than any other network."[3] DuMont's only other distribution option was to send affiliates shabby kinescopes of programs.

DuMont hoped to bypass AT&T through the Electronicam, a new device developed by DuMont's engineers to record live studio programs. The network brass expected local stations, unhappy with the technical quality of kinescopes, to run programs produced with the Electronicam, since these offerings looked as good as the live or film shows on other networks. What's more, the Electronicam was cheaper and faster than the conventional film techniques used to produce many television programs in Hollywood, so DuMont also planned to rent its studios and Electronicam equipment to outside producers. However, the Electronicam was not ready until mid-1955, when the network had already abandoned operations. Jackie Gleason used the device and Du-Mont's Adelphi Theatre to make the original thirty-nine *Honeymooners* episodes that aired on CBS during the 1955–1956 season and are still re-run today. Except for Gleason and a handful of others, however, the industry was not enticed to abandon either live production or film.[4] In 1956, the innovation of videotape, a more economical and versatile medium for recording programs, rendered the Electronicam obsolete.

In the midst of this financial chaos, DuMont made its last great programing gamble, hiring comedian Ernie Kovacs to host a late-night talk show that aired on a single station. DuMont's New York outlet, WABD, carried the Kovacs show for a year starting in April 1954. Kovacs was the biggest name ever signed by DuMont for strictly local duty. By 1954, he was a television veteran, having started as a morning talk show host on NBC's Philadelphia affiliate, WPTZ, in November 1950. Kovacs then helmed a succession of shows on NBC and CBS. The WABD programs was his debut on late-night. *Variety* reported that DuMont was spending $1 million to launch *The Ernie Kovacs Show*, though this figure may have been inflated for publicity purposes. Nevertheless, DuMont did everything it could to get value from its newest signing. In addition to providing a forum for Kovacs every night at 11:15 on the WABD talk show, DuMont put Kovacs to work on two undistinguished quiz programs that ran on the network: *One Minute Please* and *Time Will Tell*.

The late-night *Ernie Kovacs Show* gave the star an opportunity to enhance his skills and his growing reputation as early television's most creative and clever comedian. Kovacs used the WABD program to develop some of his best material, including characters and sketches that later resurfaced on prime-time shows with larger audiences on NBC and ABC. An enthusiastic *Variety* review dubbed WABD's *The Ernie Kovacs Show* "the wackiest entry (on or off TV)" since vaudeville. "There's no pretense at making sense," *Variety* explained, recognizing that Kovacs was a master at creating pandemonium on the set. "It's the only known display where the backstage clamor is more rightfully attuned to and rightfully belongs with the on-camera behavior."[5] Kovacs and his crew, including DuMont veterans Frank Bunetta (producer) and Barry Shear (director), created enchanted images unlike anything else on television. As a DuMont press release noted, "Filters, inverted lenses, and odd camera angles aid the cigar-smoking emcee in achieving such effects as sawing a woman in half, playing ball with a girl's head, swimming in a crowded fish tank, levitating, piercing a head with an arrow, and singing with two heads."[6] Kovacs reveled in the medium's possibilities while tweaking the routines and conventions that were already firmly in place by 1954.

With Kovacs, everything was an adventure. Sporting his trademark cigar and moustache, Kovacs was recognizable to many early TV fans as a performer. However, he also wrote much of the show and worked closely with his directors and technical experts on photography, lighting, sound. Kovacs was a master at using all of the technical tricks and toys that television had to offer, devising fantastic special effects to punctuate his surreal comedy. As historian William Henry wrote, "The essence of Kovacs's humor was unpredictability. He redefined the humdrum, everyday world as an unreliable place in which normal order and causality might vanish at any moment."[7] A typical, recurring skit from the NBC show employed fast gags and visual tricks while also revealing Kovacs's attitudes regarding the network brass. Kovacs would ask the audience to welcome an NBC vice-president visiting the show. Actor Al Kelly, portraying the network executive, would stride purposefully toward Kovacs, then suddenly disappear through a trap door as he was about to shake hands with the star.[8]

Regardless of where he was working, Kovacs was no fan of network executives. He constantly joked about the low salary, insufficient production budget, and inane commercials imposed by management, anxious to wring every dollar of profit possible from him and his program. Nevertheless, he was sophisticated and self-aware enough to admit that, despite its problems, commercial television offered him a good living and the best medium for his style of performance. For example, the lone remaining kinescope of Kovacs on WABD, a Tuesday evening program from March 1955, is filled will sponsor announcements and filmed advertisements. After one series of ads, the show returns to Kovacs, in the middle of a conversation with his off-camera crew, complaining about the commercials. "They could run a soap opera in that [commercial time]. They've got about twenty minutes out of every show. They're selling more commercials. They're sneaking them in there, so I can't get my hands on a percentage." The set comes alive with the crew's laughter at the frank comment about network advertising practices and the efforts of performers to secure a cut of the revenue.[9]

The WABD kinescope offers a good example of the way in which Kovacs maintained his integrity while airing the kinds of commercials that the job demanded.[10] The roster of sponsor products included a few well-known items, like *TV Guide* and Prell shampoo, which were promoted through slick films supplied by the advertisers. But the majority of the pitches were delivered by Kovacs on behalf of lesser-known products or local establishment, such as Arthur Maisel's restaurant chain, home of the $1.89 steak dinner. Kovacs was no fan of advertising; in fact, he starts his program with a parody of an ad for a toothpaste called Kodadent, a black toothpaste with an "invisible film that protects your teeth." In the WABD kinescope, for the most part, Kovacs delivers earnest pitches, perhaps out of a practical sense of duty to his patrons and the knowledge that it would be too easy for him to make fun of these small businesses and their products. Nevertheless, as somebody who thought of television as his art form, and did not like these commercial aspects of the program, he could not resist sneaking little jokes and jibes at the sponsors into his presentations. For example, Kovacs starts the ad for an inexpensive wine, Vino Paisano, with a little pun about bad food: "It goes with fowl food or poultry. Or maybe with you its foul. I don't know. It depends how you cook it." Kovacs continues, "It's one of those intermediate wines that goes with everything. It's a light wine. It's a dry wine. It's not a heavy sweet wine, and you'll find that it won't interfere with your appetite." Kovacs then stops in what appears to be the middle of the sales pitch. "I took a big whiff of cigar smoke earlier and I'm choking to death here." It is not clear whether Kovacs is choking on the cigar smoke or the exorbitant claims of the ad copy. At any rate, Kovacs loudly clears his throat and moves on to the next segment without finishing the announcement. In later ads, Kovacs forgets the name of one sponsor's restaurants and reads from the label of another sponsored product, Leprechaun Mist Suede Restorer, that the item is "used on shoes, gloves, handbags, and any members of the family who happen to be composed of suede."

Kovacs's spontaneous asides made the ads more lively and fit the tone of the program. *The Ernie Kovacs Show* had a casual, improvisational, irreverent style that anticipated much of the late-night comedy that has followed. In fact, the star even changed his program's title from *The Ernie Kovacs Show* to *The Ernie Kovacs Rehearsal* toward the end of his run at WABD, highlighting the program's shambling, unfinished quality. Whether working at DuMont or elsewhere, Kovacs had no compunctions about chatting with the crew in the middle of a program or prowling the set, exposing scenery, cue cards, and microphone wires. In a typical episode from the daily NBC morning show that he landed six months after leaving DuMont, Kovacs wanders into the studio audience and interviews shy spectators about their jobs. One reticent man admits that he feigned illness at work so that he could join Kovacs's audience. On his way back to the set, Kovacs pauses at a broken television camera and opens it up, giving many viewers their first glimpse of the inner workings of this mysterious device.[11] Kovacs's candor about the secrets of television was "both refreshing and shocking to see," explained Diana Rico in her biography of the comedian. His behind-the-scenes revelations also "equalized his relationship with the audience" and showed a respect for the curiosity and intelligence of viewers. As Sid Shalit, of the *New York Daily News*, recognized, Ernie "enjoyed a remarkable rapport with his audience, who by some strange chemistry seem to feel they are a part of what is going on. His viewers are proud when the camera trick comes off, almost as if they had something to do with it."[12]

Despite the many advertisements, the Kovacs show was not a commercial success. It attracted little attention in the industry press and had ratings of around 1.0, which put it in the middle of the pack during its 11:15 P.M. time slot.[13] In a tacit admission that the Kovacs experiment was not working, WABD made some scheduling changes to *The Ernie Kovacs Show* eight months into its run. In January 1955, WABD cut the show from a full hour every night to a half hour, and decided to air it only two nights a week: Tuesdays and Thursdays. The starting time was also moved from 11:15 to 10:30 P.M. The station made more changes in March 1955. In its final six weeks, through April 7, the re-titled *Ernie Kovacs Rehearsal* ran for an hour, starting at ten o'clock on Tuesdays and Thursdays.[14]

Kovacs remained on the air for a year by cultivating a small but loyal following. In fact, broadcasters did not expect the ratings from a late-night show that a successful prime-time program drew. Relatively few people watched television on any station after ten o'clock, and even more of the audience dropped off, and went to sleep, after eleven o'clock. Whereas 70 or 80 percent of all TV sets were in use during prime time, only 5 to 10 percent were on at midnight. This small potential audience made it very difficult for broadcasters to attract the sponsors and revenue necessary to support network production and distribution costs, including the rental of coaxial cable lines from AT&T to transmit shows from one city to another. When the Kovacs program debuted on April 12, 1954, no network offered programing after eleven o'clock. For most local stations, the goal was to air the cheapest programing possible while generating sponsor revenue from neighborhood stores and restaurants that wanted a presence on television at bargain rates. Before Kovacs came to WABD, for example, the station ran a short newscast at eleven o'clock and then signed off with a cheap movie and another newscast at 11:45. NBC did not distribute its *Tonight* show nationally until September 1954, though the prototype, hosted by Steve Allen, was somewhat successful in an earlier run that began in July 1953 on NBC's local station, WNBT in New York. Still, New York's most popular program in the 11:15 to 12:15 time slot was the CBS late movie, which aired inexpensive British films or B movies from independent American studios.

Given the small, late-night audience that may have been half asleep anyway, Kovacs and WABD did not see the need to spend a fortune on props, set design, and special effects. In fact, Kovacs enjoyed parodying other shows and genres that sported higher budgets, but still produced dull, predictable programing. For example, newspaper critic Shalit was fascinated by a running skit called "Plop," which used an ingenious, homemade device to satirize game shows. Kovacs "employed a weird Rube Goldberg contraption in which a candle burns downward toward a string," critic Shalit explained. "Through connected networks, the string supports a baseball suspended over a jar of borscht. The idea, which almost everybody seems to have lost sight of, has something to do with [awarding] prizes to the persons who guess most closely the time when the candle will burn through the string, thus releasing the baseball which will go 'plop' into the borscht." Shalit was disappointed to see the candle burn through the rope, triggering the borscht bomb, and the end of the skit, after three months.[15]

Moving beyond borscht, Kovacs created a stable of quirky and popular characters at DuMont. For example, he introduced the world to Howard, the World's Strongest Ant, who could move large objects such as tool kits. As described by biographer Rico, "Howard didn't even physically exist; this whimsical conceit consisted entirely of Ernie bending down to talk to a tabletop," while magnets and other off-camera devices were employed to actually move the items. Kovacs's wife and co-star, Edie Adams, supplied Howard's "teensy-weensy voice." According to Rico, Howard was the most popular character on the NBC shows that Kovacs produced after leaving DuMont.[16] Kovacs also developed the act for which he is most remembered today, the Nairobi Trio, while at WABD. The skit showcased three actors—usually Kovacs, Adams, and whoever else was available for the third role—dressed in bowler hats, overcoats, and rubber gorilla masks. The trio moved like mechanical toy monkeys to the tune of "Solfeggio," an obscure recording by Robert Maxwell, that Kovacs presented with a xylophone, a piano, and a silent conductor. "At a precise moment in a recurring musical phrase, the xylophonist-ape turns jerkily to the conductor-ape and bashes him on the head with his xylophone hammer," wrote Rico. "It was a sketch of modest scale, sublimely simple and exquisite in its timing."[17]

Celebrity guests sometimes appeared on the Kovacs show alongside these characters. The DuMont debut, for example, featured Morey Amsterdam, Jacqueline Susann, and comedian Sam Levenson. In later episodes, Broadway stars like Zero Mostel and Geraldine Page visited Kovacs after performing at nearby theaters.[18] However, the Kovacs program was different from most other talk and variety shows in that the guests were not a central attraction. Instead, Kovacs enjoyed talking to everyday people or, on occasion, quirky entertainers who worked the fringes of the industry. His WABD kinescope features guests who seem like parodies of show business performers, but under Kovacs's guidance, their segments are smart and charming. The first act is a group called the Four Tophatters. They sing in Italian accents on "Leave-a-My-Gal Alone," a novelty song that was released on Cadence Records, a small independent label.

The group actually boasts a fifth Tophatter for its Kovacs appearance. Cadence Records head Archie Bleyer is along to talk about the single and lend his talents on trumpet. Bleyer was not unknown to viewers. He led the orchestra and arranged the music for Arthur Godfrey at CBS from 1946 until 1953. Godfrey, perhaps the most popular talk and variety show host on radio and television, was genial and easygoing on camera but had a reputation for being irrational and mean off the air. He fired Bleyer as part of a well-publicized housecleaning in 1953, after Bleyer's record label released singles by Julius LaRosa, a singer on the Godfrey program who had fallen out of favor with that host.[19] Kovacs, who reveled in puncturing the pompous and the powerful, offers a sharp and funny imitation of Godfrey. After the Tophatters finish their number, Kovacs suddenly appears on a split screen, playing Godfrey's trademark ukulele and wearing a wig with headphones attached. Bleyer is still visible in the corner of the frame. "God bless you, Archie," starts Kovacs, as Godfrey, with a smile. "It was awfully good. I want to thank you for coming and playing for us on the program. I want to thank you, too, for your Cadence Record Company." Bleyer and the audience laugh together at this unexpected reference to the source of Bleyer's problems with Godfrey. Kovacs finishes with a savage send off, "And I hope you go bust." Kovacs then drops the God-

Kovacs with his wife and co-star, Edie Adams.
Source: Library of American Broadcasting, University of Maryland.

frey imitation and has a relaxed chat with Bleyer and the group. They
talk about the single and the Four Tophatters' sole upcoming concert:
a gig at Nick's Three Bets Restaurant in Mountain View, New Jersey.

Later in the program, Kovacs hosts an audio engineer and composer
named Jim Fassett, who recorded and manipulated everyday sounds as
the foundation for his work. Fassett enjoys a small following today
among avant garde and electronic music enthusiasts for his *Symphony of
the Birds* (1960), which pieced together field recordings of bird calls. On
the Kovacs show, Fassett plays a series of what he calls "disguised

sounds" from his album, *Strange to Your Ears*. Kovacs, who made extensive use of music and audio effects in his own comedy, listens with interest and tries to identify the sounds that Fassett has manipulated. The site of Kovacs and his well-dressed guest identifying strange sounds is, in itself, novel. However, Kovacs and director Barry Shear cannot resist giving the segment an added visual twist by matching brief film clips to the sounds. The overall effect is to create the sorts of videos that one might expect to find in a modern art museum. For example, on one track, Fassett alters the sound of a baby crying, creating a low, slow tone. Kovacs and Shear counter with an old film, running at very high speed, of cars zooming through a city street. In another clip, Fassett records the song "America" with the notes played in reverse order. "This is what it sounds like backwards," he says, as the sound plays under his explanation. In the meantime, Kovacs and Shear offer a clever visual pun, showing what an image looks like "backwards." They dig up a film negative that Shear directed and aired a few years earlier as part of a dream sequence on a DuMont crime program, *Not for Publication*. The short film clips are not introduced or commented upon by Kovacs, who is having too much fun listening to Fassett's record.

Kovacs's last WABD program aired on April 7, 1955, a few months before the network was dissolved. Neither Kovacs nor DuMont received much media attention for the WABD show and it is doubtful that anybody made money from the program. Kovacs did not, however, go unnoticed. After Kovacs left DuMont, NBC re-signed the performer for an engagement that lasted more than two years, starting with a two-week run as Steve Allen's summer substitute on the *Tonight* show. The NBC programs included many routines from the DuMont years, along with talented performers like Bill Wendell, Barbara Loden, and Peter Hanley, who started with Kovacs on WABD. NBC delivered a national line-up of affiliates and brought Kovacs better prime-time exposure than he had ever enjoyed before. The high point of his NBC run came on January 19, 1957, when Kovacs and his team created a special that was filled with innovative audio and video special effects, but included no words. The program, known as "The Silent Show," starred Kovacs as a gentle character named Eugene. It earned mountains of critical acclaim, including a cover story in *Life* magazine that anointed Kovacs "the man most likely to rouse TV comedy out of its present un-amusing rut."[20] Kovacs was working on a series of specials for ABC in January 1962 when he died in a car accident. He was forty-two years old.

The DuMont Legacy

The Ernie Kovacs Show epitomizes DuMont's diminishing national scope in its final year. The company signed a bona fide star in Kovacs and scheduled him in a late-night time slot at which he excelled; however, the network did not have the affiliate line-up or set of prospective advertisers to make a national splash with the Kovacs program. Nevertheless, Kovacs's tenure at WABD also serves as a final reminder of what DuMont did well: hiring talented people and giving them creative freedom. The Kovacs program, like many at DuMont, achieved artistic success without earning the kind of revenue that would have enabled the broadcasting company and its network to continue operating profitably. In addition, Kovacs was one of several figures who found a larger audience and greater critical acclaim after leaving the network.

This book has highlighted DuMont's experiments and concentrated on areas in which DuMont was a pioneer. DuMont developed scheduling strategies, advertising practices, production techniques, and program genres that were daring at the time, but are now standard in the television industry. It also played a pivotal role in the careers of Ernie Kovacs, Jackie Gleason, Art Carney, Morey Amsterdam, Dennis James, Bishop Fulton Sheen, and a host of other performers who starred on the network in the late 1940s and early 1950s.

Although the DuMont network did not survive beyond 1955, the DuMont name is still warmly remembered by the people who worked at the network and the many who watched its programs. Aficionados of popular culture who had no first-hand experience with the network during its mid-century heyday also continue to value DuMont for its historical importance. In 1984, the Museum of Broadcasting (now the Museum of Television and Radio) in New York celebrated DuMont's fortieth anniversary with an exhibition. The museum located rare kinescopes and showed them to the public for the first time since the programs originally aired. More recently, television shows like *The Simpsons* and *Family Guy* have referenced the DuMont network to share their knowledge of TV history with viewers, while a 2002 made-for-television movie, *The Big Time* (Turner Network Television), is set at the fictional Empire Network, a thinly veiled stand-in for DuMont. The film unconscionably portrays the head of the network, an engineer and inventor named "Doc," as a hot-blooded racist; nevertheless, *The Big Time* otherwise faithfully recreates the difficulties and excitement of live production at DuMont. On the big screen, Barry Levinson's *Avalon* (1990) recognized the importance of *Captain Video* to kids growing up in the early 1950s. Recent television history books have also credited DuMont as a pioneer, while the Internet has provided a lively forum for the study of DuMont. No other broadcaster has been rewarded with a historical Web site as informative and thorough as Clarke Ingram's tribute to DuMont. In addition, "Roaring Rockets," a comprehensive site created by Rory Coker that looks at *Captain Video* and other "space operas," rivals any Web treatment of a particular program or genre of the 1950s.[21] This recent work about DuMont demonstrates an appreciation for the network's accomplishments as the underdog, taking on the bigger and more established networks at the dawn of commercial television.

DuMont was especially willing to take risks in order to establish the new medium. The upstart network had no history in broadcasting, no radio talent or engineers under contract who could move to television, and no preconceptions about popular entertainment. Most of the people who worked at DuMont shared Allen Du Mont's fascination with the incredible new technology of television. They were also participants in the vibrant postwar popular culture, centered in New York, and they wanted to bring this culture to a nation of television viewers. Like the city itself, DuMont offered a range of cultural products for different tastes and audiences. For example, DuMont producers, crew members, directors, and performers enjoyed New York jazz clubs like Birdland, located only a few blocks from the network's offices, and sometimes plugged these nightclubs and performers on the air. Director Barry Shear used the Cy Coleman Trio as the centerpiece of a *Not for Publication* episode set in a cocktail lounge. A DuMont variety program, *Stage Entrance*, featured Charlie Parker and Dizzy Gillespie, who accepted awards from *Downbeat* magazine and performed "Hot House." Another DuMont show, *Cavalcade of Bands* was television's premiere showcase for the more mainstream big band music that was popular in New York nightclubs and hotel ballrooms. Every major orchestra from Guy Lombardo to Duke Ellington appeared on the show.

These few examples from the world of jazz are part of a seemingly endless list of cultural sources and references for DuMont's programing. The men and women who worked at DuMont were inspired by everything from pulp fiction to the Bible. They made smart use of the new television technology in crafting programs that incorporated interesting facets of the culture. In so doing, they enabled DuMont to convince millions of Americans that television was intelligent, entertaining, and worthwhile.

Allen Du Mont and Commercial Television

Allen Du Mont was unimpressed by most of the programs on television, including the offerings on the DuMont network. When he moved into the television broadcasting business in the late 1930s, Du Mont probably did not expect his network's legacy to be shows like *Captain Video* and *Cavalcade of Stars*. As the president and founder of DuMont Laboratories, Allen Du Mont was one of the people most responsible for introducing television to America after World War II. Yet, despite his accomplishments, Du Mont was conflicted. Throughout his time at DuMont Laboratories, Allen Du Mont retained a sense of wonder and respect for the magic of a technology that could transmit distant sounds and images into people's living rooms. Not only did his company build the finest TV sets on the market, but Du Mont also consistently argued before the FCC for high technical standards so that consumers could watch the best pictures that science could deliver. He expected more from television programing than what he saw as crass popular entertainment.

In almost all of his public speeches, interviews, and articles about television, Du Mont spoke enthusiastically about television's capacity to educate the public about science, the arts, and politics. In 1948, for example, Du Mont proclaimed that television's "opportunities for public service are endless. Through video, history-in-the-making will literally be brought into every home. No other medium will be able to match it in conveying pleasure and instruction to the public."[22] Four years later, Du Mont mentioned the 1952 political convention coverage as an example "of the indispensable role that television can play in the nation's life."[23]

Nevertheless, the early television networks were a far cry from PBS, CNN, or C-SPAN. DuMont produced sufficient news, religious, and assorted informational programing to help its affiliates satisfy the FCC's public interest guidelines, but, for the most part, the network did nothing more than it had to do. In this regard, DuMont was not different from its counterparts elsewhere on the dial. In the area of television news, for example, all four networks aired weekly political discussion programs; however, news budgets were small. CBS and NBC were the only networks with regular nightly newscasts. ABC joined these networks in October 1953. The news programs were subdued, 15-minute productions that relied on wire service copy, still photos, and newsreel or film footage that was at least a few hours old.[24] All networks, including DuMont, occasionally made a splash by covering political events—congressional hearings, inaugurations, party conventions, speeches—but these programs were not the norm.

Allen Du Mont's failure to realize his hopes for more serious nonfiction programing is a testament to the powerful forces of commercialism in early television. Allen Du Mont was in a difficult position. He was forced to choose between the kinds of educational, public interest programing that he personally favored, and the less highbrow fare that attracted more viewers. In considering this question of public taste and television, Du Mont was not alone. Over the years, countless high-minded reformers—FCC commissioners, industry executives, producers, on-air talent, academics, and critics across the political spectrum—have tried to elevate the level of television discourse. Many of these reformers have also recognized that their taste in television was that of a minority of viewers. A large public audience generally has not been interested in the kinds of complex programs that do a good job of presenting high art, science, religion, history, and current events. Programs like Bishop Sheen's *Life Is Worth Living*—which started as an unsponsored religious show and unexpectedly captured a mass audience—have been rare. Given the nature of the intensely competitive early television industry, and the fact that certain types of entertainment shows were attracting viewers and even enjoying critical praise, it would have been disastrous for his company if Allen Du Mont had saddled the DuMont network with a programing strategy based upon his own hopes for television.

In a 1953 speech delivered to a group of social-science teachers in

Troy, New York, Du Mont recognized these commercial limitations and was apologetic for the economic strictures of his industry. "Television stations and television networks are completely dependent for their income upon the money spent by advertisers for television time and programs . . . We've got to give the people what they want or we won't have income," he explained. Du Mont then reviewed the ratings for programs by genre, showing that comedy-variety shows were the most popular programs and "cultural and educational" shows, "unfortunately," were the least popular. Nevertheless, all was not lost. Du Mont reminded his audience of the "wide variety" of cultural programs that were available despite these commercial pressures. He singled out public interest offerings on his own network, such as *Life Is Worth Living* and *The Johns Hopkins Science Review*. But he also praised like-minded shows on other networks; for example, political discussion shows like *American Forum of the Air* and cultural offerings like *Omnibus* on NBC.[25]

By 1961, the DuMont network was long gone and DuMont Laboratories was absorbed by Fairchild Camera & Instrument. Allen Du Mont worked as a technical consultant with Fairchild. In a short speech that he made upon receiving an honorary degree from the Institute of Electrical Engineers in June 1961, four years before his death, Du Mont surveyed the state of television. "Many have been the evenings that I have gone from channel to channel on my TV receiver with the hope of seeing decent drama, important personalities and discussions, good music, contemporary or classical, dancing, or the opera." Instead, he found mayhem and violence on his TV set. "How can 47 million television sets be tuned to this kind of production five hours and more a day? My reaction has been that of the creator of Frankenstein. Yet I am here today, honored by you, because I helped to make this possible. Rather than [being honored], perhaps I should instead be censured." In a coda to this indictment of television, and his role in bringing the medium to life, Du Mont shared a melancholy thought with the electrical engineers who were honoring him. For Allen Du Mont, an inventor was ultimately powerless because he could not determine how his inventions would be used. "In our society, an engineer can create—he can develop but he cannot control the ultimate utilization. As engineers we must, I am afraid, be content with the role of the originator and leave it to those with other functions to use the developments in the best interests of mankind."[26]

Appendix

DuMont Chronology

January 29, 1901	Allen Balcom Du Mont is born in Brooklyn, New York.
1912	Allen Du Mont suffers from a polio attack that leaves him with a severe limp for the rest of his life.
1914	Du Mont's family moves to Upper Montclair, New Jersey.
1924	Du Mont graduates from Rensselaer Polytechnic Institute in Troy, New York, with a degree in electrical engineering.
1924	Du Mont joins the Westinghouse Lamp Company in Bloomfield, New Jersey, as an engineer in charge of producing receiving tubes.
October 19, 1926	Du Mont marries Ethel Martha Steadman. The couple later has two children: Allen and Yvonne.
1928	Du Mont joins the De Forest Radio Company as chief engineer. He is soon promoted to the position of vice-president in charge of engineering and manufacturing.
1931	Du Mont is fired from De Forest Radio. He establishes his own company, DuMont Laboratories, to research and manufacture cathode-ray tubes. The company starts with $1,000 and a three-person staff that works in the basement of Du Mont's Upper Montclair, New Jersey, home.
1931–1934	DuMont Laboratories gradually expands from the basement to a group of five converted retail stores in Upper Montclair.
1935	Mortimer Loewi invests in DuMont Laboratories. Loewi holds several executive positions and serves as one of Allen Du Mont's chief financial advisors through the early 1950s.

October 31, 1935	Allen B. DuMont Laboratories is incorporated. Allen Du Mont is president of the company. He remains president of DuMont Laboratories until 1955.
1937	DuMont Laboratories sells RCA the rights to one of its inventions: a cathode-ray instrument known as the "magic eye" that is used to tune radio and TV receivers. DuMont uses the $20,000 from the sale to move into a 30,000 square-foot facility that had previously served as a pickle factory in Passaic, New Jersey.
July 1938	DuMont Laboratories forms a partnership with Paramount Pictures. In exchange for approximately $200,000 in cash and loans, Paramount receives DuMont stock and the right to appoint three directors and three officers of the company.
1938	Du Mont begins manufacturing television receivers to demonstrate at department stories in the New York area.
1939	DuMont becomes one of the nation's first companies to produce commercial television receivers for the public.
April 17, 1940	DuMont receives a license to operate New York's second television station, experimental station W2XWV, on channel four. Network offices and a studio are located on the 42nd floor of a building at 515 Madison Avenue in New York. The station broadcasts throughout World War II.
May 2, 1944	DuMont is granted a commercial license for its New York station. The call letters of W2XWV are changed to WABD.
December 1944	WABD moves from channel four to channel five.
1945	Leonard Cramer is appointed director of the DuMont network, the top position at the network.
June 25, 1945	DuMont receives a permit to commence experimental television operations in Washington, D.C., over station W3XWT.
April 15, 1946	DuMont opens a new studio, located in the auditorium of the John Wanamaker department store in downtown Manhattan. It continues to use the studio at 515 Madison Avenue for smaller productions.
April 26, 1946	DuMont is granted a commercial television license for a Washington station, WTTG-TV, channel five.
Fall 1946	DuMont telecasts network programing between New York and Washington three nights a week. NBC is the only other broadcaster in the country with a regular network schedule at this time.

June 1947	Ted Bergmann joins the DuMont network as an advertising salesman.
June 1947	Chris Witting joins the DuMont network as an accountant.
1947	Lawrence Phillips replaces Leonard Cramer as director of the DuMont network.
1947	James L. Caddigan is appointed director of programing and production for the DuMont network. Caddigan serves in this position until 1955.
September 23, 1948	The Federal Communication Commission (FCC) places a so-called "freeze" on new station allocation while it creates a new system for delivering television to the nation.
November 1, 1948	DuMont introduces the country's first all-day schedule on its New York station, WABD.
1949	Chris Witting is named general manager of the network.
January 1949	Mortimer Loewi replaces Phillips as director of the network.
January 11, 1949	The coaxial cable linking cities in the East with stations as far west as St. Louis is inaugurated. DuMont marks the occasion by opening its third owned-and-operated station, WDTV (Pittsburgh), channel three.
April 21, 1949	*The Morey Amsterdam Show* debuts on DuMont, following a brief run on CBS.
June 4, 1949	*Cavalcade of Stars* debuts with Jack Carter as host.
June 27, 1949	*Captain Video* debuts.
October 12, 1949	*The Plainclothes Man* debuts.
January 14, 1950	*Rocky King, Detective* debuts.
July 8, 1950	Jackie Gleason debuts as host of *Cavalcade of Stars*.
July 1951	Mortimer Loewi leaves the DuMont network. He remains with DuMont Laboratories as an assistant to the president. Chris Witting is appointed managing director of the DuMont network.
October 5, 1951	"The Honeymooners" debuts as a skit on *Cavalcade of Stars*.
February 12, 1952	*Life Is Worth Living* with Bishop Fulton Sheen debuts.
April 11, 1952	The FCC releases its Sixth Report and Order, which ends the freeze on new station licenses and provides a plan for allocating television stations.
February 9, 1953	The FCC releases its decision that Paramount Pictures controls DuMont.

July 1953	Ted Bergmann is named general manager of the DuMont network, the highest position under Witting.
January 1, 1954	Ted Bergmann replaces Witting as managing director of the DuMont network.
April 12, 1954	*The Ernie Kovacs Show* debuts on WABD-TV in New York.
January 10, 1955	DuMont sells WDTV (Pittsburgh) to Westinghouse Broadcasting.
Summer 1955	Dumont ceases network operations but honors remaining network contracts through 1956.
October 10, 1955	The DuMont Broadcasting Corporation is spun off as a separate entity from DuMont Laboratories. WABD and WTTG, DuMont's two owned-and-operated stations, serve as the foundation for the new company. Manufacturing divisions remain part of DuMont Laboratories. Allen Du Mont is removed as president, but continues as chairman of the board of each company.
1958	Emerson Radio & Phonograph purchase DuMont Laboratories' Receiver Division.
May 12, 1958	The name of the DuMont Broadcasting Company is changed to Metropolitan Broadcasting. Allen Du Mont resigns from the board in protest of the name change.
1960	Fairchild Camera & Instrument purchases everything that remains in DuMont, including the instrument and tube businesses. Allen Du Mont serves as a technical consultant to Fairchild.
November 15, 1965	Allen Du Mont passes away in Doctor's Hospital (New York) after a short illness.

Notes

I use the following abbreviations for libraries, archives, and collections of records that are cited several times:

Arbitron-TV: Arbitron TV Collection, Hargrett Rare Book and Manuscript Library, University of Georgia, Athens, GA.

DuMont-LC: Records of the Allen B. DuMont Laboratories, Manuscript Division, Library of Congress, Washington, DC.

DuMont-SI: Allen B. Du Mont Collection, Collection Number 18, Archives Center, National Museum of American History, Smithsonian Institution, Washington, DC.

FCC Docket 10031 Proceedings: Federal Communications Commission, *Official Report of Proceedings Before the Federal Communications Commission*, Docket 10031, et al., Records of the Federal Communications Commission, RG 173, National Archives, College Park, MD.

FCC Executive Director: Entry 100B, Office of the Executive Director, General Correspondence, 1947–1956, Records of the Federal Communications Commission, RG 173, National Archives, College Park, MD.

Goldsmith-LC: Thomas T. Goldsmith Collection, Manuscript Division, Library of Congress, Washington, DC.

LAB: Library of American Broadcasting, University of Maryland, College Park, MD.

MTR-NY: Museum of Television and Radio, New York, NY.

UCLA Archive: UCLA Film and Television Archive, Los Angeles, CA.

Preface and Acknowledgments

1. Christopher H. Sterling and John M. Kitross, *Stay Tuned: A Concise History of American Broadcasting*, 2nd ed. (Belmont, CA: Wadsworth, 1990), 657; James L. Baughman, "Television Comes to America, 1947–1957," *Illinois History*, March 1993. Illinois Periodicals Online, Northern Illinois University Libraries, http://www.lib.niu.edu/ipo/ihy930341.html.

2. The figure of 400 surviving kinescopes is an educated guess based on my research trips and searches of the catalogs and databases of programs at the UCLA Film and Television Archives and the Museum of Television and Radio in New York. Many of the programs at UCLA come from the Peter Vest Collection, which consisted of approximately 325 shows. See Donald Ernest Zimmerman, "The Portrayal of Women in Mass Media, 1949 to 1956: The DuMont Television Network Versus Popular Film, Books, Magazines, and Songs," (Ph.D. diss., Union Graduate School, Cincinnati, 1979), passim.

Chapter One: My Father Was an Engineer

1. Les Brown, *Les Brown's Encyclopedia of TV*, 3rd ed. (Detroit, MI: Visible Ink Press, 1992), 164.

2. See, for example, "Du Mont's Domain," *Forbes*, 15 February 1954, 16; Also see Jeff Kisseloff, *The Box: An Oral History of Television, 1920–1961* (New York: Viking, 1995), 123; Craig Fisher and Helen Fisher, "Metromedia and the DuMont Legacy: The New York Story W2XWV, WABD, WNEW-TV," in *Metromedia and the DuMont Legacy* (New York: Museum of Broadcasting, 1980), 9.

3. All references to inflation-adjusted dollars are calculated from U.S. Department of Labor, Bureau of Labor Statistics, "CPI Inflation Calculator," http://stats.bls.gov/cpi/ and Columbia Journalism Review, "CJR Dollar Conversion Calculator," http://www.cjr.org/resources/inflater.asp.

4. Robert Rice, "The Prudent Pioneer," *New Yorker*, 27 January 1951, 36.

5. Bill Wallace, "Boatman of the Month," *Popular Boating*, November 1956, 84; also see Robert W. Marks, "He Found a Fortune in a Tube," *Coronet*, July 1947, 188.

6. Rice, "The Prudent Pioneer," 36.

7. Yvonne DuMont Stelle, telephone conversation with author, 4 November 2001.

8. Museum of Broadcast Communications, *Celebrating Television's 60th Anniversary: A Reunion of the DuMont Television Network*, seminar, 30 April 1999, videotape, Museum of Broadcast Communications, Chicago.

9. Rice, "The Prudent Pioneer," 37; Jerry Krupnick, "DuMont Regrets His Television Empire Doesn't Leave Him Time to Exploit New Ideas," *Newark Star Ledger*, 7 June 1953.

10. Wallace, "Boatman of the Month," 82.

11. Thomas T. Goldsmith, interview by Bruce DuMont, Chicago, IL, n.d., Museum of Broadcast Communications, Chicago, www.museum.tv; Stelle, telephone conversation; Les Arries Jr., interview by David Marc, Osprey, FL, 12 March 2001, Center for the Study of Popular Television, S. I. Newhouse School of Public Communication, Syracuse University.

12. *Person to Person*, June 24, 1955, videotape, B:04382, Museum of Televion and Radio, New York, NY (hereafter cited as MTR-NY).

13. See, for example, the comments of Werner Michel and Ted Bergmann in Kisseloff, *The Box*, 219.

14. Stelle, telephone conversation.

15. Ted Bergmann and Ira Skutch, *The DuMont Television Network: What Happened?* (Lanham, MD: The Scarecrow Press, 2002) 57; Kisseloff, *The Box*, 218–9.

16. Stelle, telephone conversation.

17. Thomas T. Goldsmith, telephone conversation with author, 22 October 2001.

18. Rice, "Prudent Pioneer," 50

19. Lynn Boyd Hinds, *Broadcasting the Local News: The Early Years of Pittsburgh's KDKA-TV* (University Park, PA: Pennsylvania State University Press, 1995), 21.

Chapter Two: From Basement to Broadway

1. "Allen B. Du Mont Is Dead at 64; Devised Vital TV Component," *New York Times*, 16 November 1965. Information about Allen B. Du Mont's childhood polio and early career in radio appears in several contemporary articles and official Du-Mont company biographies. See, for example, Wallace, "Boatman of the Month," 82; "Du Mont, Allen B(alcom)," *Current Biography*, June 1946, 10–1; Rice, "The Prudent Pioneer," 36; Marks, "He Found a Fortune in a Tube," 187–89; Craig Thompson, "Mr. Television," *Collier's*, 25 June 1949, 18–9, 44. Subsequent biographical information comes from these sources. Also see Federal Communications Commission, *Official Report of Proceedings Before the Federal Communications Commission*, Docket 10031 et al., 15 January 1952, 117, Records of the Federal Communications Commission, RG 173, National Archives, College Park, MD (hereafter cited as FCC Docket 10031 Proceedings).

2. Susan J. Douglas, *Inventing American Broadcasting 1899–1922* (Baltimore: Johns Hopkins University Press, 1987), 205; Hugo Gernsback, letter to *New York Times*, 29 March 1912.

3. FCC Docket 10031 Proceedings, 15 January 1952, 118.

4. FCC Docket 10031 Proceedings, 17 January 1952, 370; "Du Mont, Allen B(alcom)," *Current Biography*, 12; "Du Mont's Domain," 18; Marks, "He Found a Fortune in a Tube," 188. Du Mont put his initial investment at between $45,000 and $50,000 in a *Collier's* profile. See Thompson, "Mr. Television," 44.

5. FCC Docket 10031 Proceedings, 15 January 1952, 121, 449; Rice, "The Prudent Pioneer," 44.

6. Marks, "He Found a Fortune in a Tube," 190. Loewi became director of the DuMont network in January 1949. See "Loewi Becomes Head of DuMont Network," *The Raster*, January–February 1949, 4; "TV Station to Concentrate Signal Along East Coast," *The Miami Herald*, 28 August 1953.

7. FCC Docket 10031 Proceedings, 17 January 1952, 359; FCC Docket 10031 Proceedings, 22 January 1952, 869.

8. FCC Docket 10031 Proceedings, 17 January 1952, 360.

9. FCC Docket 10031 Proceedings, 15 January 1952, 123, 133, 138; "1939—The Television Year," *Business Week*, special report, 31 December 1938, n.p. Records of the Allen B. DuMont Laboratories, Manuscript Division, Library of Congress, Washington, DC (hereafter cited as DuMont-LC).

10. FCC Docket 10031 Proceedings, 17 January 1952, 361.

11. FCC Docket 10031 Proceedings, 22 January 1952, 867.

12. The number of directors was increased from six to eight in 1939; each class of stock elected half of the directors. Class A voters elected five of these members starting in 1946. Federal Communications Commission, "In the Matter of the Applications of Paramount Television Productions, Inc. et al.," Dockets 10031 et al.,

adopted 9 February 1953, *Federal Communications Commission Reports*, Volume 17 (Washington, DC: Government Printing Office, 1966), 274.

13. For more on the initial arrangement between DuMont and Paramount, see Gary Newton Hess, "An Historical Study of the Du Mont Television Network," (Ph.D. diss., Northwestern University, 1960; reprint, New York: Arno Press, 1979), 92–3 (citations to reprint edition); Reed Miller, "Proposed Findings and Conclusions of Law of Paramount Television Productions, Inc., Paramount Pictures, Inc., and Paramount Pictures Corporation," Docket 10031, unpublished document, 4–5, Records of the Federal Communications Commission, RG173, National Archives, College Park, MD; William A. Roberts, et al., "Proposed Findings and Conclusions of Law of Allen B. Du Mont Laboratories," Docket 10031, unpublished document, 29–31, Records of the Federal Communications Commission, RG173, National Archives, College Park, MD; FCC Docket 10031 Proceedings, 22 January 1952, 871; Marks, "He Found a Fortune in a Tube," 190.

14. Rice, "The Prudent Pioneer," 46.

15. "1939—The Television Year," n.p.; FCC Docket 10031 Proceedings, 15 January 1952, 133.

16. "New York Display Dedicated by RCA," *Broadcasting*, 1 May 1939, 21; Orrin E. Dunlap Jr., "Ceremony Is Carried by Television as Industry Makes its Formal Bow," *New York Times*, 1 May 1939. RCA at the World's Fair is covered in most histories of television. See, for example, David E. Fisher and Marshall John Fisher, *The Tube: The Invention of Television* (San Diego: Harvest, 1997), 276–9. Erik Barnouw, *The Golden Web: A History of Broadcasting in the United States* (New York: Oxford University Press, 1968), 125–6; Michael Ritchie, *Please Stand By: A Prehistory of Television* (Woodstock, NY: The Overlook Press, 1994), 57–8; Harry W. Sova, "A Descriptive and Historical Survey of American Television, 1937–1946" (Ph.D. diss., Ohio University, 1977), 208–9.

17. For more on television before and during World War II, see Ritchie, *Please Stand By*, passim; Sova, "American Television," passim; James A. Von Schilling, "Television During World War II: Homefront Service, Military Success," *American Journalism* 12 (Summer 1995): 290–303; histories of particular local stations and markets in Michael D. Murray and Donald G. Godfrey, eds., *Television in America: Local Station History from Across the Nation* (Ames, IA: Iowa State University Press, 1997). Donald G. Godfrey, *Philo T. Farnsworth: The Father of Television* (Salt Lake City: University of Utah Press, 2001), 47–156.

18. Sova, "American Television," 221.

19. Sova, "American Television," 215; "NBC Shuts Down Video Plant," *Broadcasting*, 1 August 1940, 101.

20. Von Schilling, "Television During World War II," 292–3; "Television Review 1943," *The Raster*, February 1944, 5.

21. Wanda Marvin, "DuMont Television," *Billboard*, 4 September 1943.

22. Sterling and Kitross, *Stay Tuned*, 657; J. Walter Thompson, "Where the Sets Are," rev. ed., 1 September 1953, n.p., Pamphlet 2503, Library of American Broadcasting, University of Maryland, College Park, MD (hereafter cited as LAB).

23. "DuMont Television Moves Toward Commercialization," *The Raster*, December 1943, 4.

24. For more on the reduced operations of the other stations, see Sova, "Amer-

ican Television," 241–2; "DuMont Varieties," 8 September 1943, in *Variety Television Reviews, Volume 3, 1923–1950*, ed. Howard H. Prouty (New York: Garland, 1989), n.p.; Von Schilling, "Television During World War II," 296.

25. "DuMont Television Moves Toward Commercialization," 4.

26. Harry Sova, "American Television," 224–5. For more on RCA's wartime activity, see Robert Sobel, *RCA* (New York: Stein and Day, 1986), 137–9; Von Schilling, "Television During World War II," 294–5.

27. "The War Report of the Allen B. Du Mont Laboratories," unpublished report, 6 September 1945, Thomas T. Goldsmith Collection, Manuscript Division, Library of Congress, Washington, DC (hereafter cited as Goldsmith-LC). Allen B. DuMont Laboratories, "Prospectus," 21 May 1946, Allen B. Du Mont Collection, Collection Number 18, Archives Center, National Museum of American History, Smithsonian Institution, Washington, DC (hereafter cited as DuMont-SI).

28. "Television Directory," *Television Digest*, 8 December 1945, n.p.

29. "New DuMont Station Opens in Nation's Capitol," *The Raster*, January–February 1946, 4.

30. "New York and District Linked by Television," *Washington Star*, 16 April 1946; "Bust by Television," *Newsweek*, 29 April 1946, 61; "Dedicate DuMont Studios Today in John Wanamaker N.Y. Store," *Radio Daily*, 15 April 1946, 5. While there had been numerous experimental network transmissions conducted by Farnsworth, Philco, NBC, and DuMont, this telecast marked the beginning of continuous, commercial network television operations.

31. Howard Field, "'Temporary' W3XWT Blossomed Into Indie Powerhouse, WTTG," *Television/Radio Age*, May 1985, A2–A3; Charles Kelly to Leslie G. Arries, memo, 14 June 1946, DuMont-LC.

32. Michael Woal and Linda Kowall Woal, "Forgotten Pioneer: Philco's WPTZ," in Murray and Godfrey, eds., *Television in America*, 50.

33. Field, "'Temporary' W3XWT Blossomed," A–4; Federal Communications Commission, *Second Interim Report of the Office of Network Study: Television Network Program Procurement, Part II*, Docket 12783 (Washington, DC: Government Printing Office, 1965), 160–67. Also see schedule cards for DuMont programs from early 1947 in DuMont-LC.

34. Sterling and Kitross, *Stay Tuned*, 294–5.

35. Susan Brinson, *Personal and Public Interests: Frieda B. Hennock and the Federal Communications Commission* (Westport, CT: Praeger, 2002), 53; Robert Pepper, "The Pre-Freeze Television Stations," in *American Broadcasting: A Source Book on the History of Radio and Television*, Lawrence Lichty and Malachi C. Topping, eds. (New York: Hastings House, 1975), 140.

36. Sterling and Kitross, *Stay Tuned*, 657.

37. Bergmann and Skutch, *The DuMont Television Network*, 58.

38. Federal Communications Commission, *Network Program Procurement*, 183; "No. 1 TV Problem: Thawing the 'Freeze,'" *Business Week*, 6 May 1950, 30–4.

39. Also see Federal Communications Commission, *Sixth Report and Order*, adopted 11 April 1952, reprinted in *Federal Communications Commission Reports*, Vol. 41 (Washington, DC: Government Printing Office, 1970), 148–73; 204–9.

40. "Table of Assignments," *Broadcasting Telecasting*, Part II, Final Report, 14 April 1952, 132–4; United States Senate, Committee on Interstate and Foreign

Commerce, *Allocation of TV Channels*, 85th Cong., 2d sess., 14 March 1958 (Washington, DC: Government Printing Office, 1958), 99.

41. Barry Russell Litman, *The Vertical Structure of the Television Broadcasting Industry: The Coalescence of Power* (East Lansing, MI: Michigan State University Business Studies, 1979), 22.

42. "Ultra High TV in Trouble," *Business Week*, 29 May 1954, 94–5.

43. James L. Baughman, *Television's Guardians: The FCC and the Politics of Programming 1958–1967* (Knoxville, TN: University of Tennessee Press, 1985), 38.

44. United States Senate, *Allocation of TV Channels*, 98–9.

45. House Subcommittee on Interstate and Foreign Commerce, Hearings, "Investigation of Regulatory Commissions and Agencies," Part 6, 85th Cong, 2nd Session (1958), 2399; Susan L. Brinson, "Missed Opportunities: FCC Commissioner Frieda Hennock and the UHF Debacle," *Journal of Broadcasting & Electronic Media* 44:2 (Spring 2000), 264.

46. *Television Digest*, 1 January 1949, n.p.

47. Pepper, "The Pre-Freeze Television Stations," 141.

48. DuMont Laboratories, Minutes of DuMont Management Meeting, 21 July 1949, DuMont-SI. Also see James L. Baughman, "The Weakest Chain and the Strongest Link: The American Broadcasting Company and the Motion Picture Industry, 1952–1960," in *Hollywood In the Age of Television*, ed. Tino Balio (Boston: Unwin Hyman, 1990), 95.

49. Lichty and Topping, eds., *American Broadcasting*, 155; Litman, *Vertical Structure*, 21; Stuart Lewis Long, *The Development of the Network Television Oligopoly* (New York: Arno Press, 1979), 59–60; Federal Communications Commission, *Second Interim Report of the Office of Network Study*, 165–83; the testimony of Allen B. Du Mont in *Official Verbatim Transcript of Hearings Before Social Subcommittee of the Judiciary Committee of the House of Representatives in Connection With Its Study of the Anti-Trust Laws*, 19 September 1956 (Washington, DC: Bureau of National Affairs, 1956), n.p., DuMont-LC.

50. Ted Bergmann, telephone conversation with author, 24 June 2002.

51. These nine reliable affiliates were WAAM (Baltimore), WGN (Chicago), WCPO (Cincinnati), WXEL (Cleveland), WTVN (Columbus), WABD (New York), WFIL (Philadelphia), WDTV (Pittsburgh), WTTG (Washington). See DuMont Television Network, "Anticipated Affiliate Station Program Order," week ending December 30, 1950, memo, DuMont-LC; E. B. Lyford, to C. G. Alexander, et al., Traffic Schedule, 5 March 1952, DuMont-LC; "Du Mont Television Network Projected Program Distribution Order," week ending February 7, 1954, DuMont-LC. Also see A.C. Nielsen Company, *National TV Nielsen-Ratings*, Second Report, December 1950 (Chicago: A.C. Nielsen Company, 1950), passim.

52. "Television Sets-In-Use," *Television Digest*, Special Report, 14 February 1953, n.p. Since television viewing was a group activity, each TV home represented multiple potential viewers.

53. Hess, "Historical Study," 81. Also see the testimony of Allen B. Du Mont and others before the so-called Potter Committee. U.S. Senate, Committee on Interstate and Foreign Commerce, Subcommittee on Communications, *Status of UHF and Multiple Ownership of TV Stations*, 83rd Congress, 2nd session (Washington, DC: Government Printing Office, 1954).

54. Bergmann and Skutch, *The DuMont Television Network*, 64.

55. Les Arries Jr., interview by author, tape recording, Venice, FL, 20 December 1995, LAB.

56. Robert Doyle, interview by author, tape recording, Chevy Chase, MD, 3 July 1996, LAB.

57. Baughman, *Television's Guardians*, 13; Sterling Quinlan, *The Hundred Million Dollar Lunch* (Chicago: J. Philip O'Hara, 1974), 4.

58. Bergmann and Skutch, *The DuMont Television Network*, 64–5.

59. Bergmann, telephone conversation.

60. Timothy White, "Hollywood on (Re)Trial: The American Broadcasting-United Paramount Merger Hearing," *Cinema Journal* 31 (1992), 26.

61. Paramount also operated a second station in Chicago, WBKB, from 1939 to 1950. Paramount transferred WBKB to UPT when the companies split. On March 23, 1954, DuMont made a final attempt to own and operate a fourth station by filing an application for Boston's channel five. The FCC's allocation decision did not come down until after the network had been dissolved. See Hess, "Historical Study," 83.

62. Federal Communications Commission, "Memorandum Opinion and Order," 53–589, Docket 10031, unpublished document, 18 May 1953, passim, Records of the Federal Communications Commission, RG173, National Archives, College Park, MD; Federal Communications Commission, "In the Matter of Paramount Television Productions et al.," 271–9; Hess, "Historical Study," 113.

63. Witting, "Report for the Broadcasting Division for 1952," 3 March 1953.

64. Quoted in Kisseloff, *The Box*, 218; also see Bergmann and Skutch, *The DuMont Television Network*, 66; Ralph Baruch, interview by Robert Allen, November 1990, The Cable Center, Hauser Foundation Oral and Video History Project, www.cablecenter.org.

65. William Boddy, "Building the World's Largest Advertising Medium: CBS and Television, 1940–1960," in Balio, ed., *Hollywood Television*, 70.

66. Boddy, "Building the World's Largest Advertising Medium," 68–72; *Moody's Manual of Investments: Industrials 1950* (New York: Moody's Investor Services, 1950), 1374.

67. *Moody's Industrials 1950*, 1155, 1374.

68. Harvard Business School, "Allen B. DuMont Laboratories, Inc.," BP 452 (Cambridge, MA: Harvard College, 1952), 36, DuMont-LC. Also see the FCC's summary of DuMont's attempts to raise funds in FCC, "In the Matter of Paramount Television Productions, et al.," 273.

69. Harvard Business School, "Allen B. DuMont Laboratories, Inc.," 38–9.

70. Hess, "Historical Study," 70. Also see "DuMont Sales Up," *Broadcasting Telecasting*, 15 October 1951, 74; DuMont Laboratories annual reports; minutes of Du Mont Management Meeting, 25 May 1951, DuMont-SI.

71. "Du Mont's Domain," 18.

72. Ted Bergmann, telephone conversation. Also see Chris J. Witting, to Allen B. Du Mont, memo, 1 September 1953, DuMont-LC. Witting's report argues that DuMont must spend more on network programming, but he concludes the memo humbly, asking Du Mont for support "to the extent that you believe is compatible with the economies and other factors now existing in the company."

73. *Moody's Manual of Investments: Industrials 1953* (New York: Moody's Investors Service, 1953), 1300.

74. A few of these programs also appeared on CBS or NBC.

75. "Network Television Billings: 1949–57," *Television Factbook No. 31* (New York: Television Digest, 1960); "Fall Business Divides Unevenly Among Networks," *Tide*, 22 August 1952, n.p., DuMont-SI; "ABC Tops DuM in 2nd Division Field," *Billboard*, 15 November 1952, n.p., DuMont-SI; "B-T Forecast II: Fall TV Sales Well Ahead of '52," *Broadcasting Telecasting*, 7 September 1953, 27–8.

76. Quoted in Kisseloff, *The Box*, 221. Since so many stations had multiple affiliations, it is difficult to make precise counts of network affiliates. Coverage varied from one show to another. Most networks classified a station as an affiliate if it agreed to carry even a single program.

77. Leonard H. Goldenson and Marvin J. Wolf, *Beating the Odds* (New York: Charles Scribner's Sons, 1991), 105.

78. Sterling Quinlan, *Inside ABC: American Broadcasting Company's Rise to Power* (New York: Hastings House, 1979), 37.

79. Chris J. Witting, "Report for the Broadcasting Division for 1952," memo, 3 March 1953, DuMont-LC. Also see John Bachem, memo to all salesmen, 12 September 1951, DuMont-LC; Edward R. Eadoh, to Gerry Martin, memo, 27 October 1953, DuMont-LC.

80. Quinlan, *Inside ABC*, 4, 26.

81. Goldenson and Wolf, *Beating the Odds*, 105–6.

Chapter Three: Who Is in Charge Here?

1. Thompson, "Mr. Television," 18. Also see FCC Docket 10031 Proceedings, 17 January 1952, 338; FCC Docket 10031 Proceedings, 22 January 1952, 901, 967. Paramount's stake in DuMont was closer to 50 percent in 1938, when the studio first became a partner in DuMont. This stake was diluted over the years through additional stock offerings.

2. Clark Dodge & Co., *DuMont Laboratories, Inc.* (New York: Clark Dodge & Co., 1949), 4; Federal Communications Commission, "In the Matter of Paramount Television Productions et al.," 266–77 gives a good summary of the DuMont-Paramount business relationship. Also see DuMont annual reports, 1938–1955.

3. Goldenson and Wolf, *Beating the Odds*, 106.

4. See Hess, "Historical Study," 117.

5. Quoted in Kisseloff, *The Box*, 223.

6. Quoted in Hess, "Historical Study," 118.

7. Timothy R. White, "Life After Divorce: the Corporate Strategy of Paramount Pictures Corporation in the 1950s," *Film History* 2 (1988), 109.

8. White, "Hollywood's Attempt at Appropriating Television," 149–59; "Paramount TV," *Broadcasting Telecasting*, 19 June 1950, 57.

9. See George T. Shupert, "Paramount's TV Network Plan," *1950 Radio Annual and Television Yearbook* (New York: Radio Daily, 1950), 844–5.

10. FCC Docket 10031 Proceedings, 22 January 1952, 898–9.

11. FCC Docket 10031 Proceedings, 16 January 1952, 273.

12. FCC, "In the Matter of Paramount Television Productions, et al.," 395.

13. FCC Docket 10031 Proceedings, 17 January 1952, 391–2.

14. FCC, "In the Matter of Paramount Television Productions, et al.," 299; "Balaban Picks Up Options on 40,000 Par Common, Ditto UPT at 800 G Saving," *Billboard*, 15 December 1951, DuMont-SI.

15. FCC Docket 10031 Proceedings, 22 January 1952, 906.

16. This account of the 1950 merger negotiations between Paramount and Du-Mont comes from the testimony before the FCC of the four principals: Allen Du Mont, Paul Raibourn, James Murtaugh, and Edwin Falk. See FCC Docket 10031 Proceedings, 17 January 1952, 382–403; FCC Docket 10031 Proceedings, 22 January 1952, 893–906; FCC Docket 10031 Proceedings, 24 January 1952, 1207–20, 1260–83. Except for this 1952 FCC testimony, Allen Du Mont never publicly spoke about this offer or his reasons for rejecting it. Also see White, "Life After Divorce," 102; "DuMont's $2,564,491 Loss in '49 on B'cast Operations; Ask Par to Unload," *Variety* 5 April 1950, 34. "Balaban, Weisl on DuMont Bd. Cues No Sellout," *Variety*, 12 April 1950, 3.

17. "DuMont Television Network," *Radio Annual and Television Yearbook* (New York: Radio Daily, 1949), 1053.

18. "Admiral Patten New Assistant to President," *The Raster*, July–August 1947, 7; Thomas T. Goldsmith, e-mail to author, 4 September 2002; Michel quoted in Kisseloff, *The Box*, 219.

19. "DuMont Faced With Minority Revolt," *Broadcasting Telecasting*, 9 May 1955, 94; "Network Television Billings: PIB Reports, 1949–55," *Television Factbook* 22 (1956), 26.

20. DuMont Television Network, "Minutes of the Staff Meeting," 22 September 1955, LC-DuMont.

21. Charles Henry Grant, *The DuMont Television Network*, Monograph Number 1 (Bowie, MD: The Radio History Society, 2000), 17; Tim Brooks and Earle Marsh, *The Complete Directory to Prime Time Network and Cable TV Shows 1946–Present*, 7th ed. (New York: Ballantine Books, 1999), 123.

22. "DuMont Faced With Minority Revolt," 94; "DuMont Network to Quit in Telecasting 'Spin-Off,'" *Broadcasting Telecasting*, 15 August 1955, 64; Bergmann and Skutch, *The DuMont Television Network*, 84. Timothy White discusses Paramount's role in the 1955 dissolution of the DuMont network in "Hollywood's Attempt to Appropriate Television," 117–20.

23. Quoted in Kisseloff, *The Box*, 224.

24. Quoted in Hess, "Historical Study," 88.

25. DuMont Broadcasting Company, "Minutes of Adjourned Meeting of the Board of Directors," 23 March 1958, Goldsmith-LC; Metropolitan Broadcasting Corporation, *1958 Annual Report* (New York: Metropolitan Broadcasting, 1959), n.p. Also see Thomas T. Goldsmith, quoted in Kisseloff, *The Box*, 224.

26. Bergmann and Skutch, *The DuMont Television Network*, 85; "Dr. A.B. DuMont Dead; TV Industry Pioneer," *Radio & Television Weekly*, 22 November 1965, 3; "Allen B. Du Mont Is Dead at 64."

27. Hastings talked about Du Mont at the Museum of Broadcast Communications, *Reunion of the DuMont Televisions Network*. Rice, "Prudent Pioneer," 50; Irwin Rostin, telephone conversation with author, 19 May 2001. David Hollander, telephone conversation with author, 3 June 2001.

28. Les Arries Jr., interview by Marc.

29. See DuMont Laboratories to Joseph J. Garibaldi Agency, letter, 13 March 1948, 8, DuMont-LC; "Lawrence Phillips Named Director of DuMont Web," *The Raster*, July–August 1947, 7; Also see Witting's testimony before the FCC, Docket 10031 Proceedings, 18 January 1952, 525.

30. Bergmann and Skutch, *The DuMont Television Network*, 51.

31. "TV Station to Concentrate Signal Along East Coast"; "Bergmann Seen Sure to Succeed Witting as DTN Managing Director," *Broadcasting Telecasting*, 26 October 1953, 70; Bergmann and Skutch, *The DuMont Television Network*, 51–2.

32. "Bergmann Seen Sure to Succeed Witting as DTN Managing Director," 70; "We've Proved the Skeptics Wrong," *Television*, April 1954, 24

33. C. G. Alexander, "Television's False Prosperity," *Radio-Television Daily*, 2 August 1951, 103.

34. Chris J. Witting, "Low Cost Production Emphasized," *Radio Daily*, 22 August 1950, 31.

35. Bergmann, telephone conversation.

36. "Fall Business Divides Unevenly Among Nets," clipping, *Tide*, 22 August 1952, n.p., DuMont-LC. Also see DuMont trade journal ads from this period, for example, *Radio-Television Daily*, 30 July 1953, 78; *Radio-Television Daily*, 2 August 1954, 86.

37. Bergmann and Skutch, *The DuMont Television Network*, 70–71; "We've Proved the Skeptics Wrong," 23.

38. Bergmann, telephone conversation; also see Ted Bergmann to Allen B. Du Mont, memo, 6 May 1954, DuMont-LC.

39. Hal Cooper, interview by author, tape recording, Los Angeles, CA, 6 December 2001. For more on the role of the sponsor in early television, see Lawrence R. Samuel, *Brought to You By: Postwar Television Advertising and the American Dream* (Austin, TX: University of Texas Press, 2001), xvii; Erik Barnouw, *The Sponsor: Notes on a Modern Potentate* (New York: Oxford University Press, 1978), 41–55; Erik Barnouw, *Tube of Plenty*, 2nd rev. ed. (New York: Oxford University Press, 1990), 163–71; Christopher Anderson, *Hollywood TV: The Studio System in the Fifties* (Austin, TX: University of Texas Press, 1994), 71, 87.

40. Chris J. Witting, "Dare to Telecast the Unusual," *Radio-Television Daily*, 14 July 1952, 77.

41. Bergmann and Skutch, *The DuMont Television Network*, 70; Witting, "Low Cost Production Emphasized," 31; FCC Docket 10031 Proceedings, 18 January 1952, 638.

42. "How to Save Money," *Newsweek*, 8 December 1952, 53–4; Jack Gould, "Television in Review," *New York Times*, 13 April 1953; "Television News From DuMont," 22 December 1952, 1, Entry 100B, Office of the Executive Director, General Correspondence, 1947–1956, Records of the Federal Communications Commission, RG 173, National Archives, College Park, MD (hereafter cited as FCC Executive Director).

43. Stan Epstein, telephone conversation with author, 18 May 2001.

44. Don Russell, interview by author, Stamford, CT, 20 April 2001; Bergmann, telephone conversation.

45. FCC Docket 10031 Proceedings, 18 January 1952, 631–5.

46. Howard Rubin, telephone conversation with author, 20 May 2001.

47. Epstein, telephone conversation.

48. Epstein, telephone conversation.

49. Arthur Forrest, interview by author, Chevy Chase, MD, 7 July 2003.

50. Arthur Forrest, interview.

51. Wes Kenney, telephone conversation with author, 14 May 2001.

52. Epstein, telephone conversation.

53. Rostin, telephone conversation.

54. David Hollander, telephone conversation.

55. Rubin, telephone conversation.

56. Don Hastings, interview by author, New York, NY, 3 October 2001.

57. Hollander, telephone conversation.

58. Norman Baer, telephone conversation with author, 31 August 2001.

Chapter Four: The DuMont Daytime Experiment

1. "All-Day Looker," *Time*, 22 November 1948, 46–9. Through 1949, WABD maintained its daytime schedule, but gradually dropped some early morning shows. Network offerings fluctuated. By November 1949, DuMont premiered a more stable network schedule from 2:30 to 4:30 daily. See "Daytime TV in the Network Jigsaw," *Television Digest*, 15 January 1949, 1; "Daytime Video," *Broadcasting Telecasting*, 28 November 1949, 31; "Daytime Network for Local Sponsors," *Television Digest*, 26 November 1949, 1.

2. James L. Caddigan, "DuMont's Daytime Programming Experiment," *Television*, September 1948, 24; Gerald Lyons, "Sterling Products Buys Eastern Net for James's 'Okay Mother' Program," *The Raster*, December 1949, 5.

3. Caddigan, "DuMont's Daytime Programming Experiment," 19, 24; "Round-Clock Schedule Here to Stay as DuMont Makes Programming Good," *Variety*, 10 November 1948, 38; Chris Witting, "Analysis of Results of Operation of WABD Nighttime Versus Daytime for 12th Period Ending 12/5/48," memo, n.d., DuMont-LC; Edward J. McCrossin, "Minutes of Staff Meeting," memo, 8 November 1948, DuMont-LC; James Caddigan, "As Television Enters 1950," *Televiser*, December 1949, 20.

4. James L. Caddigan, "Daytime Programming," *Television*, January 1949, 17; Caddigan, "As Television Enters 1950," 20.

5. James L. Caddigan, "Program Planning for Daytime Schedule," *The Raster*, December 1948, 5.

6. Caddigan, "Daytime Programming," 17; Caddigan, "Program Planning for Daytime Schedule," 5.

7. "Round-Clock Schedule Here to Stay," 38. *Time* magazine also noted the similarity of DuMont's daytime programing to that on radio. See "All-Day Looker," 46–9.

8. "DuMont's 15 Hours of Daily Programming Excites Producers," *Televiser*, September 1948, 47.

9. Caddigan, "Program Planning for Daytime Schedule," 5.

10. "DuMont's Daytime Programming Experiment," 24.

11. Adelaide Hawley, "Women's Interest," *Television Guide* (New York), 18 June 1949, n.p; see the list of sponsors in Caddigan, "Daytime Programming," 19.

12. "All Day Television," *Newsweek*, 4 October 1948, 52; "DuMont's Daytime Programming Experiment," 24. *Okay Mother*, discussed below, began in an 11:00 A.M. slot, but was soon moved to the early afternoon.

13. Caddigan, "Daytime Programming," 17; Caddigan, "Program Planning for Daytime Schedule," 5.

14. Cooper, interview.

15. Cooper, interview.

16. "Round-Clock Schedule Here to Stay," 38; Jack Gould, "Programs in Review," *New York Times*, 7 November 1948.

17. Cooper, interview.

18. Judith Crist, "'Magic Cottage': Unique Children's TV Program," *New York Herald Tribune*, 7 March 1954; McNeil, *Total Television*, 506; DuMont Television Network, Press Release, 2 June 1955, 1, FCC Executive Director.

19. Hawley, "Women's Interest," n.p; "Inside Television," *Variety*, 14 April 1948, in *Variety Television Reviews, Volume 3, 1923–1950*, ed. Howard H. Prouty (New York: Garland, 1990), n.p.

20. Kathi Norris, "Shopping's a Snap Now," *TV Guide* (New York), 25 March 1950, 20.

21. Bruce Robertson, "Kathi's Daytime Success," *Broadcasting Telecasting*, 7 November 1949, 52, 59.

22. Mortimer W. Loewi, "Is the Rating Worth the Rate?" *Televiser*, May 1949, 29.

23. See, for example, "DuMont's 'Tele-Auction' Show Seen as Spur in Wooing Fashion Accounts," *Variety*, 24 December 1947, in *Variety Television Reviews, 1946–1956*, n.p.; "Advertising and Merchandising," *Televiser*, July–August 1946, 33; Mary Gannon, "Ten Men On a Horse," *Television*, July 1948, 24–5; Television and the Sponsor Today," *Sponsor*, November 1946, 62; "Department Store TV," *Sponsor*, 24 April 1950, 30–1, 58–61; Lynn Spigel, *Make Room for TV* (Chicago: University of Chicago Press, 1992), 78.

24. "DuMont's Daytime Programming Experiment," 24; "DuMont's 15 Hours of Daily Programming Excites Producers," 47.

25. For more on these fears, see Spigel, *Make Room for TV*, 87.

26. Jack Gould, "Programs in Review," *New York Times*, 7 November 1948.

27. "Mama Put That Duster Down, Gable's on at 4:30 P.M.," *Television Guide* (New York), 13 November 1948, 16.

28. Dennis James, "Report From Mothers, Incorporated," *Television Guide* (New York), 2 April 1949, 16.

29. "A Housewife Audience," *Televiser*, November 1949, 11; Lyons, "Sterling Products," 4; Mortimer W. Loewi to Allen B. Du Mont, memo, 10 February 1950, DuMont-LC.

30. Kisseloff, *The Box*, 67.

31. Bob Jamieson, "The Cue Sheet," *The Raster*, Fall 1946, 6; Bob Jamieson, "The Cue Sheet," *The Raster*, Summer 1947, 5.

32. Quoted in Kisseloff, *The Box*, 133.

33. Dennis James, "A Show Is Born," *TV Show*, June 1951, 41.

34. James, "A Show Is Born," 41.

35. "Okay Mother," videotape, author's collection.

36. "Okay Dennis, or At Home With a 'Mother's Boy,'" *Television World*, 6 February 1949, n.p; James, "A Show Is Born," 40.

37. "Tops of the TV Glamour Boys," *TV Digest* (Pittsburgh), 10 January 1953, 29.

38. Karal Ann Marling, *As Seen on TV: The Visual Culture of Everyday Life in the 1950s*, paperback ed. (Cambridge: Harvard University Press, 1996), 148–9; Patricia Coffin, "Julia Meade: Small Parts Pay Off," *Look*, 22 September 1953, 94–7.

39. James, "Report From Mothers, Incorporated," 16.

40. "Oceans of Empathy," *Time*, 27 February 1950, 77–8. Also see William A. Henry III, *The Great One: The Life and Legend of Jackie Gleason* (New York: Doubleday, 1992), 105.

41. "Daytime TV as an Advertising Medium," *Televiser*, December 1950, 107.

42. Harry Castleman and Walter Podrazik, *The TV Schedule Book: Four Decades of Network Television, From Sign-On to Sign-Off* (New York: McGraw Hill, 1984), 43–84; Robert C. Allen, *Speaking of Soap Operas* (Chapel Hill, NC: University of North Carolina Press, 1985), 124–5. "All Day Long," *Newsweek*, 24 September 1951, 57.

Chapter Five: Captain Video

1. In addition to the daily episodes, *Captain Video* also aired on Saturdays from February 1950 to November 1950. For more on ratings, see "Telestatus," *Broadcasting*, 5 December 1949, 56; "Telestatus," *Broadcasting Telecasting*, 30 January 1950, 61; "Telestatus," *Broadcasting Telecasting*, 13 October 1952, 84; "New York May Report Released by Pulse," *Broadcasting Telecasting*, 29 May 1950, 68. In a sampling of New York ratings books, *Captain Video* was the highest rated program at 7 P.M. in October 1952, with a 12 rating. In October 1953, the 15-minute program was second behind the local CBS station's early movie with a 6 rating. By October 1954, the program was still competitive, usually scoring a rating of 3 or 4, which put it in the upper half of the seven-station market. See reports from the American Research Bureau, "The New York Television Audience," for the weeks beginning October 1, 1952, October 8, 1953, October 7, 1954. Also see the similar figures in the American Research Bureau ratings books for the Washington, D.C., market from October of each year, 1952–1954. The American Research Bureau ratings books are held in the Arbitron TV Collection, Hargrett Rare Book and Manuscript Library, University of Georgia, Athens, GA (hereafter cited as Arbitron-TV). For more on the stations carrying *Captain Video*, see "Du Mont Television Network Projected Program Distribution Order," week ending February 7, 1954, DuMont-LC.

2. The figure of 3.5 million appears in "Captain Video," *TV Digest*, 2 August 1952, 12. It may have come from network or sponsor publicists. Media historians have also used this figure, without clear attribution. See Mark Siegel, "Science Fiction and Fantasy TV," in *TV Genres*, Brian Rose, ed. (Westport, CT: Greenwood Press, 1985) 92. Suzanne Hurst Williams cites the figure for 1951 in "Captain Video and His Video Rangers," *Encyclopedia of Television*, vol. 1, ed. Horace Newcomb (Chicago: Fitzroy Dearborn, 1997), 309.

3. See "Outer Space Promotion," *Electrical Dealer*, December 1954, n.p., clipping, DuMont-SI.

4. "America's No. 1 Bachelor—of 1955," *TV Digest* (Pittsburgh), 9 August 1952, 8.

5. Other space-themed TV programs that aired nationally included *Space Patrol* (ABC, 1950–1955), *Buck Rogers* (ABC, 1950–1951), *Flash Gordon* (syndicated, 1953), *Captain Z-Ro* (syndicated, 1955), *Johnny Jupiter* (DuMont and ABC, 1953–1954), *Rocky Jones, Space Ranger!* (syndicated, 1954–1955), and *Tom Corbett, Space Cadet* (all four networks, 1950–1955). Several local stations also introduced space captains on their children's programs throughout the 1950s.

6. The precise authorship of the program is murky. Rory Coker, who has conducted the best research on the origins of *Captain Video*, credits only Caddigan and Menkin as the show's creators. See Rory Coker, "The Space Hero Files," *Roaring Rockets*, http://www.slick-net.com/space/text/index.phtml. M. C. Brock is named as the program's "creator" in an early *New York Times* article. See Jack Gould, "Television in Review," *New York Times*, 20 November 1949.

7. Murray Robinson, "Planet Parenthood," *Collier's*, 5 January 1952, 63. A later DuMont press release described Captain Video as a "free agent" who worked for the good of a federation of planets called the Solar Council. See DuMont Television Network, press release, 5 November 1954, 2, FCC Executive Director.

8. The prop budget was between fifteen and twenty-five dollars a week. See Kisseloff, *The Box*, 453; Donald F. Glut and Jim Harmon, *The Great Television Heroes* (Garden City, NY: Doubleday, 1975), 7.

9. "Electronic Age of Captain Video," *TV Forecast* (Chicago), 10 June 1950, 6.

10. Quoted in Kisseloff, *The Box*, 453.

11. Harvey Kurtzman, *Mad Strikes Back* (New York: Ballantine, 1955; reprint, New York: Ballantine, 1975), 28 (page citations are to the reprint edition).

12. Thanks to Rory Coker for his e-mails to the author explaining *Captain Video*'s tools and weapons.

13. John Javna, *The Best of Science Fiction TV* (New York: Harmony Books, 1987), 64.

14. Gould, "Television in Review," 20 November 1949.

15. Al Hodge, "I Can't Escape Being Captain Video," *TV Digest* (Philadelphia), 20 October 1951, 25.

16. Listed as "Maurice C. Brockhauser" in George W. Woolery, *Children's Television: The First Thirty-Five Years, 1946–1981; Part II: Live, Film, and Tape Series* (Metuchen, NJ: The Scarecrow Press, 1985), 107.

17. Gould, "Television in Review," 20 November 1949.

18. Olga Druce, interview by author, New York, NY, 2 September 2000.

19. Hastings, interview.

20. Druce, interview, 2 September 2000; also see Coker, "The Space Hero Files."

21. "7 M.P.S.; Zero 3," *Time*, 25 December 1950, 45.

22. "Out of the World Guy," *TV Forecast* (Chicago), 9 February 1952, 7.

23. "7 M.P.S; Zero 3," 45. Robinson, "Planet Parenthood," 63.

24. *Captain Video*, untitled episode, circa 1950, videotape, author's collection.

25. "General Foods Signs on Capt. Video for Five Years," *Tide*, 23 March 1951, n.p., clipping, DuMont-SI.

26. See, for example, "Here's What Captain Video Rangers Will Wear This Season," *Chicago Sun-Times*, 14 October 1951.

27. DuMont Television Network, "Official Captain Video Merchandise," cata-

log, n.d., Toni Mendez Collection, Cartoon Research Library, Ohio State University, Columbus, OH (hereafter cited as Mendez Collection).

28. Philip Santora, "Out of This World," *New York Daily News*, 11 August 1954, Mendez Collection.

29. See Joe Sarno's episode guide to *Captain Video*. Joe Sarno, "Captain Video: Daily Episodes," *Joe Sarno's Comic Kingdom*, http://home.earthlink.net/~joesarno/tvscifi/captainvdaily.htm. Contemporary articles did not specifically note the change, but this date is consistent with other published materials listing the program's cast.

30. Hastings, interview.

31. Val Adams, "Coogan Finds Role of 'Captain Video' Requires Steady Nerves," *New York Times*, 26 March 1950. Also see Gould, "Television in Review," 20 November 1949; Kisseloff, *The Box*, 454.

32. The best biographical essay about Hodge is Rory Coker's "Al Hodge: Before and After Captain Video," *Roaring Rockets*, http://www.slick-net.com/space/text/index.phtml. Also see Jim Harmon, *Radio Mystery and Adventure and Its Appearance in Film, Television, and Other Media* (Jefferson, NC: McFarland, 1992), 18, 41, 106; Woolery, *Children's Television*, 108; "Al Hodge Is the Real Man Behind Captain Video," *TV Guide* (New York), 17 October 1952, 28; "Captain Video," *TV Digest* (Philadelphia), 12.

33. Hastings, interview.

34. Glut and Harmon, *The Great Television Heroes*, 6.

35. Hodge, "I Can't Escape Being Captain Video," 25.

36. Jack Gaver, "Daddy of All Space Shows Will Accent More Action," *Paterson Evening News*, 16 August 1954, clipping, DuMont-SI.

37. Hodge, "I Can't Escape Being Captain Video," 25.

38. "Captain Video Teaches School," *Television News* (Pittsburgh), 25 February 1951, n.p., clipping, DuMont-SI. Also see Hodge, "I Can't Escape Being Captain Video," 25; "Al Hodge Is the Real Man Behind Captain Video," 28.

39. Al Hodge, "Captain Video's Toughest Mission," *Faith Made Them Champion*, ed. Norman Vincent Peale (Carmel, NY: Guideposts Associates, 1954), 165.

40. Bergmann and Skutch, *The DuMont Television Network*, 40; "Gen. Foods Takes DuMont's 'Capt. Video' for Over 7 Yrs.," *Billboard*, 3 March 1951, n.p. clipping, DuMont-SI. DuMont Television Network, "Network Sales Meeting Notes," unpublished meeting notes, 15 June 1953, DuMont-LC; Olga Druce, telephone conversation with author, 28 December 2000. A 1954 report by the National Association for Better Radio and Television lists the sponsor as Mishawanka Rubber Company, a children's shoe manufacturer. It is not clear whether this was a local Los Angeles sponsor or a national one. See National Association for Better Radio and Television, "Fourth Annual Report on Children's Radio and Television Programs," unpublished manuscript, circa 1954, 5, Subcommittee to Investigate Juvenile Delinquency, Judiciary Committee of the Senate, 1953–1961, Records of the U.S. Senate, Record Group 46, National Archives, Washington, DC (hereafter cited as Senate Juvenile Delinquency).

41. Olga Druce, telephone conversation with author, 2 July 2000.

42. Druce, interview, 2 September 2000.

43. "Short Takes," *Variety*, 25 April 1951, in *Variety Television Reviews, Volume 4, 1951–1953*, ed. Howard H. Prouty (New York: Garland, 1990), n.p.

44. Olga Druce, "TV's Responsibility to Children," *Radio-Television Daily*, 14 July 1952, 107. An abridged version of this article appears in Olga Druce, "On Our Cover: Producing Children's Shows for TV," *TV Today* (Detroit), 18 October 1952, 2.

45. Druce, interview, 2 September 2000.

46. General Foods also had other expenses, such as Druce's salary and a fee to DuMont for the network's airtime. Its total cost was higher than the $6,500 production budget cited by Druce. Druce's figure is consistent with budget figures that appeared in contemporary sources. Robert Stewart reported that the fall 1952 costs for *Captain Video* were $5,000 per week. See Robert Hammel Stewart, "The Development of Network Television Program Types to January, 1953" (Ph.D. diss., Ohio State University, 1954), 255, 346. When General Foods decided to discontinue sponsorship in June 1953, DuMont estimated that the new, 15-minute episodes of *Captain Video* would be offered to sponsors at a net cost of $9,500 per week. This figure included a few expenses, such as a producer's salary, that had been assumed by General Foods. See "Network Sales Meeting Notes," 15 June 1953. These figures are strictly production costs.

47. Druce, interview, 2 September 2000.

48. See, for example, Jack Cluett, "Rocket-Bye Baby," *Woman's Day*, August 1953, 113–4; Robinson, 64; Harriet Van Horne, "Space Rocket Kick," *Theatre Arts*, December 1951, 40–2.

49. Cluett, "Rocket-Bye Baby," 114.

50. Druce, "TV's Responsibility to Children," 107.

51. Druce, interview, 2 September 2000; Frederik Pohl, "Forward," *Science Fiction of the 50's*, Martin Harry Greenberg and Joseph Olander, eds. (New York: Avon, 1979), xii.

52. Jack Vance, *Captain Video and his Video Rangers*, unpublished script, 18 May 1953, 3, Mugar Memorial Library, Boston University, Boston, MA. The other Vance scripts cited below are also located at Mugar Memorial Library. Each script is dated, but the actual air dates varied according to the scheduling needs of DuMont and its affiliates, who ran the programs live or on kinescope.

53. Vance, *Captain Video*, 18 May 1953, 3.

54. Vance, *Captain Video*, 18 May 1953, 17

55. Vance, *Captain Video*, unpublished script, 20 May 1953, 11.

56. Vance, *Captain Video*, unpublished script, 21 May 1953, 32.

57. Vance, *Captain Video*, unpublished script, 25 May 1953, 29.

58. Vance, *Captain Video*, unpublished script, 27 May 1953, 10.

59. "Move Over, Don Hastings," *TV Digest* (Pittsburgh), 28 February 1953, 25.

60. *Captain Video*, untitled episode, circa 1950, videotape, author's collection.

61. See "Telestatus," *Broadcasting Telecasting*, 15 October 1951, 76; National Association for Better Radio and Television, "Fourth Annual Report," 3.

62. James Gilbert, *A Cycle of Outrage: America's Reaction to the Juvenile Delinquent in the 1950s* (New York: Oxford University Press, 1986), 8–10, 89.

63. National Association for Better Radio and Television, *Look and Listen: "NAF-BRAT" Radio and Television Guide to Better Programming*, Spring 1954 (Los Angeles: NAFBRAT, 1954), n.p., Senate Juvenile Delinquency.

64. National Association for Better Radio and Television, "Fourth Annual Report," 5.

65. Druce, interview, 2 September 2000.

66. United States Senate, Committee on the Judiciary, Subcommittee to Investigate Juvenile Delinquency, *Juvenile Delinquency (Television Programs)*, 83rd Congress, 2nd sess., June 5, October 19 and 20, 1954, (Washington, DC: Government Printing Office, 1954), 131.

67. Robinson, "Planet Parenthood," 63.

68. "Captain Video," *Variety*, 13 July 1955, in *Variety Television Reviews, Volume 5, 1954–1956*, ed. Howard H. Prouty (New York: Garland, 1990), n.p.; "Captain Video and His Cartoon Rangers," *Variety*, 28 March 1956, in *Variety Television Reviews, 1954–1956*, n.p; Coker, "Al Hodge: Before and After Captain Video."

69. "Al Hodge," *Variety Obituaries, Volume 8, 1975–1979* (New York: Garland, 1988), n.p.; Richard Lamparski, *Whatever Became Of . . . ?*, Fourth Series (New York: Crown, 1973), 133; Coker, "Al Hodge: Before and After Captain Video."

Chapter Six: What'd He Say?

1. Joe Cohen, "Texaco Star Theatre," *Variety*, 23 June 1948, in *Variety Television Reviews, 1923–1950*, n.p.

2. "Back at the Palace," *Time*, 23 August 1948, 74.

3. "46% of TV Viewers Prefer Vaudeo; Snub News, Kids, Quiz, Musical Shows," *Variety*, 17 November 1948, 29; also see ratings books from this time period.

4. See McNeil, *Total Television*, 1143.

5. "Network TV Sponsorships," *Television Digest*, 22 January 1949, n.p.

6. "*School House*," *Variety*, 26 January 1949, in *Variety Television Reviews, 1923–1950*, n.p. There is one episode of *School House* circulating among collectors. All references are to this undated episode.

7. *Window on the World*, March 25, 1949, videotape, VA9728T, UCLA Film and Television Archive, Los Angeles, CA (hereafter cited as UCLA Archive).

8. Tim Brooks, *The Complete Directory to Prime Time TV Stars, 1946–Present* (New York: Ballantine Books, 1987), 804.

9. "Network TV Sponsorships," *Television Digest*, 11 February 1950, 3; Campbell-Ewald Company, "'Famous Guests' Proposal," unpublished proposal, 30 December 1953, 3, DuMont-LC.

10. A lawsuit later claimed that the song's melody was lifted from a Trinidanian calypso piece originally written in 1906. Amsterdam and his publisher settled the plagiarism case with Maurice Baron, the original publisher of the song. See John Sforza, *Swing It! The Andrews Sisters* (Lexington: University of Kentucky Press, 1999), 75–6.

11. "Morey Amsterdam," *Tele Vision Guide* (New York), 19 February 1949, 12; Cindy Adams, "Morey: From Al Capone to Dick Van Dyke, He Always Leaves Them Laughing," *TV Guide*, 3 August 1963, 15–7; Brooks, *The Complete Directory to Prime Time TV Stars*, 22.

12. "Morey Amsterdam Is Top Receiver Salesman," *The Raster*, May 1950, 19.

13. Barbara Seaman, *Lovely Me: The Life of Jacqueline Susann*, rev. ed. (New York: Seven Stories Press, 1996), 201–2. Also see episodes of the CBS Amsterdam show at UCLA Archive.

14. Scott Yanow, "Johnny Guarneiri," *All Music Guide*, http://www.allmusic.com/cg/amg.dll.

15. *The Morey Amsterdam Show*, 12 October 1950, videotape, author's collection.

16. Audrey Meadows, *Love, Alice: My Life as a Honeymooner* (New York: Crown, 1994), 36. "A New Perspective for Art Carney," *TV Guide* 28 November 1959, 7; "Va, Va, Va, VOOM!" *Tele Vision Guide* (New York), 27 August 1949, 16; "Who's King of Television Stooges?" *TV Digest* (Philadelphia), 25 March 1950, 5; Michael Starr, *Art Carney: A Biography* (New York: Fromm, 1997), 47–50.

17. *The Morey Amsterdam Show*, 12 October 1950.

18. *The Morey Amsterdam Show*, 5 October 1950, videotape, author's collection.

19. Michael Alexander, *Jazz Age Jews* (Princeton, NJ: Princeton University Press, 2001), 141

20. *The Morey Amsterdam Show*, circa 1950, videotape, author's collection.

21. Spigel, *Make Room for Television*, 39.

22. The print advertisement appeared in *Saturday Evening Post*, 19 August 1950, 15. The program description is from an episode of *The Morey Amsterdam Show*, circa 1950, videotape, author's collection.

23. DuMont Laboratories, "Minutes of DuMont Management Meeting," unpublished document, 2 February 1950, DuMont-SI.

24. DuMont did have a longer-running public affairs program, *Court of Current Issues*, which aired from February 1948 to June 1951.

25. Brooks and Marsh, *Directory to Prime Time*, 1244.

26. See Arthur Frank Wertheim, "The Rise of Milton Berle," in *American History/American Television*, ed. John E. O'Connor (New York: Ungar, 1983), 74–6; David Marc, *Comic Visions* (Boston: Unwin Hyman, 1989), 43–4; Susan Murray, "Lessons From Uncle Miltie," in *Small Screens, Big Ideas*, ed. Janet Thumin (New York: I.B. Tauris, 2002), 84–5.

27. "Video Audience Switches From Caviar to Bread 'n Butter!" *Tele Vision Guide* (New York), 19 November 1949, 12–3; Abel Green, "Too Much Borscht?" *Variety*, 28 February 1951, 28; Spigel, *Make Room for Television*, 147–51; Sam Levenson, "The Dialect Comedian Should Vanish," *Commentary*, August 1952, 168–9.

Chapter Seven: And Away He Went . . .

1. "Network TV Billings," *Broadcasting Telecasting*, 4 July 1949, 54; Lichty and Topping, *American Broadcasting*, 257.

2. C. J. Witting to Commander M. W. Loewi, memo, 24 November 1950, DuMont-LC.

3. "Estimated Weekly Network TV Program Costs," *Variety*, 14 November 1951, 26. Also see Stewart, "Network Program Types," 320.

4. *Cavalcade of Stars*, no date, videotape, B:17806, MTR-NY.

5. Bergmann and Skutch, *The DuMont Television Network*, 27; Bergmann, telephone conversation; "Television's Growing Pains," *Business Week*, 12 November 1949, 51–2; Samuel, *Brought to You By*, 38; Henry, *The Great One*, 124.

6. "Tele Follow-up Comment," *Variety*, 31 August 1949, in *Variety Television Reviews, 1923–1950*, n.p.

7. "Network TV Sponsorships," *Television Digest*, 11 February 1950, 3; McNeil, *Total Television*, 1143.

8. *Cavalcade of Stars*, 1950, videotape, author's collection. The tape, one of two in circulation featuring Lester as host, may combine two episodes of *Cavalcade* from 1950. The second half of the tape fits a description from a *Variety* review of a May 20, 1950, episode. See "Tele Follow-up Comment," *Variety*, 24 May 1950, in *Variety Television Reviews, 1923–1950*, n.p.

9. "Life With Lester," *Newsweek*, 18 September 1950, 58.

10. "The Jerry Lester-Dagmar Feud," *TV Guide* (New York), 28 April 1951, 8.

11. Ronald Sullivan, "Jerry Lester Early TV Host and Comedian Is Dead at 85," *New York Times*, 25 March 1995.

12. Henry, *The Great One*, 87–8.

13. Karen Adir, *The Great Clowns of American Television* (Jefferson, NC: McFarland, 1988), 116.

14. Bishop cites these figures for a 1948 engagement at Slapsie Maxie's. He also notes that the *Cavalcade of Stars* job, even at the low starting rate, gave Gleason more money than he was making at Slapsie Maxie's. See Jim Bishop, *The Golden Ham* (New York: Simon and Schuster, 1956), 176–7, 200.

15. Bishop, *The Golden Ham*, 160.

16. Bishop, *The Golden Ham*, 199–202; Henry, *The Great One*, 93–4; Bergmann and Skutch, *The DuMont Television Network*, 28. Donna McCrohan and Peter Crescenti report that Gleason signed to *Cavalcade* under slightly different terms: $1,000 a week for two weeks. See Donna McCrohan and Peter Crescenti, *The Honeymooners Lost Episodes* (New York: Workman, 1986), 30.

17. Bishop, *The Golden Ham*, 27.

18. "Tele Follow-up Comment," *Variety*, 12 July 1950, in *Variety Television Reviews, 1923–1950*, n.p. "Tele Follow-up Comment," *Variety*, 9 August 1950, in *Variety Television Reviews, 1923–1950*, n.p. "Tele Follow-up Comment," *Variety*, 13 September 1950, in *Variety Television Reviews, 1923–1950*, n.p. "Tele Follow-up Comment," *Variety*, 15 November 1950, in *Variety Television Reviews, 1923–1950*, n.p.

19. *Cavalcade of Stars*, September 8, 1950, videotape, author's collection.

20. Critic Gilbert Seldes described Gleason as "a heavy man with the traditional belief of heavy men in their own lightness and grace." See Seldes, *The Public Arts* (New York: Simon and Schuster, 1956), 161.

21. Henry, *The Great One*, 97–102. Along with Ralph Kramden, the Loudmouth may have been created by the new writers in the second season. Don Russell introduces the skit starring "a hilarious new character." See *Cavalcade of Stars*, 12 October 1951, videotape, B: 20143, MTR-NY.

22. Quoted in Kisseloff, *The Box*, 214–5.

23. Val Adams, "Not Tough at All: Jackie Gleason Decries the Terrors of TV," *New York Times*, 20 May 1951.

24. Henry, *The Great One*, 97.

25. Jackie Gleason, "The Truth About My Characters," *TV Guide* (New York), 9 November 1951, 21.

26. Harold Clemenko, "The Armchair Spectator Meets Jackie Gleason," *TV Guide* (New York), June 13, 1952, 5, 36.

27. Dick Cavett, "An Interview with Jackie Gleason," in *Jackie Gleason: "The Great One"* (New York: Museum of Broadcasting, 1987), 37.

28. Quoted in Larry Wilde, *The Great Comedians Talk About Comedy* (New York: The Citadel Press, 1968), 25.

29. Sam Boal, "The Many Sides of Jackie Gleason," *Coronet*, May 1953, 61.

30. For more on Gleason's suite, see the authorized biography by James Bacon, *How Sweet It Is: The Jackie Gleason Story* (New York: St. Martin's Press, 1985), 101.

31. David Marc, *Demographic Vistas: Television in American Culture* (Philadelphia: University of Pennsylvania Press, 1984), 102.

32. Jackie Gleason, "Confessions of a Bachelor," *TV Guide* (New York), 20 January 1951, 24.

33. Henry, *The Great One*, 111.

34. *Cavalcade of Stars*, September 8, 1950, videotape.

35. Tom Shales, "How Sweet it Was!" *Washington Post*, 25 July 1988.

36. *Cavalcade of Stars*, October 26, 1951, videotape, author's collection.

37. The most widely cited story about the show's origins is from Joe Cates, who credits Gleason with coming up with the idea. In another account, writer Harry Crane claims that he created the skit based on his own experiences. See Kisseloff, *The Box*, 215–6; Henry, *The Great One*, 112–3; McCrohan and Crescenti, *The Honeymooners Lost Episodes*, 38–51. In his authorized biography of Gleason, Bishop credits Gleason. See Bishop, *The Golden Ham*, 217.

38. McCrohan and Crescenti, *The Honeymooners Lost Episodes*, 45.

39. Marc, *Demographic Vistas*, 113

40. Marc, *Demographic Vistas*, 102.

41. Henry, *The Great One*, 123.

42. American Business Consultants, *Red Channels: The Report of Communist Influence in Radio and Television* (New York, NY: American Business Consultants, 1950), 92. For more on blacklisting and television, see Thomas Doherty, "Blacklisting," in *The Encyclopedia of Television*, ed. Horace Newcomb, on-line edition, Museum of Broadcast Communications, http://www.museum.tv/archives/etv/index.html.

43. Cooper, interview.

44. Bergmann and Skutch, *The DuMont Television Network*, 74; Bergmann, telephone conversation. In his autobiography, Bergmann does not discuss *The Hazel Scott Show*, a music program starring the well-known pianist, which aired on WABD starting in March 1950. The show moved to the network that summer. According to Scott, potential sponsors shunned her after she was listed in *Red Channels* in June 1950. DuMont kept Scott on the air without a sponsor until September 29, 1950. See Donald Bogle, *Prime Time Blues: African Americans on Network Television* (New York: Farrar, Strauss and Giroux, 2001), 17–9; "Gypsy, Scott & Wicker in Red Denials," *Billboard*, 23 September 1950, 16.

45. Henry, *The Great One*, 112.

46. Hoberman, "Ralph and Alice and Ed and Trixie," 22.

47. "The Honeymooners: The Really Lost Debut Episodes," The Disney Channel, circa 1993, videotape, author's collection.

48. Accounts differ over who recommended Carney first. Joseph Cates, assistant producer of *Cavalcade of Stars*, credits one of the writers (he is not sure which one) with the idea to use Carney. Arthur Forrest, a cameraman on the Adelphi Theatre

214 Notes to Chapter Seven

production crew, remembers his colleague Hal Bowden telling the producer about Carney during a rehearsal break. See Kisseloff, *The Box*, 214; Forrest, interview with author.

49. McCrohan and Crescenti, *The Honeymooners Lost Episodes*, 64.

50. "The Honeymooners: The Really Lost Debut Episodes," videotape.

51. E. B. Lyford to C. G. Alexander, et al., "TV Network 1952," memo, 5 March 1952, DuMont-LC.

52. Also see American Research Bureau, "The New York City Television Audience," October 1–8, 1951 (New York: American Research Bureau, 1951), 35, Arbitron-TV. American Research Bureau, "The Washington Television Audience," October 12–21, 1951 (New York: American Research Bureau, 1951), 31, Arbitron-TV.

53. "Colgate Comedy Hour," *Variety*, 5 September 1951, in *Variety Television Reviews, 1951–1953*, n.p.

54. McCrohan and Crescenti, *The Honeymooners Lost Episodes*, 38–9.

55. *Cavalcade of Stars*, November 2, 1951, videotape, T:28247, MTR-NY.

56. Henry, *The Great One*, 69–70.

57. "Gleason Gets Girls and Awa-a-ay He Goes!" *Life*, 29 September 1952, 89; Boal, "The Many Sides of Jackie Gleason," 63.

58. Henry, *The Great One*, 103.

59. Henry, *The Great One*, 83, 105, 128–9.

60. *Cavalcade of Stars*, November 2, 1951, videotape.

61. Henry, *The Great One*, 141.

62. See James L. Baughman, "Take Me Away From Manhattan: New York City and American Mass Culture, 1930–1990," in *Capital of the American Century: The National and International Influence of New York City*, ed. Martin Shefter (New York: Russell Sage Foundation, 1993), 128.

63. Richard A. Schwartz, *Cold War Culture: Media and the Arts, 1945–1990*, paperback ed. (New York: Checkmark Books, 2000), 237.

64. Quoted in David Halberstam, *The Fifties* (New York: Villard Books, 1993), 573.

65. Bishop, *The Golden Ham*, 235–6. In a story that has become part of Gleason lore, repeated in at least one cable television biography of Gleason, assistant producer Joe Cates claims that Gleason offered to sign a three-year contract extension with DuMont at the start of the second season in exchange for a $30,000 advance, but that Caddigan decided not to make this deal. Instead, the DuMont programing executive invested the $30,000 in a program starring actor Joseph Schildkraut. See Kisseloff, *The Box*, 217. However, it seems unlikely that Gleason would have actually re-signed with DuMont for such a low figure. No other sources confirm Cates's story. The Schildkraut program did not debut on DuMont until more than two years after Gleason allegedly made his offer. In addition, both DuMont and Gleason knew that the star would cost more than a $30,000 advance by the start of the 1951–52 season. CBS was in a bidding war with NBC for Gleason's services, with one trade magazine prematurely reporting that Gleason had signed a $300,000 deal with NBC in October 1951. "Gleason's $300,000 NBC Deal for TV," *Variety*, 17 October 1951, n.p., DuMont-SI.

66. Henry, *The Great One*, 92.

67. Bergmann, telephone conversation.

Chapter Eight: Law and Order, DuMont Style

1. "Murder Most Foul," *Life*, 28 April 1952, 95–6; TV *Digest* also counts 29 crime shows in "The Plainclothes Man," *TV Digest* (Pittsburgh), 28 June 1952, 8.

2. "Down-to-Earth Rocky King," *TV Digest* (Pittsburgh), 17 January 1953, 28. Also see DuMont distribution schedules and memos: E. B. Lyford to C. G. Alexander, et al., "TV Network 1952," memo, 5 March 1952, DuMont-LC; DuMont Television Network, "Network Traffic Department Report, corrected to February 1, 1953," DuMont-LC; "Du Mont Television Network Projected Program Distribution Order," week ending February 7, 1954, DuMont-LC. Also see American Research Bureau ratings books in the Arbitron-TV collection. *Rocky King* cost $6,000 per episode and *The Plainclothes Man* $5,000. CBS ran *The Fred Waring Show* ($35,000/episode) and NBC alternated two live theater programs: *Philco TV Playhouse* ($25,000/episode), and *Goodyear TV Playhouse* ($25,000/episode). Program costs are from Stewart, "Network Television Types," and "Estimated Weekly Program Costs," *Variety*, 14 November 1951, 26.

3. Forrest, interview.

4. "The Plainclothes Man," *TV Digest* (Pittsburgh), 2 February 1952, 7. Also see William Marceau, "Plainclothes Man," *TV Digest* (Philadelphia), 27 September 1952, 28. A nearly identical article was published under Ken Lynch's byline in *TV Digest* (New England), 17 October 1952, 9.

5. "The Plainclothes Man," *TV Digest* (Pittsburgh), 2 February 1952, 6.

6. Forrest, interview.

7. "Tele Follow-up Comment," *Variety*, 5 July 1950, in *Variety Television Reviews, 1923–1950*, n.p.

8. Marceau, "Plainclothes Man," 28.

9. See J. Fred Macdonald, *Don't Touch That Dial* 1996. (Chicago: Nelson-Hall, 1979), 162; John Dunning, *On the Air: The Encyclopedia of Old-Time Radio* (New York: Oxford University Press, 1998), 8–9. DuMont similarly melded the whodunit and quiz show for a short time an a program called *Crawford Mystery Theatre* (re-titled *Public Prosecutor*, 1951–52). Brooks and Marsh, *Directory to Prime Time*, 216.

10. "The Plainclothes Man," *TV Digest* (Pittsburgh), 2 February 1952, 6.

11. "The Plainclothes Man," *TV Digest* (Pittsburgh), 2 February 1952, 6.

12. Sergeant Brady, "What's Wrong With TV Mysteries?" *TV Guide* (Washington-Baltimore), 20 January 1952, 22.

13. Christopher P. Wilson, *Cop Knowledge: Police Power and Cultural Narrative in Twentieth-Century America* (Chicago: University of Chicago Press, 2000), 63; also see Thomas Doherty, *Cold War, Cool Medium: Television, McCarthyism, and American Culture* (New York: Columbia University Press, 2003), 135–6.

14. *The Plainclothes Man*, July 26, 1953, videotape, B:33388, MTR-NY.

15. *The Plainclothes Man*, no date, videotape, B:33064, MTR-NY.

16. See *The Plainclothes Man*, July 26, 1953.

17. *The Plainclothes Man*, July 26, 1953. Also see the film insert in *The Plainclothes Man*, no date, videotape, B:33064, MTR-NY. Director Barry Shear uses a similar technique in an episode of another DuMont detective show. See *Not for Publication*, "88 Keys for Escape," April 1, 1952, videotape, VA17403T, UCLA Archive.

18. The description is from *The Plainclothes Man*, July 26, 1953.

19. "Screen Star Roscoe Karns Portrays Rocky King, Detective," *TV Digest* (Philadelphia), 21 October 1951, 16–7.

20. Other DuMont crime shows with a similar sensibility included *Colonel Humphrey Flack* and *Not for Publication*.

21. "The Housewife Audience," *Televiser*, November 1949, 12.

22. "Screen Star Roscoe Karns Portrays Rocky King, Detective," 16–7. Also see "Roscoe Karns Has Outlasted All Other Detectives," *TV Guide*, 31 July 1953, 21.

23. "Rocky King, Detective," *TV Forecast* (Chicago), 4 October 1952, 8.

24. "Real Cops vs. TV Sleuths," *TV Guide*, 16 October 1954, 8–9.

25. "Rocky King, Detective," *TV Forecast* (Chicago), 8.

26. *Rocky King, Detective*, "Murder by Natural Death," no date, videotape, author's collection.

27. Roscoe Karns, "Why You Never See My TV Family," *TV Guide* (New York), 7 December 1951, 24.

28. "Rocky King, Detective," *TV Forecast* (Chicago), 8.

29. Todd Karns replaced Hammond with a new character, Detective Hart, during the show's final 1953–1954 season.

30. Kenney, interview.

31. Kenney, interview.

32. *Rocky King, Detective*, "Murder in Advance," circa 1953–1954, videotape, author's collection. This conversation is also cited on Clarke Ingram's informative and well-researched Web site. See Ingram, "Appendix Seven: Rocky King," *The Du-Mont Television Network*, http://members.aol.com/cingram/televisoin/dumonta7.htm. Ingram offers a good discussion of Rocky King, including other examples of the way the show broke the so-called "fourth wall" between camera and audience.

Chapter Nine: A Bishop for Berle Fans

1. Ken Auletta, "Vox Fox," *New Yorker*, 26 May 2003, 71.

2. The ratings are for the 1951–1952 season. McNeil, *Total Television*, 1143. For the two weeks ending February 23, Berle was rated fourth behind Godfrey, *Red Skelton*, and *I Love Lucy*. "News Digest," *Ross Reports*, 23 March 1952, 4.

3. Mary Ann Watson, "And They Said Uncle Fultie Didn't Have a Prayer," *Television Quarterly* 30 (1999), 81.

4. The viewer numbers are for the New York and Washington markets. American Research Bureau, "The New York City Television Audience," October 1–8, 1951 (New York: American Research Bureau, 1951), 19, Arbitron-TV. American Research Bureau, "The Washington Television Audience," October 12–21, 1951 (New York: American Research Bureau, 1951), 15, Arbitron-TV. Also see Brooks and Marsh, *Directory to Prime Time*, 1243.

5. "Sheen on TV Screen," *Life*, 24 March 1952, 92–6.

6. "Bishop Sheen's Monumental Mail," *TV Digest* (Pittsburgh), 4 April 1953, 36.

7. Brooks and Marsh, *Directory to Prime Time*, 581.

8. "Bishop Sheen's Monumental Mail," 8.

9. DuMont Television Network, "Fact Sheet: Life Is Worth Living," 20 October 1954, press release, FCC Executive Director; "Wider TV Coverage Seen for Sheen," *New York Times*, 21 July 1953; "Life Is Worth Living," *Variety*, 21 October 1953, in *Variety Television Reviews*, 1951–53, n.p.

10. Forrest, interview.

11. "Microphone Missionary," *Time*, 14 April 1952, 78.

12. James C. G. Conniff, *The Bishop Sheen Story* (New York: Fawcett, 1953), 31. Thomas C. Reeves, *America's Bishop: The Life and Times of Fulton J. Sheen* (San Francisco: Encounter Books, 2001), 225. Also see photographs of Sheen from this time.

13. Edwin Broderick, telephone conversation with author, 17 March 2003.

14. Gretta Palmer, "Bishop Sheen on Television," *The Catholic Digest*, February 1953, 79.

15. "Microphone Missionary," 78.

16. John Crosby, "Radio and Television," *New York Herald Tribune*, 22 December 1952.

17. Marya Mannes, "Channels: Comments on TV," *The Reporter*, 20 January 1953, 38; Doherty, *Cold War, Cool Medium*, 153–4.

18. Bergmann and Skutch, *The DuMont Television Network*, 41–2.

19. "Microphone Missionary," 72.

20. Thomas Doherty provides a good discussion of Sheen's ironic style in *Cold War, Cool Medium*, 157.

21. Palmer, "Bishop Sheen on Television," 76.

22. *Life Is Worth Living*, n.d., videotape, B:03971, MTR-NY.

23. "The Man Who Toppled Berle," *TV Forecast* (Chicago), 14 June 1952, 13.

24. Martin E. Marty, *Modern American Religion*, Volume 3, *Under God, Indivisible, 1941–1961* (Chicago: University of Chicago Press, 1986), 323.

25. Mark S. Massa, *Catholics and American Culture* (New York: Herder and Herder, 1999), 83.

26. Reeves, *America's Bishop*, 211.

27. Joseph Roddy, "A Talk With Bishop Sheen," *Look*, 27 January 1953, 41.

28. Fulton J. Sheen, "Why I Am on Television," *TV Guide* (New York), 11 April 1952, 8.

29. David Weinstein, "DuMont in Washington, D.C.: Out on a Limb," *Quarterly Review of Film and Video* 16 (1999): 380–1.

30. Edwin Broderick, telephone conversation.

31. See Ellen Caddigan Lyner, interview with Rory Coker, February 2001, posted on Coker, "Roaring Rockets."

32. The Eye and Ear Department, "Pat on the Back for DuMont," *Advertising Age*, 19 May 1952, 74.

33. Jack Gould, "Radio and Television," *New York Times*, 22 February 1952.

34. Broderick, telephone conversation.

35. "Microphone Missionary," 72.

36. The million dollar figure was reported in "Admiral Sponsor of Sheen TV Talks," *New York Times*, 22 October 1952; "A Sponsor for the Bishop," *Time*, 3 November 1952, 79. Ted Bergmann remembered the figure as $25,000 for twenty-six weeks ($15,000 a week to Sheen's Society for the Propagation of the Faith and $10,000 a week to DuMont for the network's time and facilities). See Bergmann and Skutch, *The DuMont Television Network*, 43.

37. Brooks and Marsh, *Directory to Prime Time*, 470. Also see Hal Erickson, *Religious Radio and Television in the United States, 1921–1991* (Jefferson, NC: McFarland, 1992). The program moved from 10:00 to 10:30 p.m. for its final season.

38. Bergmann and Skutch, *The DuMont Television Network*, 42.

39. Lawrence M. Hughes, "Bishop Sheen's Sponsor," *The Catholic Digest*, May 1956, 17–8.

40. Jack Gould, "Video Departure: Bishop Sheen's Program to be Sponsored," *New York Times*, 26 October 1952; John Crosby, "Bishop Sheen's Second Year," *New York Herald Tribune*, 22 December 1952.

41. See, for example, *Life Is Worth Living*, n.d., videotape, B:03971, MTR-NY.

42. *Life Is Worth Living*, "Prayer," circa 1952–53, videotape, author's collection. This is one of several episodes of *Life Is Worth Living* that was regularly rerun on the Eternal Word Television Network in 2002 and 2003. Also see Fulton J. Sheen, *Life Is Worth Living, Second Series* (New York: McGraw-Hill, 1954), 209–17. The published version of this talk does not include the portion about Admiral quoted.

43. Also see Conniff, *The Bishop Sheen Story*, 15; Reeves, *America's Bishop*, 227; Doherty, *Cold War, Cool Medium*, 156.

44. Conniff, The Bishop Sheen Story, 15; Michael Sheridan, "How Bishop Sheen Inspires Millions," *TV Carnival*, April 1954, 7.

45. Crosby, "Bishop Sheen's Second Year."

46. Everett C. Parker, David W. Barry, and Dallas W. Smythe, *The Television-Radio Audience and Religion* (New York: Harper and Brothers, 1955), 21, 212.

47. Robert S. Ellwood, *The Fifties Spiritual Marketplace: American Religion in a Decade of Conflict* (New Brunswick, NJ: Rutgers University Press, 1997), 9.

48. Marty, *Modern American Religion*, passim. Also see Doherty, *Cold War, Cool Medium*, 156–60 for more on how television supported this growing consensus view of America as a Judeo-Christian nation.

49. Reeves, *America's Bishop*, 231; Doherty, *Cold War, Cool Medium*, 271–2.

50. Thomas O'Malley, "Bishop Fulton J. Sheen: A TV Star Is Born," *TV Forecast* (Chicago), 21 June 1952, 28.

51. See "Letters," *Time*, 28 April 1952, 4–5; "Letters," *Time*, 5 May 1952, 12.

52. Ellwood, *The Fifties Spiritual Marketplace*, 13.

53. Steven Stark, *Glued to the Set* (New York: The Free Press, 1997), 39.

54. Joseph Roddy, "A Talk With Bishop Sheen," *Look*, 27 January 1953, 38.

55. Christopher Owen Lynch, *Selling Catholicism: Bishop Sheen and the Power of Television* (Lexington, KY: University Press of Kentucky, 1998), 89.

56. *Life Is Worth Living*, "Something Higher," 1952, videotape, author's collection. Fulton J. Sheen, *Life Is Worth Living* (New York: McGraw-Hill, 1953), 171–80.

57. *Life Is Worth Living*, "Prayer," videotape. Sheen, *Life Is Worth Living, Second Series*, 209–17.

58. See the interviews in Parker et al., *The Television-Radio Audience and Religion*, 274–315.

59. Doherty, *Cold War, Cool Medium*, 157–8.

60. Life Is Worth Living, "How Mothers Are Made," 1952, videotape, author's collection. Also see Sheen, *Life Is Worth Living* (New York: McGraw-Hill, 1953), 51–9.

61. *Life Is Worth Living*, "Comparison of Soviet and American Constitutions," 1952, videotape, T:51059, MTR-NY.

62. Sheen, *Life Is Worth Living*, (New York: McGraw-Hill, 1953), 149–58.

63. Sheen, *Treasure in Clay*, 74.

64. Donald Crosby, *God, Church, and Flag: Senator Joseph R. McCarthy and the Catholic Church, 1950–1957* (Chapel Hill, NC: University of North Carolina Press), 15–6.

65. Reeves, *America's Bishop*, 234.

66. Doherty, *Cold War, Cool Medium*, 160.

67. See "Admiral, Sheen Calling It Quits?" *Variety*, 21 March 1956, 19.

68. Reeves, *America's Bishop*, 255.

69. Brooks and Marsh, *Directory to Prime Time*, 580; Reeves, *America's Bishop*, 285; Richard F. Shepard, "A.B.C. Outlet Bars a Critic of Queen," *New York Times*, 19 October 1957.

Chapter Ten: Ernie Kovacs and the DuMont Legacy

1. Castleman and Podrazik, *The TV Schedule Book*, 67, 73. Allen B. DuMont Laboratories, *1955 Annual Report*, 16, DuMont-SI; Val Adams, "DuMont Cutting Its Network," *New York Times*, 29 December 1954; The figures for network losses are from Booz, Allen & Hamilton, "Survey of the Broadcasting Division: Allen B. DuMont Laboratories," unpublished report, 4 February 1955, Dumont-LC. Westinghouse actually took possession of the Pittsburgh station on January 10, 1955.

2. Bergmann and Skutch, *The DuMont Television Network*, 80.

3. Quoted in Hess, "Historical Study," 147; also see Boddy, *Fifties Television*, 53.

4. The Electronicam was also used to film The Les Paul and Mary Ford Show, Modern Romances, Broadway TV Theatre, and several commercials. See Allen B. DuMont Laboratories, *1955 Annual Report*, 8.

5. "Ernie Kovacs Show," *Variety*, 14 April 1954, in *Variety Television Reviews, Volume 5, 1954–1956*, n.p.

6. "Television News From DuMont," 21 February 1955, 1, FCC Executive Director.

7. William A. Henry, "Topsy-Turvy in the Everyday World: The Unsurpassed Career of Ernie Kovacs," in *The Visions of Ernie Kovacs* (New York: Museum of Broadcasting, 1986), 11.

8. Diana Rico, *Kovacsland: A Biography of Ernie Kovacs* (San Diego: Harcourt, Brace, Jovanovich, 1990), 185; see, for example, *The Ernie Kovacs Show*, July 9, 1956, NBC, re-broadcast, Comedy Central, 1991.

9. *The Ernie Kovacs Rehearsal*, March 22, 1955, videotape, T:85:0619, MTR-NY; David G. Walley, *The Ernie Kovacs Phile* (New York: Bolder Books, 1975), 93.

10. *The Ernie Kovacs Rehearsal*.

11. *The Ernie Kovacs Show*, July 9, 1956.

12. Sid Shalit, "Is Ernie Kovacs Crazy? Yes Crazy Like a Fox, *New York Daily News*, 14 November 1954; Rico, Kovacsland, 158.

13. See American Research Bureau, *The New York Television Audience, October 8–14, 1953* (Washington, DC: American Research Bureau, 1953), passim; American Research Bureau, The *New York Television Audience, November 7–13, 1954* (Washington, DC: American Research Bureau, 1954), passim, in Arbitron-TV.

14. Rico, *Kovacsland*, 338.

15. Shalit, "Is Ernie Kovacs Crazy?"

16. Rico, *Kovacsland*, 180.

17. Rico *Kovacsland*, 154–5; Walley, *The Ernie Kovacs Phile*, 96.

18. Rico, *Kovacsland*, 157.

19. "Oceans of Empathy," 72; Dunning, *The Encyclopedia of Old-Time Radio*, 46.

20. Rico, *Kovacsland*, 209; "An Electronic Comic and His TV Tricks," *Life*, 15 April 1957, 167.

21. Ingram, *The DuMont Television Network*, http://members.aol.com/cingram/television/dumont.htm; Coker, *Roaring Rockets*, http://www.slick-net.com/space/. Three recent books do a good job of situating DuMont within the broader history of television, starting in the late 1930s. See Kisseloff, *The Box;* R. D. Heldenfels, *Television's Greatest Year: 1954* (New York: Continuum, 1994); James Von Schilling, *The Magic Window: American Television, 1939–1953* (New York: Haworth Press, 2003). Ted Bergmann's memoir, published in 2002, is a lively and informative account of the rise and fall of the network from the perspective of a long-time executive. See Bergmann and Skutch, *The DuMont Television Network*. The older, standard histories of network television are excellent surveys of the programs and strategies of NBC and CBS, but they neglect DuMont. See, for example, Barnouw, *Tube of Plenty;* J. Fred MacDonald, *One Nation Under Television: The Rise and Decline of Network Television*, rev. ed. (Chicago: Nelson-Hall, 1994); Boddy, *Fifties Television;* Max Wilk, *The Golden Age of Television: Notes from the Survivors* (New York: Moyer Bell, 1989).

22. Allen B. Du Mont, "Television's Future," unpublished typescript, circa 1948, DuMont-LC; Allen B. Du Mont, "Stop, Look, Listen," *Safety Education*, February 1948, 10; Allen B. Du Mont, "The Television Industry," reprint of address delivered before the Industrial Council, Rensselaer Polytechnic Institute, Troy, New York, 30 October 1953, 12, DuMont-LC.

23. Allen B. Du Mont, "Television's Unlimited Opportunities for Public Service," *Academy*, November 1952, 11.

24. All of the networks, including DuMont, experimented with short-lived news programs and formats during the late 1940s. For more on early news, see Edward Bliss Jr., *Now the News: The Story of Broadcast Journalism* (New York: Columbia University Press), 226–36.

25. Du Mont, "The Television Industry," 11–2.

26. Allen B. Du Mont, address, annual summer meeting, American Institute of Electrical Engineers, unpublished typescript, 19 June 1961, n.p., DuMont-SI.

Index

Pages with photos are shown in italic.

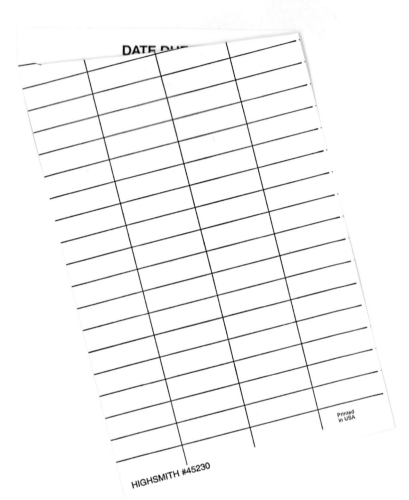

DATE DUE

Printed
in USA

HIGHSMITH #45230